Religious Prose
of Seventeenth-Century
England

The Borzoi Anthology
of 17th-Century English Literature

GENERAL EDITOR

Joseph A. Mazzeo
Columbia University

Seventeenth-Century English Poetry (*Vols. I & II*)
EDITED BY *MIRIAM K. STARKMAN*
Queens College of The City University of New York

Seventeenth-Century English Prose (*Vol. III*)
EDITED BY *DAVID NOVARR, Cornell University*

Literary Criticism of Seventeenth-Century England (*Vol. IV*)
EDITED BY *EDWARD W. TAYLER, Columbia University*

Religious Prose of Seventeenth-Century England (*Vol. V*)
EDITED BY *ANNE DAVIDSON FERRY, Harvard University*

Religious Prose

of Seventeenth-Century

England

EDITED BY

Anne Davidson Ferry

HARVARD UNIVERSITY

ALFRED·A·KNOPF

NEW YORK

1967

Acknowledgments

Acknowledgments are due to the following publishers for permission to use these standard editions:

John Donne. *Devotions Upon Emergent Occasions,* ed. by John Sparrow. Cambridge: The Cambridge University Press, 1923.

John Milton. *The Works of John Milton,* ed. by F. A. Patterson and others. New York: Columbia University Press, 1931–8.

John Bunyan. *Grace Abounding to the Chief of Sinners,* ed. by Roger Sharrock. Oxford: the Clarendon Press, 1962.

The Pilgrim's Progress, ed. by James Blanton Wharey; 2nd Edition revised by Roger Sharrock. Oxford: the Clarendon Press, 1960.

Thomas Traherne. *Centuries, Poems and Thanksgivings,* ed. by H. M. Margoliouth. Oxford: the Clarendon Press, 1958.

For assistance in preparation of the other texts in this volume I am indebted to the staffs of the Houghton Library and the Harvard University Library Photographic Service.

To Mary Ann Youngren, Instructor part time in the Humanities, and to William Youngren, Assistant Professor of English both at the Massachusetts Institute of Technology, I am indebted for their generously attentive criticisms of the introductory essay, and to my husband, David Ferry, Associate Professor of English at Wellesley College, for innumerable improvements in the introduction itself, and for approaches to criticism which have become an inseparable part of my own thinking. To the memory of Doris Russell, late Professor of English at Vassar College, with whom I first studied seventeenth-century prose, this volume is lovingly dedicated.

A. D. F.

Cambridge, Massachusetts

Contents

INTRODUCTION 3

John Donne 30

Second Sermon on Psal. 38.4 31
FROM *Devotions Upon Emergent Occasions* 42

Sir Thomas Browne 59

FROM *Religio Medici:* THE FIRST PART 60

Jeremy Taylor 116

FROM *The Rule and Exercises of Holy Dying* 117

John Milton 139

FROM *Of Reformation in England* 140
FROM *Animadversions* 143
FROM *The Reason of Church-government urg'd
against Prelaty* 150
FROM *An Apology* 160

John Bunyan 164

FROM *Grace Abounding to the Chief of Sinners* 165
FROM *The Pilgrim's Progress* 175

Thomas Traherne 214

FROM *Centuries of Meditations:* THE THIRD CENTURY 215

A MISCELLANY

Augustine Baker   233

FROM *Treatise of the Venerable Father Augustin Baker
concerning his own Life*   233

Lancelot Andrewes   236
FROM *A Sermon Preached before the King's Majestie*   236

Edward Lord Herbert   239
FROM *The Life of Edward Lord Herbert of Cherbury*   239

George Herbert   241
FROM *A Priest to the Temple*   241

Isaac Barrow   244
FROM *A Sermon: Of the Goodness of God*   244

Thomas Sprat   245
FROM *A Sermon Preached before the King at White-Hall* 245

John Tillotson   247
FROM *A Sermon: The Precepts of Christianity not
Grievous*   247

Benjamin Whichcote   248
FROM *Moral and Religious Aphorisms*   248

Richard Baxter   250
FROM *The Saints Everlasting Rest*   250

George Fox   253
FROM *The Journal of George Fox*   253

BIBLIOGRAPHY   255

Religious Prose
of Seventeenth-Century
England

Introduction

In order to read with discrimination the religious literature of the seventeenth century, we must educate ourselves in some unfamiliar assumptions, must learn to recognize certain historical conditions which are foreign to us because we live in the twentieth century, nourished by a literature largely secular, irreligious, or religious, if at all, in ways which would be quite incomprehensible to seventeenth-century readers.

We must recognize, first, that religious writings of the types included in this volume—sermons, devotions, confessions of faith, manuals of piety, polemical tracts, spiritual autobiographies, moral allegories, meditations, aphorisms—were not a literary by-path of the seventeenth century, not exclusively the interest of special groups, specially learned or devout. Religious words were written, published and read by all sorts of people. The two greatest poets of the period, John Donne and John Milton, spent more years of their lives writing religious works in prose than composing poems, Donne as a priest of the Church of England, Milton as a would-be priest whose conscience drove him out of that Church. Not only poets and priests, but men of almost every profession were engaged in this activity. Among the other religious writers in this volume, Sir Thomas Browne was a physician, Lord Herbert a courtier and ambassador as well as a philosopher, John Bunyan a tinker, Isaac Barrow a mathematician and teacher of

Isaac Newton (who considered his own interpretation of the Book of Revelation to be his most important writing). Works of religious literature engaged the energies of a vast variety of writers, and were read as eagerly as they were composed, by as wide a variety of men. Religion was interesting to everyone in England in the seventeenth century; the writer who concerned himself with theological doctrine or forms of devotion or ecclesiastical organization could be sure of engaging the attention of a vast and varied audience. Sir Thomas Browne's *Religio Medici* was circulated in two pirated editions before an authorized version appeared in 1642, the first of eight English editions to be printed during the author's lifetime. The writings of George Herbert, Jeremy Taylor, Bunyan, and Richard Baxter had an immensely wide audience in their own period, along with works equally popular with readers of that time but long since forgotten. Two such, for example, were those mentioned in *Grace Abounding* among the meager possessions of Bunyan's wife— Dent's *Plain Man's Pathway to Heaven* and Bayly's *Practice of Piety*—works surpassed in popularity only by the Bible itself.

This energetic interest in religious doctrine, religious institutions, or religious experience is expressed in every work included in this volume. It is reflected, for example, in assumptions about the reader which, to secular modern minds, are sometimes disconcerting. The audiences for these works were assumed to be thoroughly familiar with Scripture, to have a solid knowledge of orthodox Christian doctrine, to be capable of following a theological argument, and to be faithful *believers* (whatever their behavior might be). These assumptions were made about them, not as learned specialists or a pious elite, but as ordinary men, Protestants, Englishmen, members of a Christian society. These assumptions were shared by all the writers represented in this volume (except Augustine Baker to whom only Roman Catholics were true believers), a few of whom assumed additional, more special kinds of knowledge. Donne, for example, preaching before the lawyers of Lincoln's Inn with whom he had once studied, or Lancelot Andrewes, preaching to the King at Whitehall, played upon a knowledge of Latin and logic which only special congregations could be expected to appreciate; not George Herbert's parishioners at Bemerton or Bunyan's at Bedford. Taylor, in the selection printed here, used only one Greek word but made numerous allusions to ancient literature and history. Browne seemed to assume in his readers (and surely he intended his work to be read, despite conventional protests against publicity in its preface) some familiarity with all sorts of esoteric learning. But the religious writers of the period did not *need* to make exclusive or snobbish assumptions about their audiences, because, as Milton asked in *An Apology,* "who almost of the meanest Christians hath not heard the Scriptures often read from his childhood, besides so many Sermons and Lectures more in number than any student hath heard in Philosophy?" In the seventeenth century this could safely be asked as a rhetorical question.

The intensity of interest in religious matters is reflected in another special quality of this literature—its conviction, its commitment, even what could be called its contentiousness. Concerning religion there seem to have been no "academic questions" (a term which would, I think, have been quite incomprehensible to most of these writers), nothing of indifference, no dead issues. In an age when men were willing to go to war or to prison to defend their faith, they argued with passion questions which a modern reader might too easily dismiss as indifferent. So compelling was the urge to battle that, paradoxically, even when Sir Thomas Browne pleaded for an end to religious argument, he was himself arguing contentiously:

> Every man is not a proper Champion for Truth, nor fit to take up the Gauntlet in the cause of Verity: Many from the ignorance of these Maximes, and an inconsiderate Zeal unto Truth, have too rashly charged the Troops of Error, and remain as Trophies unto the enemies of Truth: A man may be in as just possession of Truth as of a City, and yet be forced to surrender; 'tis therefore far better to enjoy her with peace, than to hazzard her on a battle. . . . (page 64)

To write this in the 1630's was to take sides in a bitter argument over religious toleration, an issue which actively entered the lives of most seventeenth-century Englishmen (virtually all the writers in this volume were imprisoned, ejected from their livings, or persecuted in some way by their religious opponents).

Seventeenth-century writers expressed passionate conviction, and in a variety of tones of voice—not always solemn but often scornful, sarcastic, furious, playful, ironic, sophisticated, sweet

—sometimes in accents which to the modern reader less secure in his attitude toward religion seem indecorous, even irreverent. In controversy or in preaching or in prayer they were remarkably free to speak in the accents of individual human beings who themselves felt the pressure of what they wrote. Within a single paragraph, then, we often hear tones of exalted reverence mingling with the expression of what Milton in *Animadversions* called "those two most rationall faculties of humane intellect anger and laughter."

The intensity of concern with religion was a symptom and perhaps also a cause of another historical condition which the twentieth-century reader of these works must come to recognize. Religion in the seventeenth century was virtually inseparable from other systems of thought, other institutions, other kinds of experience. At least until the late years of the century, religious concerns were reflected in every form of literature, appeared in almost every piece of writing. There was virtually no consistent division between "sacred" and "secular" matters because all experience was permeated by religion and religion included all experience. The interest rates to be charged by money-lenders was a religious question; the tenure of kings and magistrates was argued on theological grounds; the theatres of London were the subject of pious attack; the defeat of the Armada was attributed (by Browne among others) to direct heavenly intervention, and the imprisonment of George Fox was thought to have infected his enemies with the plague. The areas of experience which we distinguish as "secular" were interpreted in religious terms, and conversely, religious concerns penetrated, *became,* finance, politics, philosophy, science. The existence of bishops involved economic interests (as the Presbyterians liked to point out); willingness to take the Holy Communion according to the rites of the Anglican Church was for a time the test for eligibility to hold public office; the existence of God was a premise of all systems of knowledge (perhaps excepting the philosophy of Thomas Hobbes, which was therefore almost universally abhorred and attacked); Genesis was a chief source of geological fact.

The absence of anything consistently like a modern separation of "sacred" and "secular" matters explains (or is explained by) another characteristic of seventeenth-century religious thought.

Religion not only pervaded or included the whole of experience. It was the interpreter of all experience. Until the late seventeenth century, for almost all Englishmen, religion was not one possible source of truth among alternatives, but the Truth, by which all other possible sources were to be judged. The fundamentals of the faith were unquestioned assumptions: the existence of God, his creation of Adam and Eve in his own image, their fall and promised redemption by Christ. These beliefs were shared by every writer in this volume, and by their readers. These were the givens in any system or argument (perhaps again excepting that of Hobbes, who yet pretended at least to accept them).

For example, in the following passage from the first part of the *Religio Medici*, Sir Thomas Browne speculated about the nature of the soul. Browne was an admirer of Sir Francis Bacon and a physician trained at the universities most advanced in medical studies—Montpellier, Padua, and Leyden. He was here self-consciously attempting to use the sort of observation or experiment (here specifically anatomical dissection), urged by Bacon as a source of truths about God's creation, in support of what turns before our eyes into a kind of logical proof of a tenet of faith:

In our study of Anatomy there is a mass of mysterious Philosophy, and such as reduced the very Heathens to Divinity; yet amongst all those rare discoveries and curious pieces I find in the Fabrick of man, I do not so much content my self, as in that I find not, there is no Organ or Instrument for the rational soul: for in the brain, which we term the seat of reason, there is not any thing of moment more than I can discover in the crany of a beast: and this is a sensible and no inconsiderable argument of the inorganity of the Soul, at least in the sense we usually so receive it. (page 95)

Scientific experiment, it is evident here, had nothing like its modern priority, was by no means the test of religious truth or an alternative to it (as William Harvey, a somewhat earlier seventeenth-century physician, must have recognized when his medical practice declined after his shockingly unorthodox demonstration of the circulation of the blood). Browne's experimental knowledge of anatomy did not challenge the axioms of his religion, but by a piece of faulty logic was made to support them. The existence of the soul was unquestioned truth; the absence of any experimental evidence for its existence simply proved its immateriality.

Or, to take another illustration, Thomas Traherne, in the following passage from paragraph 8 of "The Third Century" of his *Meditations,* was attempting to define the nature of man in the light of his own experience, but his own experience was characteristically interpreted in Biblical images:

> From whence I clearly find how Docible our Nature is in natural Things, were it rightly entreated. And that our Misery proceedeth ten thousand times more from the outward Bondage of Opinion and Custom, then from any inward corruption or Depravation of Nature: And that it is not our Parents Loyns, so much as our Parents lives, that Enthrals and Blinds us. Yet is all our Corruption Derived from Adam: inasmuch as all the Evil Examples and inclinations of the World arise from His Sin. But I speak it in the presence of GOD and of our Lord Jesus Christ, in my Pure Primitive Virgin Light, while my Apprehensions were natural, and unmixed, I can not remember, but that I was ten thousand times more prone to Good and Excellent Things, then evil. But I was quickly tainted and fell by others. (pages 218–219)

We find in this passage the intensity of conviction (in the repeated exaggeration of "ten thousand times" for example, or the solemn testimony before God and Christ) and also the contentiousness characteristic of seventeenth-century religious writing. For Traherne was here fighting against the traditional interpretation of man's nature, set forth in this volume most elaborately in Donne's *Second Sermon on Psal. 38.4.* Traherne was attempting to refute the orthodox view that "Adams punishment is pardoned in *no man,* in this world" because we are all born into this world "under the weight of Originall sinne." By arguing that his own recollections of childhood contradicted this view of human nature, he seems in a sense to have rejected religious assumptions which did not survive the test of experience, and therefore to make experience itself the highest authority for truth. Yet even that immediate experience itself was seen in Biblical images: "all our Corruption Derived from Adam," and "I was quickly tainted and fell by others." In attempting to adjust his definition of human nature to his own sense of himself, Traherne reinterpreted religious doctrine without rejecting it. He did not substitute a "secular" for a "sacred" view of man's nature. He transposed Biblical images without questioning their historical truth or their relevance to himself. He was therefore arguing against Donne's view of man at the same time that he shared many of Donne's unquestioned assumptions. He too believed, for example, that man in his original condition could not have been as stupid and vicious as he now is, because man was created by God, and God could create only what is good. Like Donne (and the other writers in this anthology) Traherne believed that Adam was the first man in history and the archetype of all men, that Adam "fell," that his fall was both the cause and the pattern for the experience of all other men, that our condition is "Misery" because we follow Adam.

Religious writers of the seventeenth century, then, shared with each other and their readers certain habits of mind and feeling which distinguish them from most of their modern readers. The expression of these habits of mind and feeling in a language very different from our own is what strikes us most forcibly about much of this writing. We are also struck, however, by lively differences among the works themselves, differences which can be explained in various ways, by reference to various sorts of causes.

Most obviously, the religious writers of the seventeenth century differed from one another in spiritual temperament. Browne's whimsy sounds quite different from Donne's wit, Taylor's melancholy from the meditative sweetness of Traherne, the earnestness of Baxter from the urgency of Bunyan, George Herbert's gravity from Whichcote's. Other differences among religious writings can be attributed to demands of genre. Devotions and meditations could more easily accommodate intimate uses of language than could a public sermon. A spiritual autobiography like *Grace Abounding* differed in shape and emphasis from an autobiographical treatise (written in the third person) like the life of Augustine Baker or from a journal such as that of Fox. Polemical tracts like those of Milton persuaded with a rhetoric different from Baxter's in his exhortations to virtue.

Such varieties of spiritual temperament or of genre can explain many of the differences among the works included in this volume. Other differences can be explained only as expressions of the revolutionary changes in the religious life of Englishmen, changes that took place within the experience of these writers. From the distance of several hundred years it is possible to look back upon the religious upheavals in England without realizing their impact upon individual men. It is easy to recall in large terms England's break with the Church of Rome in the sixteenth century, and the Puritan revolt against the Church of England in the seventeenth century without imagining how such movements shaped the lives and attitudes of men who experienced them. Yet we must perform this imaginative act in order to respond to the differences in their language which express these revolutionary changes.

Although none of these writers was yet living in 1533–4, when Henry VIII made the Church of England finally independent of the Pope, Lancelot Andrewes was born during the return to the Roman Church under Mary Tudor (1553–1558) while many others, themselves born during the reign of Elizabeth (1558–1603), must have had a mixed religious training something of the kind described by Augustine Baker, the only one of these writers to remain in the Roman Catholic Church of his forbears. In Baker's memory, twelve years or so after the succession of Elizabeth, his parents,

. . . with thousands of others that likewise in their younger years had bin professors of the Catholick religion (besides those that proved enemies thereto, as being Protestants) in tract of time and *sensim,* and indeed as it were unawares to themselves, became neutrals in religion, viz. neither indeed true Catholicks, for perfect knowledg, belief, and practice, nor yet meer Protestants or otherwise hereticks in their belief, though schismaticall, by their external accommodation of themselves to the schismaticall service of the English Church. (page 234)

Therefore although among these writers only Baker and Donne (before his conversion) were themselves Roman Catholics, most of them were the children or grandchildren of Christians who had worshipped in what to their descendants was the church of the enemy. Andrewes, George Herbert, eventually Donne, became priests of the Church of England in the flourishing period after its Settlement, and they spoke with a conscious sense of belonging to the established Church that continued to characterize Anglican writing during and even after the Civil Wars (a consciousness evident in this volume in the language of Browne,

Taylor, Barrow, Sprat, and Tillotson). They spoke characteristically as members of an order more extensive than the individual conscience—a national ecclesiastical order which in its own terms reflected the relation of individual men to the larger order of the creation. When Donne in Meditation 17 of the *Devotions* wrote of his relationship to this order, his metaphors were borrowed from Scripture and the Creed and his deepest assumptions may have been those of virtually all seventeenth-century Christians, but his emphasis was distinctively Anglican:

> The *Church* is *Catholicke, universall,* so are all her *Actions; All* that she does, belongs to *all.* When she *baptizes a child,* that action concerns mee; for that child is therefore connected to that *Head* which is my *Head* too, and engraffed into that *body,* whereof I am a *member.* And when she *buries a Man,* that action concernes me: All *mankinde* is of one *Author,* and is one *volume* . . . No man is an *Iland,* intire of it selfe; every man is a peece of the *Continent,* a part of the *maine* . . . (pages 52–53)

This consciousness of identification with an inclusive order— natural, social, political, as well as spiritual—is (to generalize rashly) a distinguishing mark of seventeenth-century Anglican writers, inherited from their predecessor, Richard Hooker (1554– 1600), the first great spokesman for the established Church. In *Of the Laws of Ecclesiastical Polity* he celebrated the larger order of which Anglicans felt themselves to be members, an order which benevolently included the whole of creation within its law. Book I concludes with what is almost a hymn to universal harmony:

> Wherefore that here we may briefly end: of Law there can be no less acknowledged, than that her seat is the bosom of God, her voice the harmony of the world: all things in heaven and earth do her homage, the very least as feeling her care, and the greatest as not exempted from her power: both Angels and men and creatures of what condition soever, though each in different sort and manner, yet all with uniform consent, admiring her as the mother of their peace and joy.

Despite the assurance of Hooker's style, however, even in the 1590's this order seemed to promise no easy security. Even the Church's first spokesman felt its foundations shaken by the impulse to reformation that soon exploded in England. The opening sentence of the Preface to Hooker's work was a forboding preface to the seventeenth century:

> Though for no other cause, yet for this; that posterity may know we have not loosely through silence permitted things to pass away as in a dream, there shall be for men's information extant thus much concerning the present state of the Church of God established amongst us, and their careful endeavour which would have upheld the same.

Already in 1593 Hooker spoke of the Anglican Establishment as an order belonging to the past, which its supporters "would have upheld" had they been able to withstand the forces of reform. Hooker's foreboding was truly prophetic. The impulse that (to generalize even more rashly) distinguished Milton, Baxter, Bunyan, Fox, and in some sense Benjamin Whichcote as dissenters from the Anglican Church was not to be resisted. No order however inclusive could withstand their insistence on the inwardness of religion, the sanctity of the private conscience, the authority of the inner light.

This impulse was irresistible; the direction in which it moved men can be illustrated by the religious history of John Milton. Born in 1608, Milton was baptized (like all Englishmen then except the children of a few stubborn Catholic families such as Donne's) a member of the Church of England, "to whose service," he said in the *Reason of Church Government:*

> . . . by the intentions of my parents and friends I was destin'd of a child, and in mine own resolutions, till comming to some maturity of yeers and perceaving what tyranny had invaded the Church, that he who would take Orders must subscribe slave, and take an oath withall, which unlesse he took with a conscience that would retch, he must either strait perjure, or split his faith, I thought it better to preferre a blamelesse silence before the sacred office of speaking bought, and begun with servitude and forswearing. (page 159)

Thus "Church-outed by the Prelates" who were enacting the program of Archbishop Laud, Milton moved toward the position of the Presbyterians (for whose cause he wrote the anti-prelatical tracts quoted in this anthology) in opposing episcopacy. But he came to distrust his party, which seemed to him as much the enemy of freedom for the private conscience as had the Anglicans. His conscience drove him then to join the more liberal independents, and finally to the position of extreme separatism: the believer's conscience became church, priest, and congregation to itself. This was his final position, expressed in the opening words of his theological treatise *Of Christian Doctrine:* "John Milton Englishman to all the Churches of Christ."

This was the farthest extreme to which the reforming impulse could drive men's consciences. It was the extreme which Hooker foresaw and feared, and his prevision came true. Once the appeal to inward conviction was allowed, or in the hostile words of Hooker, "when the minds of men are once erroneously persuaded that it is the will of God to have those things done which they fancy," there were no foreseeable limits to religious individualism. Milton could declare himself a Church, Bunyan could declare himself a Preacher. Moreover Bunyan, even after he became a preacher, could continue to identify himself as a representative of a humble, semi-literate rural class who in the early seventeenth century might have had preachers like George Herbert (Rector of Bemerton) to direct their spiritual lives, but who had to survive the revolution of the mid-seventeenth century to find spokesmen (such as Bunyan and Fox) to express their own attitudes in their own language. The movement which carried Milton and Bunyan away from the Anglican Church to the extreme position of dissent was irreversible. The possibility of such an order as Hooker had celebrated, which would include the entire nation as members of one *"Catholicke, universall"* Church, was destroyed forever.

Religious writers of the seventeenth century were involved in these large movements of history, and their involvement helps to explain many of the differences we find among their works, which cannot simply be explained by differences in spiritual temperament or variations of literary genre. Such differences in their works distinguish these writers as belonging to different traditions of religious language and attitude which separated and hardened into enemy factions during the upheavals of the seventeenth century. They are the expression of deep and deeply felt disagreements among religious parties (which were also political alliances and even social classes) that shattered forever the order whose destruction Richard Hooker had prophesied.

.   .   .

There are, however, certain other differences among the works included in this volume which can be explained neither by the writer's disposition nor choice of genre, nor by his allegiance to one of the factions dividing English believers of the seventeenth century. These are recognizable differences between early seventeenth-century prose style and the language of writers after the Restoration, and they are large differences. Donne, Andrewes, and Herbert, for example, wrote a language quite unlike our own, while Barrow, Sprat, and Tillotson sound far less foreign to us, as though a much longer time than half a century had passed between them and the earlier writers. That is to say, we have seen that these writers are all unlike us in their habits of thought as in their enthusiasms, yet we can also see the seventeenth century as a period divided not only by sectarian battles that now seem remote, but by profound changes in attitude that have continued to affect language even to our own time. The implication is that whatever religious assumptions these writers may have shared as seventeenth-century Englishmen, as Protestants, as priests of the Anglican Church, they must have differed in other of their presuppositions. Some transformations of thought and feeling in the seventeenth century must have wrought these changes in language; in certain of their fundamental notions Barrow or Tillotson must have differed from Donne and Andrewes even as we do (though far less radically).

To define some of these changes and the transformations of attitude they express, it will be illuminating to contrast in detail a passage written in the first quarter of the century with a passage from a later work, to set Meditation 10 of Donne's *Devotions* (page 49) beside a quotation from Barrow's sermon "Of the Goodness of God" (page 244).

Donne's tenth Meditation begins with a generalization about the order of the universe, and proceeds through a series of assertions about the nature of that order. Yet the language in which these generalized assertions are made does not have the qualities we have come to expect of philosophical (or theological) discourse. The Meditation begins abruptly, like many of Donne's poems, as if in the middle of things. And at once we are surrounded by metaphor:

This is *Natures nest of Boxes;* The Heavens containe the *Earth,* the *Earth, Cities, Cities, Men.* And all these are *Concentrique;* the common *center* to them all, is *decay, ruine;* only that is *Eccentrique,* which was never made; only that place, or garment rather, which we can *imagine,* but not *demonstrate* . . .

Metaphor is not used here to illustrate some abstract proposition, as it would be, for example, if the sentence read: "Nature is a nest of boxes because the heavens contain the earth, the earth contains cities, cities contain men." In such a sentence, the statement "Nature is a nest of boxes" actually means to us, "Nature may be spoken of as a nest of boxes." Virtually no literal force is given to the equation because metaphor is only a "way of talking"; it has no necessity of its own. Donne's metaphors, however, have quite different implications. They are not merely a "way of talking," of illustrating some prior meaning. For when Donne asserted that "the frame of the heavens, the states upon earth, and men in them" are all *"Concentrique,"* he used metaphor because he conceived the physical order he was describing to be naturally charged with moral or theological meaning. All things in creation are *in fact* concentric; that fact is not neutral, not in itself empty of meanings other than physical, and therefore cannot be talked about in neutral terms. When he lamented that the center of this circular universe is "ruine," his metaphor coincided with the *fact* of universal decay, for the earth is its center —the earth which was ruined by Adam's fall and which will be annihilated with all things earthly at the end of time.

The implications of this style may seem obscure, because modern prose does not use words this way, but in a later passage of the *Devotions* Donne gave a kind of explanation of his own figurative style which reveals its foundation. In the nineteenth Expostulation he exclaimed:

My God, my *God,* Thou art a *direct God,* may I not say a *literall God,* a *God* that wouldst bee understood *literally,* and according to the *plain sense* of all thou saist? But thou art also (*Lord* I intend it to thy *glory,* and let no *profane misinterpreter* abuse it to thy *diminution*) thou art a *figurative,* a *metaphoricall God* too: A *God* in whose words there is such a height of *figures,* such *voyages,* such *peregrinations* to fetch remote and precious *metaphors* . . . as all profane *Authors,* seemed the seed of the *Serpent* that creepes, thou art the

Dove, that flies. . . . Neither art thou thus a *figurative,* a *metaphori-call God* in thy *word* only, but in thy *works* too. The *stile* of thy *works,* the *phrase* of thine *actions,* is *metaphorical.*

Metaphor was justified not only by the exemplary figures of the Bible, but by the metaphorical "stile" of the creation. Not only Scripture—the Book of God's Words—but the universe—the Book of God's Works—provided the writer with true metaphors, because God was its Author and therefore everything in the universe was intended (as we think of works of literature to be intended) by a Mind whose plan endowed everything with inherent meaning. Donne's metaphors are therefore not illustrations but assertions, definitions. In fact, the entire passage is metaphorical; even the connections between one stage of the argument and another depend less upon logic than upon repetitions and variations of metaphor. For example, the first section of the Meditation expands the metaphor of a universe of concentric circles whose center is ruin. The second section opens with another general statement about the nature of this universe:

In all these (the *frame of the heavens,* the *States upon earth,* and *Men in them,* comprehend all) Those are the greatest mischifs, which are least discerned: the most insensible in their *wayes* come to bee the most sensible in their *ends.*

The reference of the phrase "all these" is the only explicit connection between this general proposition and the opening metaphor, and it is a grammatical connection that only appears to be a logical connection. For there is no necessary logical connection between the fact that all things by nature sink to annihilation and the notion that hidden dangers are worse than recognized threats. As the second proposition is developed, however, certain other kinds of connections with the opening metaphor are expanded. The identification of dangers in nature—"flood" and "fire"—with sickness, the reiteration of the words "dropsie" and "fever," then their parallel with "deadly" secrets in societies, and with hidden "diseases" of the body, repeats the pattern of concentric circles whose center is "decay, ruine." This way of developing an argument by associated patterns of metaphor imitated the connections among creatures in the universe and also the movement of the mind as it apprehended those connections. That is to say, the mind of man who is inside *"Natures nest of boxes"* itself works metaphorically. Because he is not *"Eccentrique"* to the world of created things, man can think only in its terms and its terms are metaphorical. Even when he attempts to define what is outside the *"Concentrique"* circles of created things, he can do so only in metaphorical language. In Donne's words:

> . . . only that is *Eccentrique,* which was never made; only that place, or garment rather, which we can *imagine,* but not *demonstrate,* That light, which is the very emanation of the light of *God,* in which the *Saints* shall dwell, with which the *Saints* shall be appareld, only that bends not to this *Center,* to *Ruine;* that which was not made of *Nothing,* is not threatned with this annihilation.

Because man thinks metaphorically, he thinks feelingly. He apprehends the meanings inherent in the universe not by his powers of abstract reasoning but by what he can *"imagine,"* his feelings, his response to sights and sounds. Donne's argument moves then by patterns of imagery supported by sound effects ("the *f*ire, the *f*ever, shall burne the *f*urnace itsel*f*e") designed to express the changing feelings of the speaker and to evoke answering changes of feeling in the reader. To apprehend meanings in God's creation one must not be dispassionate, for the creation itself is charged with moral or theological significance, and therefore also with feeling.

The passage from Barrow makes a pointed contrast because it concerns roughly the same large subject, the order of the universe and man's relation to it. Like Donne, Barrow assumed that there *is* an order to the universe because it was created by God, that man was appointed to a place in that order which has moral significance, that this significance is revealed to him in the nature of the creation itself (of which he is both member and observer) and in the supernatural revelations of Scripture. These assumptions, we have said, were shared by all religious writers and their readers throughout the seventeenth century. What concerns us now are the transformations of attitude which must have taken place between the first quarter of the seventeenth century and its later years, for despite the common assumptions which they reveal, Donne and Barrow are remarkably unlike, and in ways that cannot be explained by differences in temperament, choice of genre, or religious affiliation. The significant contrasts between Donne's language and Barrow's could be made in almost the same terms between a great many early and late seventeenth-century texts (for example, in this volume, between the style of Herbert or Andrewes and that of Sprat or Tillotson).

The passage from Barrow's sermon opens, as Donne's tenth Meditation opens, with a general assertion about the order of creation:

There is no argument from natural effects discernible by us, which proveth God's existence (and innumerable such there are, every sort of things well studied may afford some), the which doth not together persuade God to be very kind and benign; careful to impart to us all befitting good, suitable to our natural capacity and condition; and unwilling that any considerable harm, any extreme want or pain should befall us.

We are in a different world from Donne's concentric universe. Although we could not mistake this for a piece of modern writing, it fulfills many of our expectations about the kind of language suited to generalized assertions about philosophical (or theological) questions. Most obviously this language is not essentially figurative. The diction is for the most part abstract—"natural effects" have replaced *Natures nest of boxes.* In the entire passage from Barrow's sermon printed on pages 244–245, there are in fact only four expressions, unconnected with one another, which could be called metaphorical: "footsteps of admirable wisdom, skill, and design," "undistempered mind," "blind chance, or as blind necessity," and "dim sight." Of these, the last three have virtually no force as metaphors. In fact, "undistempered" may mean literally "free from sickness," but even if it is understood figuratively, Barrow's expression works as if it were an abstract statement meaning "the state of being well." He seems deliberately to have avoided the evocative qualities with which Donne charged his metaphors of infection and disease. The one surely metaphorical phrase in this passage—"the manifold and manifest footsteps of admirable wisdom, skill, and design apparent in the general order"—has dimly Biblical connotations, but we are not otherwise encouraged to respond to "footsteps" except as an abstract expression meaning "imprint" or "remaining sign."

This avoidance of evocative suggestions in Barrow's language can perhaps most easily be seen if we compare his metaphor with its ancestor in Bacon's "The Plan of the Work" attached to *The Great Instauration:*

> For God forbid that we should give out a dream of our own imagination for a pattern of the world; rather may he graciously grant to us to write an apocalypse or true vision of the footsteps of the Creator imprinted on his creatures.

Bacon's "footsteps" convey an impression of vastness and power because they suggest some gigantic figure striding across, then leaving, a world of his own making. But Barrow avoided all such suggestions by attaching "footsteps" to "admirable wisdom, skill, and design" which have no suggestions of shape or motion, evoke no impressions dependent upon their physical nature.

Barrow's assertions about the order of the universe are not dependent on metaphor, like Donne's. Characteristically they are abstract statements, and they are correspondingly less charged with feeling. The speaker seems almost to present himself as a dispassionate observer, as if impassioned conviction and personal commitment were no longer felt to be guarantees of, but rather obstacles to, the service of truth. His statements are measured, never extravagant, continually qualified: "unwilling that any *considerable* harm, any *extreme* pain," "*Most* of them," "*some* beneficial tendency." He modifies and explains his statements in a number of parentheses, and repeatedly claims support for his assertions from trained observation or logical induction: "discernible," "well studied," "all things being duly stated and computed," "no less convincing than obvious," "it is hardly possible that," "no less evident," "be reasonably presumed," "as upon consideration." His appeal is to the "unprejudiced and undistempered mind" or to "any man not careless or stupid," and the structure of his sentences supports this appeal. They are calmly balanced with logical connections between ideas made explicit, and their effect is of rational control. We hear admiration and even awe in Barrow's praise of order, but the passage also suggests detachment, freedom from the pressures of feeling characteristically expressed by the speaker in Donne's *Devotions.*
This distinction cannot be simply charged to the differing de-

mands of meditations and sermons, as a comparison with the following quotation from Donne's *Second Sermon on Psal. 38.4* makes clear:

> And what a cloud upon the best serenity of my conscience, what an interruption, what a dis-continuance from the sincerity and integrity of that joy, which belongs to a man truly reconciled to God, in the pardon of his former sins, must it needs be still to know, and to know by lamentable experiences, that though I wash my selfe with Soap, and Nitre, and Snow-water, mine own cloathes will defile me again, though I have washed my selfe in the tears of Repentance, and in the blood of my Saviour, though I have no guiltiness of any former sin upon me at that present, yet I have a sense of a *root* of sin, that is not grub'd up, of *Originall sinne,* that will cast me back again. (page 33)

Barrow seems deliberately to have avoided the impression of an individual voice speaking feelingly out of particular "experiences," not simply because he was writing a public sermon rather than a private meditation, not because he was (though this is obviously true) temperamentally quite unlike Donne, but for the same reason that he did not use Donne's kind of metaphorical language. He had a quite different view of the creation and man's relation to it as creature and observer, and this view distinguishes him as a late seventeenth-century writer.

Barrow's language is not essentially figurative because the order which he was attempting to define was not conceived to be a book written by God in a metaphorical "style." It was conceived as a vast arrangement of "natural effects" of causes which may not be easily "discernible," but which may be "reasonably presumed" to work according to regular laws. Man, according to Barrow, cannot know every particular of this system because he is one of the creatures within it, not its creator, but he can observe its order, as Donne's speaker can exist within, yet at the same time define *"Natures nest of boxes."* Their modes of observation are quite unlike, however. Barrow does not "imagine" this order by its definition in metaphor; he tries to induce it according to logical principles based upon "unprejudiced" observation. The order of God's creation, to Barrow, can best be defined by abstract statements: the mind by its powers of abstract reasoning traces the nature of that order from the concrete, visible signs which are its "natural effects," and defines it by laws or categories.

. . .

The large contrasts between Donne's language and Barrow's represent the large differences between early and late seventeenth-century prose. Any generalization of course immediately suggests exceptions, and we may think at once of two religious writers—Thomas Traherne and John Bunyan—whose characteristic uses of language seem to challenge this generalization. For the *Centuries of Meditations* and *Pilgrim's Progress* by their richly figurative prose suggest affinities with Donne's style rather than Barrow's. Yet attention to the precise nature of Traherne's images, of Bunyan's allegory, reveals that these writers shared habits of language and therefore assumptions more closely resembling those of Barrow, their contemporary, than of Donne and the earlier religious writers. Traherne and Bunyan are perhaps the most surprising, but therefore perhaps also the most convincing illustrations of the pervasive influence of new preconceptions on the language of later seventeenth-century writers.

Traherne, perhaps because he wrote devotional lyric poetry as well as prose, has usually been studied in relation to his predecessors—Donne, George Herbert and Henry Vaughan—rather than to his later seventeenth-century contemporaries. Even his prose style, especially in those paragraphs most often reprinted, seems at first to contradict our description of later seventeenth-century language, not only by its rapturous tone, but its profuse imagery. The best known example is paragraph 3 of "The Third Century" (page 216) beginning with a radiant metaphor: "The Corn was Orient and Immortal Wheat, which never should be reaped, nor was ever sown." The rest of the passage is full of images, but it is not metaphorical in anything like the way in which Donne's prose is metaphorical. To begin with, there are only two more formal metaphors in the entire paragraph, and one of them—"The Gates were at first the End of the World"—is so qualified by the words "at first" that we read it as a non-metaphorical statement meaning "The Gates then *seemed to me* to be the End of the World." Our attention is thus called to the metaphor as a "way of talking," a point of view, not a definition of the actual nature of created things in the Book of God's Works. The other expression is in form a metaphor: "Boys and Girls tumbling in the Street, and Playing, were moving Jewels." It works, however, almost as Barrow's "footsteps" works, to illustrate rather than to

vented to represent are distinctly separate, so that they cannot be apprehended simultaneously, as the terms in Donne's metaphors must be apprehended. For Donne, physical experiences naturally and inevitably implied moral or theological meanings. Sickness was sin, sin was sickness, so that the story of his sickness and recovery was *at the same time* the story of his fall and redemption: the same language must be used for both. In contrast, the allegorical style of *Pilgrim's Progress* does not encourage us to see physical experiences as inevitably, by their nature, expressing inherent moral or theological meanings. On the contrary, we are made to see the events of the story as signs *pointing* to meanings outside themselves, or as pictures, emblems, *representing* something other than themselves.

The distinction can be illustrated by the first incident of Christian's journey, his struggle in the Slough of Dispond (pages 179–181). The episode is presented in simple narrative terms: two men, walking along a plain, fail to look where they are going and so fall into a bog, from which one escapes but into which the other nearly sinks until a third man pulls him out. The language here refers consistently to physical things. Only the names—Dispond, Christian, Pliable, Help—refer to moral qualities or conditions, but their moral or theological meanings are apparently unknown to the characters who fall in the mire. The incident is treated by them and initially by the narrator as if it were a morally meaningless though disturbing accident. But of course the meanings of the names tell the reader that this is actually not a neutral report of an accident that happened to two travellers; it is a moral allegory in which nothing is neutral, in which everything was invented to *illustrate* a meaning. What these meanings are we can guess partly by the names themselves, but the detailed interpretation is worked out for us in several paragraphs following the episode: we learn about "conviction for sin," the sinner's "lost condition," his "many fears, and doubts, and discouraging apprehensions" and various other moral and theological qualities or conditions. The episode and the explanation of it are given in different kinds of language and the distinction between them is absolute. To maintain the distinction, the character to whom the accident happened must be sent away before the interpretation can be given: the narrator then illogically enters his own dream-story to ask Help for an explanation of the episode. Between the episode and its meaning the connection can only exist in the mind of the author, who first invented the "similitude," and then in the mind of the reader who, by retranslating, discovers its meaning. No necessary connection with the moral or theological meaning exists in the literal events of the story itself (we are not intended to think that Christian falls into the mud as a result of feeling sinful nor that because he falls into the mud he feels sinful in consequence) and the abstract meaning can be apprehended in its own terms without necessary definition in "similitudes." The allegory is therefore only a "way of talking" about the prior meanings which it illustrates.

Again the contrast with Donne's *Devotions* is illuminating. There we are asked to believe in the *fact* of the speaker's illness as well as its meaning. (Donne actually did have such an experience, but it is characteristic of his writing elsewhere to pretend that the dramatic situation is really happening in present time.) The physical fact of illness is naturally charged with moral or theological meaning precisely because the illness was not a literary invention of the author, but of God, a metaphor in the Book of His Works. Bunyan's reader, in contrast, is continually discouraged from accepting the physical terms of the allegory as anything but inventions of the writer pointing to meanings beyond themselves. The story is only a dream; it is full of unexplained coincidences and fantastic adventures, and even those episodes which could actually happen (if travellers fail to look where they are going they do sometimes fall into bogs) are not told with the sort of substantiating detail that a writer uses when he intends to persuade the reader of their physical actuality. As a result, the reader is continually reminded of the need to go beyond the literal story in order to discover the moral or theological meanings which it was invented (not by God but by the writer) to represent. Like Barrow's rare uses of metaphor, like Traherne's descriptive comparisons, Bunyan's allegory is an illustration of prior meaning, existing outside itself, not a necessary definition of meanings inherent in the metaphorical order of creation.

Some of the far-reaching implications of this transformation of attitudes in later seventeenth-century writings are suggested by another passage from *Pilgrim's Progress*—the curious episode in which Christian is mysteriously relieved of his burden. The passage is especially revealing because of its peculiarities, which show the pressure of what we have called later seventeenth-century habits of mind upon the form of Bunyan's allegory:

> He ran thus till he came at a place somewhat ascending; and upon that place stood a *Cross,* and a little below in the bottom a Sepulcher. So I saw in my Dream, that just as *Christian* came up with the *Cross,* his burden loosed from off his Shoulders, and fell from off his back; and began to tremble; and so continued to do, till it came to the mouth of the Sepulcher, where it fell in, and I saw it no more.
>
> Then was *Christian* glad and lightsom, and said with a merry heart, He hath given me rest, by his sorrow; and life, by his death. Then he stood still a while, to look and wonder; for it was very surprizing to him, that the sight of the Cross should thus ease him of his burden.

This passage could not have been written early in the seventeenth century. It could only be the work of a religious writer whose language had been transformed by new attitudes such as those implied also in the writing of Barrow and Traherne. In this episode, the separation in Bunyan's mode of thinking between physical "similitude" and its moral or theological meaning has some extraordinary effects. One such effect is characteristic of the whole work wherever Bunyan is consistent in following the demands of his allegorical form. It is characteristic that Christian should "wonder" and find "surprizing" an event which is understandable to the reader, because the reader can translate it into its theological meaning as Christian, by the logic of the allegory, cannot. For Christian is logically confined (as we saw in the first episode) within the physical world of the narrative: as a "similitude" himself, he cannot properly know the moral or theological meanings which he and his experiences were invented to represent, without ceasing to be a figure in an allegory. The curious result, here as in other passages where Bunyan follows the demands of his form, is that Christian goes through what is supposed to be a momentous religious experience, without being capable of understanding its moral meaning.

This is not to say that the "similitude" named *Christian* is a blank. On the contrary, here and throughout the book, Bunyan's hero is a lively and attractive figure who with admirable practical energy confronts the trials of his world and responds to his experiences freshly, "with a merry heart," with "wonder," tears, fright, joy, annoyance, comprehension, a range of believable human responses. What is curious is that they are responses to the physical world of the narrative, but not to the moral or theological meanings for which that world is a "similitude." In the first episode, for example, Christian learns that it is dangerous to walk "heedless" of your way because you may "fall suddenly into the bogg," and if you have a burden on your back weighing you down, you may not be able to climb out. He learns that this is a frightening experience. He does not learn anything about the nature of "Dispond." There is no dramatic connection possible in this allegorical language between immediate experience and such moral or theological qualities or conditions as "Dispond." As a result, Bunyan found it necessary as the narrative advanced to violate more and more often the formal demands of his allegory. Increasingly often, Christian is allowed to listen to moral or theological interpretations of his physical experiences; more and more often he is made to demonstrate knowledge of the religious meanings for which he and his world are "similitudes." The intention of these violations of the allegorical form, it appears, is to transform Christian into a morally responsible figure who shares with the reader and the author a knowledge of the meanings represented by the allegory. It seems to me, however, that Bunyan's allegorical form finally prevents this transformation. Even in later episodes, when illogically Christian is made to demonstrate knowledge of the moral or theological significance of the allegory, he is still involved in physical events which, by their improbability and by their definition as images in a dream, are seen as inventions of the author, not to be taken as literally true. Therefore, however much Christian may be allowed to know about the moral meaning of his physical experiences, those experiences, and even the figure of Christian himself, are not actually to be believed. They are still recognizable as inventions of the author designed to illustrate meanings outside themselves.

The separation between "similitude" and meaning has still other effects, still more curious, which make this passage peculiarly revealing of Bunyan's assumptions. Here, as usual, the reader is repeatedly reminded to translate narrative details into abstractions by devices designed to make the episode itself seem improbable. The abruptness of the beginning and the phrase "just as *Christian* came up" heighten our sense of the magical or coincidental nature of the events: Christian happened to come upon a cross, which happened to stand above a sepulchre. We are not even told whether Christian's burden fell off just by coincidence when he came up to the cross, or because the cross had some mysterious power to loosen his burden. We are encouraged, therefore, to translate these invented improbabilities into moral or theological meanings, as we are throughout *Pilgrim's Progress*. What is extraordinary here, however, is that the Cross and the Sepulchre as physical objects in the narrative are made to seem part of the fantastic world of the dream—inventions which illustrate or point to some prior theological meanings. This effect surely could not have been intended by Bunyan (who unquestionably believed in the historical actuality of the Crucifixion) but it shows how compelling was the separation in his mode of thinking between physical "similitudes" and their moral or theological meanings. Even traditional Christian symbols divided for him into illustrations of abstractions with which they were connected only by authors who invent allegories, and their readers.

When Bunyan in his prefatory poem cited the style of Scripture as his model he was, it appears, expressing very different attitudes from those of Donne. Scripture was a model of style for Bunyan because of the meanings to which its figures pointed, not because its metaphors were in themselves a necessary definition of those meanings. By implication, then, for Bunyan there was a certain arbitrariness in the metaphors even of the Bible itself, as there was in the figurative inventions of human writers:

> *I find that holy Writ in many places,*
> *Hath semblance with this method, where the cases*
> *Doth call for one thing to set forth another* . . .

Metaphors to Bunyan were "feigned" words which could be arbitrarily selected to point to something else, which could be altered, therefore, or even omitted without damage to the definition of moral or theological meanings.

For Bunyan, as for Donne, Scripture provided a model for style, but no longer for a style in which language used about physical objects and experiences—metaphors in the Book of God's Works—inevitably expressed their inherent moral or theological meanings. Bunyan's mode of thinking could not be expressed in such a style. Instead he thought of Scripture as the model for a language in which "similitudes" drawn from the physical world of familiar daily trial could be used, almost arbitrarily, as a means of teaching less easily or pleasantly recognizable moral and theological meanings. Paradoxically, then, the writer whose prose is perhaps the most thoroughly saturated with Biblical echoes and quotations suggests some reasons why, with the passing of the seventeenth century, the language of Scripture ceased to represent the model for metaphorical definition of the meanings inherent in God's creation. Still more paradoxically, the period's most famous religious work in prose suggests, by the peculiar effects of its allegorical style, some of the reasons why after the late seventeenth-century religious literature ceased to be a chief imaginative expression of English writers. For in *Pilgrim's Progress* we can see, perhaps more strikingly than in any other work, the power of certain attitudes emerging in the later seventeenth century to transform earlier modes of metaphorical vision, and to transform them into ways of thinking that have continued to inform English prose style to our own time.

John Donne

*John Donne was born in London in 1572 of a Roman Catholic family.
He studied at Hart Hall, Oxford, from 1584 to 1587 and transferred
to Trinity College, Cambridge, in 1587, but received a degree from
neither university because of his religion. From 1592 he spent two
years studying law at Lincoln's Inn, London. He sailed with Essex's
expeditions against Cadiz and the Azores (1596, 1597), the following
year becoming Secretary to the Lord Keeper, Sir Thomas Egerton. In
1602 he was dismissed and imprisoned after the discovery of his
secret marriage to Egerton's niece, Anne More. From 1605, he spent
a decade first assisting Thomas Morton (later Bishop of Chichester,
Litchfield, Durham) in anti-Catholic polemical works, then writing
his own controversial prose:* Biathanatos, *composed in 1608;* Pseudo-
Martyr, *published in 1610;* Ignatius His Conclave, *published in 1611;
and* Essays in Divinity, *probably written in 1615. He was ordained
priest in the Church of England in 1615, acted as Reader in Divinity
at Lincoln's Inn from 1616 to 1622, was appointed Dean of St. Paul's
Cathedral in 1621, and, in 1624, Vicar of St. Dunstan's in the West.
Having lost his wife in 1617, he suffered a severe illness himself in
1623, which led to the composition of the* Devotions Upon Emergent
Occasions, *and a final illness in 1631.*

Second Sermon on Psal. 38.4

For mine iniquities are gone over my head,
as a heavy burden, they are too heavy for me.

As the Philosopher says, if a man could see *vertue*, he would
love it, so if a man could see *sin*, he would *hate* it. But the *eye*
sees every thing but *it selfe*, so does *sinne*, too. It sees *Beauty*,
and *Honour*, and *Riches*, but it sees not it selfe, not the sinfull
coveting, and compassing of all these. To make, though not sin,
yet the *sinner* to see himselfe, for the explication, and application of these words, we brought you these two lights; first, the
Multiplicity of sin, in that elegancy of the holy Ghost, *supergressæ sunt, Mine iniquities are gone over my head*, and the *weight*,
and *oppression* of sin, in that, *Gravatæ nimis, As a heavy burden
they are too heavy for me;* In the first, how *numerous*, how manifold they are, in the other, how grievous, how insupportable;
first, how many hands, then how fast hold sinne lays upon me.
The first of these two, was our exercise the last day, when we
proposed and proceeded in these words, in which we presented
to you, the dangerous multiplicity of sinne, in those pieces,
which constituted that part. But because, as men, how many
soever, make but a Multitude, or a Throng, and not an Army,
if they be unarmed, so sin, how manifold, and multiform so
ever, might seem a passable thing, if it might be easily shaked
off, we come now to imprint in you a sense of the *weight* and
oppression thereof, *As a heavy burthen, they are too heavy for
mee;* The particular degrees whereof, we laid down the last day,

in our generall division of the whole Text, and shall now pursue them, according to our order proposed then.

First then, sinne is *heavy*. Does not the sinner finde it so? No marvail, nothing is heavy in his proper place, in his own Sphear, in his own Center, when it is where it would be, nothing is heavy. He that lies under water finds no burthen of all that water that lies upon him; but if he were out of it, how heavy would a small quantity of that water seem to him, if he were to carry it in a vessel? An *habituall sinner* is the naturall place, the Center of sinne, and he feels no weight in it, but if the grace of God raise him out of it, that he come to walke, and walke in the ways of godlinesse, not onely his watery Tympanies,[1] and his dropsies, those waters which by actuall and habituall sinnes he hath contracted, but that water, of which he is properly made, the water that is in him naturally, infused from his parents, *Originall sinne*, will be sensible to him, and oppresse him. Scarce any man considers the weight of Originall sinne; And yet, as the strongest tentations fall upon us when wee are weakest, in our *death-bed*, so the heavyest sinne seises us, when wee are weakest; as soon as wee are any thing, we are sinners, and there, where there can be no more tentations ministred to us, then was to the Angels that fell in heaven, that is, in *our mothers womb*, when no world, nor flesh, nor Devill could present a provocation to sinne to us, when no faculty of ours is able to embrace, or second a provocation to sin, yet there, in that weaknesse, we are under the weight of Originall sin. And truly, if at this time, God would vouchsafe mee my choice, whether hee should pardon me all those actuall and habituall sins, which I have committed in my life, or extinguish Originall sinne in me, I should chuse to be delivered from Originall sin, because, though I be delivered from the *imputation* thereof, by *Baptism*, so that I shall not fall under a condemnation for Originall sin onely, yet it still remains in me, and practises upon me, and occasions all the other sins, that I commit: now, for all my actuall and habituall sins, I know God hath instituted meanes in his Church, the *Word*, and the *Sacraments*, for my reparation; But with what a holy alacrity, with what a heavenly joy, with what a cheerfull peace, should I come to the participation of these meanes and seals of my reconciliation, and pardon of all my sins, if I knew my selfe to

1 Tympanies: tumors, swellings

be delivered from Originall sinne, from that snake in my bosome, from that poyson in my blood, from that leaven and tartar
in all my actions, that casts me into Relapses of those sins which
I have repented? And what a cloud upon the best serenity of my
conscience, what an interruption, what a dis-continuance from
the sincerity and integrity of that joy, which belongs to a man
truly reconciled to God, in the pardon of his former sins, must
it needs be still to know, and to know by lamentable experiences, that though I wash my selfe with Soap, and Nitre, and
Snow-water, mine own cloathes will defile me again, though I
have washed my selfe in the tears of Repentance, and in the
blood of my Saviour, though I have no guiltinesse of any former
sin upon me at that present, yet I have a sense of a *root* of sin,
that is not grub'd up, of *Originall sinne,* that will cast me back
again. Scarce any man considers the weight, the oppression of
Originall sinne. No man can say, that an Akorn weighs as much
as an Oak; yet in truth, there is an Oak in that Akorn: no man
considers that Originall sinne weighs as much as Actuall, or
Habituall, yet in truth, all our Actuall and Habituall sins are in
Originall. Therefore Saint *Pauls* vehement, and frequent prayer
to God, to that purpose, could not deliver him from Originall sin,
and that *stimulus carnis,* that provocation of the flesh, that *Messenger of Satan,* which rises out of that, God would give him
sufficient grace, it should not worke to his destruction, but yet
he should have it: Nay, the infinite merit of Christ Jesus himself, that works so upon all actuall and habituall sins, as that
after that merit is applyed to them, those sins are no sins, works
not so upon Originall sin, but that, though I be eased in the
Dominion, and *Imputation* thereof, yet the same Originall sin is
in me still; and though God doe deliver me from eternall death,
due to mine actual and habituall sins, yet from the temporall
death, due to Originall sin, he delivers not his dearest Saints.

Thus sin is heavy in the *seed,* in the *grain,* in the *akorn,* how
much more when it is a *field* of Corn, a *barn* of grain, a *forest*
of Oaks, in the multiplication, and complication of sin in sin?
And yet wee consider the weight of sin another way too, for as
Christ feels all the afflictions of his children, so his children will
feel all the wounds that are inflicted upon him; even the sins
of other men; as *Lots* righteous soule was grieved with sins of
others. If others sin by my example and provocation, or by my

connivence and permission, when I have authority, their sin lies
heavyer upon me, then upon themselves; for they have but the
weight of their own sinne; and I have *mine,* and *theirs* upon me;
and though I cannot have *two souls* to suffer, and though there
cannot be two *everlastingnesses* in the torments of hell, yet I
shall have two measures of those unmeasurable torments upon
my soul. But if I have no interest in the sins of other men, by
any occasion ministred by me, yet I cannot chuse but feel a
weight, a burthen of a holy anguish, and compassion and indignation, because every one of these sins inflict a new wound
upon my Saviour, when my Saviour says to him, that does but
injure me, *Why persecutest thou me,* and feels the blow upon
himselfe, shall not I say to him that wounds my Saviour, *Why
woundest thou me,* and groane under the weight of my brothers
sin, and my Fathers, my Makers, my Saviours wound? If a man
of my blood, or allyance, doe a shamefull act, I am affected with
it; If a man of my calling, or *profession,* doe a scandalous act,
I feel my self concerned in his fault; God hath made all *mankinde* of *one blood,* and all *Christians* of *one calling,* and the
sins of every man concern every man, both in that respect, that
I, that is, *This nature,* is in that man that sins that sin: and *I,*
that is, *This nature,* is in that Christ, who is wounded by that
sin. The weight of sin, were it but Originall sin, were it but the
sins of other men, is an insupportable weight.

But if a sinner will take a true balance, and try the right
weight of sin, let him goe about to leave his sin, and then he
shall see how close, and how heavily it stook to him. Then one
sin will lay the weight, of *seelinesse,* of *falshood,* of *incon-
stancy,* of *dishonour,* of *ill nature,* if you goe about to leave it:
and another sin will lay the weight of *poverty,* of *disestimation*
upon you, if you goe about to leave it. One sin will lay your
pleasures upon you, another your *profit,* another your *Honour,*
another your *Duty* to wife and children, and weigh you down
with these. Goe but out of the water, goe but about to leave a
sin, and you will finde the weight of it, and the hardnesse to
cast it off. *Gravatæ sunt, Mine iniquities are heavy,* (that was
our first) and *gravatæ nimis,* they are *too heavy,* which is a second circumstance.

Some weight, some *balast* is necessary to make a ship goe
steady; we are not without advantage, in having *some sinne;*

some *concupiscence*, some *tentation* is not too heavy for us. The greatest sins that ever were committed, were committed by them, who had *no former sinne*, to push them on to that sin: The first *Angels* sin, and the sin *of Adam* are noted to be the most desperate and the most irrecoverable sins, and they were committed, when they had no former sin in them. The *Angels* punishment is pardoned in *no part; Adams* punishment is pardoned in *no man*, in this world. Now such sins as those, that is, sins that are never pardoned, no man commits now; not now, when he hath the weight of former sins to push him on. Though there be a heavy guiltinesse in *Originall sin*, yet I have an argument, a plea for mercy out of that, *Lord, my strength is not the strength of stones, nor my flesh brasse; Lord, no man can bring a clean thing out of uncleannesse; Lord, no man can say after, I have cleansed my heart, I am free from sinne*, I could not be borne cleane, I could not cleanse my selfe since. It magnifies Gods glory, it amplifies mans happinesse, that he is subject to tentation. If man had been made *impeccable*, that he could not have sinned, he had not been so happy; for then, he could onely have enjoyed that state, in which he was created, and not have risen to any *better;* because that better estate, is a reward of our willing obedience to God, in such things, as we might have disobeyed him in. Therefore when the Apostle was in danger, of growing too light, *lest he should be exalted out of measure, through the abundance of revelation*, (says that Scripture) he had a weight hung upon him; There was something *given him*, therefore it was a benefit, *a gift*; And it was *Angelus, an Angel*, that was given him; But it was not a good Angel, a Tutelar, a Gardian Angel, to present *good motions* unto him, but it was *Angelus Satanæ, a messenger of Satan, sent*, as he says, *to buffet him;* and yet this hostile Angel, this *messenger of Satan* was a benefit, a *gift*, and a fore-runner, and some kind of *Inducer* of that *Grace*, which was *sufficient for him;* and it would not have appeared to us, no nor to himselfe, that he had had so much of that grace, if he had not had this tentation. God is as powerfull upon us when he delivers us *from* tentation, that it doe not overtake us; but not so apparent, so evident, so manifest, as when he delivers us *in* a tentation, that it doe not overcome us: some weight does but *ballast* us, as some enemies never doe us more harme, but occasion us, to arme and to stand upon our gard.

Therefore, this weight that is complained of here, is not *In carne,* in our naturall flesh; (though in *that* be no *goodnesse*) it is nothing that God from the beginning hath imprinted in our nature, not that *peccability,* and *possibility* of sinning; nor it is not *in stimulo carnis,* in these accessary tentations, and provocations which awaken, and provoke the malignity of this flesh, and put a sting into it; we doe not consider this heavy weight to be the *naturall possibility* which was in man, *before Originall sinne* entred, nor to be that naturall pronenesse to sinne, which is *originall sinne it selfe.* But it is, when we our selves whet that sting, when we labour to breake hedges, and to steale wood, and gather up a stick out of one sin, and a stick out of another, and to make a fagot to load us, in this life, and burne us in the next, in multiplying sins, and aggravating circumstances, so it is *Heavy,* so it is *too heavy, It is too heavy for me,* (for that's also another circumstance) *for David himselfe,* for any man even in *Davids* state.

Though this consideration might be enlarged, and usefully carried into this expostulation, can sin be too heavy for *me,* any burden of sin sink *me* into a dejection of spirit, that am wrapped up in the *Covenant,* borne of *Christian Parents,* that am bred up in an *Orthodox,* in a *Reformed Church,* that can perswade my selfe sometimes, that I am of the *number of the elect;* Can any sin be too heavy for *me,* can I doubt of the execution of his *first purpose* upon me, or doubt of the efficacy of his *ordinances* here in the Church, what sin soever I commit, can any sins be too heavy for me? yet it is enough that in this Sea, God holds no man up by the chin so, but that if he sin in confidence of that sustentation, he shall sink. But in this personall respect in our text, we consider onely with what weights *David* weighed his sins, when hee found here that they were too heavy for him. He weighed his sin with his punishment, and in his punishment hee saw the anger, and *indignation of God,* and when we see sin through that spectacle, through an *angry God,* it appears great, and red, and fearefull unto us; when *David* came to see himselfe in his infirmity, in his deformity, when his body could not bear the punishment here in this world, he considered how insupportable a weight the sin, and the anger of God upon that sin, would be in the world to come. For *me* that rise to preferment by my sin, for *me* that come to satisfie my *carnall appe-*

tites by my sin, my sin is not too heavy; But for *me* that suffer *penury* in the bottome of a plentifull state exhausted by my sin, for *me* that languish under *diseases* and putrefaction contracted by my sin, for *me* upon whom the hand of God lies heavy in any *affliction* for my sin, for *me*, my sins are too heavy. Till I come to hear that voice, *Come unto me all you that labour, and are heavy laden, and I will refresh you,* till I come to consider my sin in the mercy of God, and not onely in his justice, in his punishments, my sins will be too heavy for me; for, though that be a good way, to consider the justice of God, yet it is not a good *end;* I must *stop,* but not *stay* at it, I must consider my sin in his justice, how *powerfull* a God I have provoked; but I must passe through his justice to his mercy; his justice is my *way,* but his mercy is my *lodging;* for wee cannot tell by the construction and origination of the words, whether *Cain* said, *My sin is greater then can bee pardoned,* or, *my punishment is greater then can bee borne:* But it needes not bee disputed; for it is all one; He that considers *onely* the anger of God in the *punishment,* will thinke his sin unpardonable, *his sinne will be too heavy for him.* But as a *feaver* is well spent, when the patient is fit to take physick, so if God give me physick, if I take his corrections as *medicines,* and not as *punishments,* then my disease is well spent, my danger is well overcome; If I have buryed my sins in the wounds of my Saviour, they cannot be too heavy for me, for they are not upon me at all; But if I take them out again, by relapsing into them, or imagine them to rise again, by a suspicion and jealousie in God, that he hath not forgiven them, because his hand lies still upon me, in some afflictions, so, in such a relapse, so, in such a jealous *mis-interpretation* of Gods proceeding with me, *my sins are too heavy for me;* for *me,* because I do not sustain my self by those helps that God puts into my hands.

It is *heavy, too heavy, too heavy for me,* says *David;* if you consider the *elect themselves,* their election will not beare them out in their sins. But here we consider the insupportablenesse, in that, wherein the holy Ghost hath presented it, *Quia onus,* because it lies upon me, in the nature and quality of a *Burden, Mine iniquities are as a burden, too heavy for me.* When all this is packed up upon me, that I am first under a *Calamity,* a *sicknesse,* a *scorne,* an *imprisonment,* a *penury,* and then upon that

calamity, there is laid the *anger* and *indignation of God,* and
then upon that, the *weight of mine own sinnes;* this is too much
to settle me, it is enough to sinke me, it is a burden, in which
the danger arises from the last addition, in that, which is last
laid on: for, as the *sceptique Philosopher* pleases himselfe in
that argumentation, that either a penny makes a man rich, or
he can never be rich, for says he, if he be not rich yet, the addition of a penny more would make him rich: or if not that penny,
yet another, or another, so that at last it is the *addition of a
penny* that makes him rich; so without any such fallacious or
facetious circumvention in our case, it is the last addition, that
that we look on last, that makes our burden insupportable, when
upon our calamity we see the anger of God piled up, and upon
that, *our sin,* when I come to see my sin, in that glasse, not in
a Saviour bleeding for me, but in a Judge frowning upon mee;
when my sins are so far off from me, as that they are the *last
thing* that I see; for, if I would look upon my sins, first, with a
remorseful, a tearfull, a repentant eye, either I should see no
anger, no calamity; or it would not seem strange to me, that God
should bee angry, nor strange, that I should suffer calamities,
when God is angry; Therefore is sin heavy as a burden, because
it is the last thing that I lay upon my selfe, and feel not that till
a heavy load of calamity and anger be upon me before. But
then, as when we come to be unloaded of a burden, that that was
last laid on, is first taken off, so when we come, by any meanes,
though by the sense of a calamity, or of the anger of God, to a
sense of our sin, before the calamity it selfe be taken off, the sin
is forgiven. When the Prophet found *David* in this state, the first
act that the Prophet came to was the *Transtulit peccatum, God
hath taken away thy sinne,* but the calamity was not yet taken
away. The *child* begot in sin *shall surely die,* though the sin be
pardoned. The *fruit* of the tree may be preserved and kept, after
the tree it selfe is cut down and burnt; The fruit, and off-spring
of our sin, calamity, may continue upon us, after God hath removed the guiltinesse of the sin from us. In the course of civility, our parents goe out before us, in the course of Mortality, our
parents die before us; In the course of God's mercy, it is so too;
The sin that begot the calamity, is dead, and gone, the calamity,
the child, and off-spring of that sin, is alive and powerfull upon
us. But for the most part, as if I would lift *an iron chain* from

the ground, if I take but the first linke, and draw up that, the whole chain follows, so if by my repentance, I remove the uppermost weight of my load, *my sin,* all the rest, the declaration of the anger of God, and the calamities that I suffer, will follow my sin, and depart from me. But still our first care must be to take off the last weight, the last that comes to our sense, *The sin.*

You have met, I am sure, in old *Apophthegms,* an answer of a Philosopher celebrated, that being asked, *what was the heaviest thing in the world,* answered, *Senex Tyrannus, An old Tyran;* For a Tyran, at first, dares not proceed so severely; but when he is established, and hath continued *long,* he prescribes in his injuries, and those injuries become *Laws.* As sin is a *Tyran,* so he is got *over our head, in Dominio,* as we shewed you in the *supergressæ sunt,* in our former part; As he is an *old Tyran,* so he is *the heaviest burden* that can be imagined; An inveterate sin, is an inveterate sore, we may hold out with it, but hardly cure it; we may slumber it, but hardly kill it. Weigh sin in *heaven;* heaven could not *beare* it, in the *Angels;* They fell: In the *waters;* The Sea could not *beare* it in *Jonas;* He was cast in: In the *earth;* That could not *beare* it in *Dathan,* and *Abiram;* They were swallowed: And because all the inhabitants of the earth are sin it selfe, *The earth it selfe shall reel to and fro, as a Drunkard, and shall be removed like a Cottage, and the transgression thereof shall be heavy upon it, and it shall fall and not rise againe;* There's the totall, the finall fall, proper to the wicked; they shall *fall;* so shall the godly; And *fall every day;* and fall *seven times a day;* but they shall *rise againe* and *stand in judgement; The wicked shall not doe so;* They shall *rise,* rise to judgement; and they shall stand, *stand* for judgement, stand *to receive* judgement; and then, *not fall,* but *be cast out,* out of the presence of God, and *cast down,* down into an impossibility of rising, for ever, for ever, for ever. There is a lively expressing of this deadly weight, this burden in the Prophet *Zechary.* First, there was a certaine vessell, a measure shewed, and the Angel said, *Hic est oculus, This is the sight,* (says our first translation) *This is the resemblance through all the earth,* (says our second) That is, to this measure, and to that that is figured in it, every man must look, this every man must take into his consideration; what is it? In this measure sate *a woman whose name was Wickednesse;* At first, this woman, this wickednesse, *sate up* in this vessell, she

had not filled the measure, she was not laid securely in it, she
was not prostrate, not groveling, but her nobler part, *her head,*
was yet out of danger, *she sate up in it.* But before the Vision departs, she is plunged wholly into that measure; (into *darknesse,*
into *blindnesse*) and not for a time; for, then, *there was a cover,*
(says the text) and *a great cover,* and *a great cover of Lead put
upon that vessell;* and so, a perpetuall imprisonment, no hope to
get out; and *heavy fetters,* no ease to be had within; Hard ground
to tread upon, and heavy burdens to carry; first a *cover,* that is,
an *excuse; a great cover,* that is, a *defence,* and a *glory;* at last, *of
Lead;* all determines in *Desperation.* This is when the multiplicity
and indifferencie to lesser sins, and the habituall custome of
some particular sin, meet in the aggravating of the burden: for
then, they are *heavyer then the sand of the Sea,* says the holy
Ghost: where he expresses the greatest weight by the least thing;
Nothing lesse than a graine of *sand,* nothing *heavyer then the
sands of the Sea,* nothing easier to resist then a *first tentation,* or
a *single sinne* in it selfe, nothing heavyer, nor harder to devest,
then *sinnes complicated* in one another, or then *an old Tyran,*
and *custome* in any one sin. And therefore it was evermore a
familiar phrase with the *Prophets,* when they were to declare the
sins, or to denounce the punishments of those sins upon the people, to call it by this word, *Onus visionis, Onus Babylonis, Onus
Ninives, O the burden of Babylon, the burden of Nineveh.* And
because some of those *woes,* those *Iudgments,* those *burdens,*
did not always fall upon that people presently, they came to mock
the Prophets, and say to them, *Now, what is the burden of the
Lord, What Burden have you to preach to us,* and to talke of
now? Say unto them, says God to the Prophet there; *This is the
Burden of the Lord, I will even forsake you.* And, as it is elegantly, emphatically, vehemently added, *Every mans word shall
be his burden;* That which he *says,* shall be that that shall be laid
to his charge; His *scorning,* his idle questioning of the Prophet,
What burden now, what plague, what famine, what warre now?
Is not all well for all your crying The burden of the Lord? *Every
mans word shall be his burden,* the *deriding* of Gods Ordinance,
and of the denouncing of his Judgements in that Ordinance, shall
be their burden, that is, aggravate those Judgements upon them.
Nay, there is a heavyer weight then that, added; *Ye shall say no
more* (says God to the Prophet) *the burden of the Lord,* that is,

you shall not bestow so much care upon this people, as to tell them, that the Lord threatens them. Gods presence in anger, and in punishments, is a heavy, but God's absence, and dereliction, a much heavyer burden; As (if extremes will admit comparison) the everlasting losse of the sight of God in hell, is a greater torment, then any lakes of inextinguishable Brimstone, then any gnawing of the incessant worme, then any gnashing of teeth can present unto us.

Now, let no man ease himself upon that fallacy, *sin cannot be,* nor sin cannot induce such burdens as you talk of, for many men are come to *wealth,* and by that *wealth,* to *honour,* who, if they had admitted a tendernesse in their consciences, and forborn some sins, had lost both; for, are they without burden, because they have *wealth,* and *honour?* In the Originall language, the same word, that is here, a *burden, Chabad,* signifies *honour,* and *wealth,* as well as a *burden.* And therefore says the Prophet, *Woe unto him that loadeth himselfe with thick clay. Non densantur nisi per laborem;* There goes much pains to the laying of it thus thick upon us; The multiplying of riches is a laborious thing; and then it is a new pain to bleed out those riches for a *new office,* or a *new title; Et tamen lutum,* says the Father, when all is done, we are but roughcast with durt; All those *Riches,* all those *Honours* are a *Burden,* upon the *just* man, they are but a multiplying of *fears,* that they shall lose them; upon the *securest* man, they are but a multiplying of *duties* and *obligations;* for the more they have, the more they have to answer; and upon the *unjust* they are a multiplying of everlasting torments. *They possess months of vanity, and wearisom nights are appointed them.* Men are as weary of the *day,* upon *Carpets* and *Cushions,* as at the plough. And the labourers wearinesse, is to a good end; but for these men, *They weary themselves to commit iniquity.* Some doe, and some doe not; All doe. *The labour of the foolish wearieth every one of them;* Why? *Because he knows not how to goe to the City.* He that directs not his labours to the right end, the glory of God, he goes not to Jerusalem, the City of holy peace, but his sinfull labours shall bee a burden to him; and his Riches, and his Office, and his Honour hee shall not be able to put off, then when he puts off his body in his death-bed; He shall not have that happinesse, which he, till then, thought a misery, *To carry nothing out of this world,* for his Riches, his Office, his Honour shall follow him into the next world, and clog his soule there. But we proposed this consideration of this Metaphor, *That sinne is a burden,* (as there is an infinite sweetnesse, and infinite latitude in every Metaphor, in every elegancy of the Scripture, and therefore I may have leave to be loath to depart from it) in some particular inconveniences, that a *burden* brings, and it is time to come to them.

FROM

Devotions Upon Emergent Occasions,

AND SEUERALL STEPS IN MY SICKNES

1. Insultus Morbi Primus; *The first alteration, the first grudging of the sicknesse.*

I. *Meditation.* Variable, and therfore miserable condition of Man; this minute I was well, and am ill, this minute. I am surpriz'd with a sodaine change, and alteration to worse, and can impute it to no cause, nor call it by any name. We study *Health,* and we deliberate upon our *meats,* and *drink,* and *ayre,* and *exercises,* and we hew, and wee polish every stone, that goes to that building; and so our *Health* is a long and a regular work; But in a minute a Canon batters all, overthrowes all, demolishes all; a *Sicknes* unprevented for all our diligence, unsuspected for all our curiositie; nay, undeserved, if we consider only *disorder,* summons us, seizes us, possesses us, destroyes us in an instant. O miserable condition of Man, which was not imprinted by *God,* who as hee is *immortall* himselfe, had put a *coale,* a *beame* of *Immortalitie* into us, which we might have blowen into a *flame,* but blew it out, by our first sinne; wee beggard our selves by hearkning after false riches, and infatuated our selves by hearkning after false knowledge. So that now, we doe not onely die, but die upon the Rack, die by the torment of sicknesse; nor that onely, but are preafflicted, super-afflicted with these jelousies and suspitions, and apprehensions of *Sicknes,* before we can cal it a sicknes; we are not sure we are ill; one hand askes the other by the pulse, and our eye asks our urine, how we do. O multiplied misery! we die, and cannot enjoy death, because we die in this torment of sicknes; we are tormented with sicknes, and cannot stay till the torment come, but preapprehensions and presages, prophecy those torments, which induce that *death* before either come; and our dissolution is conceived in these *first changes,* *quickned* in the *sicknes* it selfe, and *borne* in *death,* which beares date from these first changes. Is this the honour which Man hath by being a *litle world.* That he hath these *earthquakes* in him selfe, sodaine shakings; these *lightnings,* sodaine flashes; these *thunders,* sodaine noises; these *Eclypses,* sodaine offuscations, and darknings of his senses; these *Blazing stars,* sodaine fiery exhalations; these *Rivers of blood,* sodaine red waters? Is he a *world* to himselfe onely therefore, that he hath inough in himself, not only to destroy, and execute himselfe, but to presage that execution upon himselfe; to assist the sicknes, to antidate the sicknes, to make the sicknes the more irremediable, by sad apprehensions, and as if he would make a fire the more vehement, by sprinkling water upon the coales, so to wrap a hote fever in cold Melancholy, least the fever alone should not destroy fast enough, without this contribution, nor perfit the work (which is *destruction*) except we joynd an artificiall sicknes, of our owne *melancholy,* to our natural, our unnaturall fever. O perplex'd discomposition, O ridling distemper, O miserable condition of Man.

I. *Expostulation.* If I were but meere *dust* and *ashes,* I might speak unto the *Lord,* for the *Lordes* hand made me of this *dust,* and the *Lords* hand shall recollect these *ashes;* the *Lords* hand was the wheele, upon which this vessell of clay was framed, and the *Lordes hand* is the *Urne,* in which these ashes shall be preserv'd. I am the *dust,* and the *ashes* of the *Temple* of the *H. Ghost;* and what Marble is so precious? But I am more then *dust* and *ashes;* I am my best part, I am my *soule.* And being so, the *breath* of *God,* I may breath back these pious *expostulations* to my *God. My God, my God,* why is not my *soule,* as sensible as my *body?* Why hath not my *soule* these apprehensions, these presages, these changes, these antidates, these jealousies, these suspitions of a *sinne,* as well as my body of a *sicknes?* why is there not alwayes a *pulse* in my *soule,* to beat at the approch of a tentation to sinne? why are there not always *waters* in mine eyes, to testifie to my spiritual sicknes? I stand in the way of tentations, (naturally, necessarily, all men doe so: for there is a *Snake in every path,* tentations in every vocation) but I go, I run, I flie into the wayes of tentation, which I might shun; nay, I breake into houses, wher the plague is; I presse into places of tentation, and tempt the *devill* himselfe, and solicite and importune them, who had rather be left unsolicited by me. I fall sick of *Sin,* and am bedded and bedrid, buried and putrified in the practise of *Sin,* and all this while have no presage, no pulse, no sense of my *sicknesse;* O heigth, O depth of misery, where the first *Symptome* of the sicknes is *Hell,* and where I never see the fever of lust, of envy, of ambition, by any other light, then the darknesse and horror of *Hell* it selfe; and where the first Messenger that speaks to me doth not say, *Thou mayst die,* no nor *Thou must die,* but *Thou art dead:* and where the first notice, that my *Soule* hath of her sicknes, is *irrecoverablenes, irremediablenes:* but, O my God, *Job did not charge thee foolishly,* in his temporall afflictions, nor may I in my spirituall. Thou hast imprinted a *pulse* in our *Soule,* but we do not examine it; a voice in our conscience, but we do not hearken unto it. We talk it out, we drinke it out, we sleepe it out; and when we wake, we doe not say with *Jacob, Surely the Lord is in this place, and I knew it not:* but though we might know it, we do not, we wil not. But will *God* pretend to make a *Watch,* and leave out the *springe?* to make so many various wheels in the faculties of the soule, and in the organs of the body, and leave out *Grace,* that should move them? or wil *God* make a *springe,* and not *wind* it up? Infuse his first *grace,* and not second it with more, without which we can no more use his first *grace,* when we have it, then wee could dispose our selves by *Nature,* to have it? But alas, that is not our case; we are all *prodigall sonnes,* and not *disinherited;* wee have received our portion, and misspent it, not bin denied it. We are *Gods tenants* heere, and yet here, he, our *Land-lord* payes us *Rents;* not yearely, nor quarterly; but hourely, and quarterly; *Every minute he renewes his mercy,* but wee *will not understand, least that we should bee converted, and he should heale us.*

·   ·   ·

1. *Prayer.* O Eternall, and most gracious *God,* who, considered in thy selfe, are a *Circle,* first and last, and altogether; but considered in thy working upon us, art a *direct line,* and leadest us from our *beginning,* through all our wayes, to our end, enable me by thy grace, to looke forward to mine end, and to looke backward to, to the considerations of thy mercies afforded mee from my beginning; that so by that practise of considering thy mercy, in my beginning in this world, when thou plantedst me in the *Christian Church,* and thy mercy in the beginning in the other world, when thou writest me in the *Booke of life* in my *Election,* I may come to a holy consideration of thy *mercy,* in the beginning of all my actions here: that in all the beginnings, in all the accesses, and approaches of spirituall sicknesses of *Sinn,* I may heare and hearken to that voice, *O thou Man of God, there is death in the pot,* and so refraine from that, which I was so hungerly, so greedily flying to. *A faithfull Ambassador is health,* says thy wise servant *Solomon.* Thy voice received, in the beginning of a sicknesse, of a sinne, is true health. If I can see that light betimes, and heare that voyce early, *Then shall my light breake forth as the morning, and my health shall spring forth speedily.*

Deliver mee therefore, O my God, from these vaine imaginations; that it is an overcurious thing, a dangerous thing, to come to that tendernesse, that rawnesse, that scrupulousnesse, to feare every *concupiscence,* every offer of *Sin,* that this suspicious, and jealous diligence will turne to an inordinate dejection of spirit, and a diffidence in thy care and providence; but keep me still establish'd, both in a constant assurance, that thou wilt speake to me at the beginning of every such sicknes, at the approach of every such *sinne;* and that, if I take knowledg of that voice then, and flye to thee, thou wilt preserve mee from falling, or raise me againe, when by naturall infirmitie I am fallen: doe this, O *Lord,* for his sake, who knowes our naturall infirmities, for he had them; and knowes the weight of our sinns, for he paid a deare price for them, thy *Sonne,* our *Saviour, Chr: Jesus, Amen.*

2. Actio Laesa. *The strength, and the function of the Senses, and other faculties change and faile.*

2. *Meditation.* The *Heavens* are not the less constant, because they move continually, because they move continually one and

the same way. The *Earth* is not the more constant, because it lyes stil continually, because continually it changes, and melts in al parts thereof. *Man,* who is the noblest part of the *Earth,* melts so away, as if he were a *statue,* not of *Earth,* but of *Snowe.* We see his owne *Envie* melts him, he growes leane with that; he will say, anothers *beautie* melts him; but he feels that a *Fever* doth not melt him like *snow,* but powr him out like *lead,* like *yron,* like *brasse* melted in a furnace: It doth not only *melt* him, but *calcine* him, reduce him to *Atomes,* and to *ashes;* not to *water,* but to *lime.* And how quickly? Sooner than thou canst receive an answer, sooner than thou canst conceive the question; *Earth* is the *center* of my *Bodie, Heaven* is the *center* of my *Soule;* these two are the naturall places of those two; but those goe not to these two in an equall pace: My *body* falls downe without pushing, my *Soule* does not go up without pulling: *Ascension* is my *Soules* pace and measure, but *precipitation* my *bodies:* And, even *Angells,* whose home is *Heaven,* and who are winged too, yet had a *Ladder* to goe to *Heaven,* by steps. The *Sunne* who goes so many miles in a minut, the *Starres* of the *Firmament,* which go so very many more, goe not so fast, as my *body* to the *earth.* In the same instant that I feele the first attempt of the disease, I feele the victory; In the twinckling of an eye, I can scarse see, instantly the tast is insipid, and fatuous; instantly the appetite is dull and desirelesse: instantly the knees are sinking and strengthlesse; and in an instant, sleepe which is the *picture,* the *copie of death,* is taken away, that the *Originall, Death* it selfe may succeed, and that so I might have death to the life. It was part of *Adams* punishment, *In the sweat of thy browes thou shalt eate thy bread:* it is multiplied to me, I have earned bread in the sweat of my browes, in the labor of my calling, and I have it; and I sweat againe, and againe, from the brow, to the sole of the foot, but I eat no bread, I tast no sustenance: Miserable distribution of *Mankind,* where one halfe lackes meat, and the other stomacke.

3. Decubitus sequitur tandem. *The Patient takes his bed.*

3. *Meditation.* We attribute but one privilege and advantage to Mans body, above other moving creatures, that he is not as

others, groveling, but of an erect, of an upright form, naturally
built, and disposed to the contemplation of *Heaven*. Indeed it is
a thankfull forme, and recompences that *soule*, which gives it,
with carrying that soule so many foot higher, towards *heaven*.
Other creatures look to the *earth;* and even that is no unfit object, no unfit contemplation for *Man;* for thither hee must come;
but because, *Man* is not to stay there, as other creatures are, *Man*
in his naturall forme, is carried to the contemplation of that
place, which is his *home, Heaven*. This is *Mans* prerogative; but
what state hath he in this *dignitie?* A fever can fillip him downe,
a fever can depose him; a fever can bring that head, which yesterday caried a *crown* of gold, five foot towards a *crown* of glory,
as low as his own foot, today. When *God* came to breath into
Man the breath of life, he found him flat upon the ground; when
he comes to withdraw that breath from him againe, hee prepares
him to it, by laying him flat upon his bed. Scarse any prison so
close, that affords not the prisoner two, or three steps. The *An-
chorites* that barqu'd themselves up in hollowe trees, and im-
mur'd themselves in hollow walls; that perverse man, that bar-
rell'd himselfe in a Tubb, all could stand, or sit, and enjoy some
change of posture. A sicke bed, is a grave; and all that the patient
saies there, is but a varying of his owne *Epitaph*. Every nights
bed is a *Type* of the *grave:* At night wee tell our servants at what
houre wee will rise; here we cannot tell our selves, at what day,
what week, what moneth. Here the head lies as low as the foot;
the *Head* of the people, as lowe as they, whome those feete trod
upon; And that hande that signed Pardons, is too weake to begge
his owne, if hee might have it for lifting up that hand: Strange
fetters to the feete, strange Manacles to the hands, when the
feete, and handes are bound so much the faster, by how much
the coards are slacker; So much the lesse able to doe their Offices,
by how much more the Sinewes and Ligaments are the looser. In
the *Grave* I may speak through the stones, in the voice of my
friends, and in the accents of those wordes, which their love may
afford my memory; Here I am mine owne *Ghost,* and rather
affright my beholders, then instruct them; they conceive the
worst of me now, and yet feare worse; they give me for dead now,
and yet wonder how I doe, when they wake at midnight, and aske
how I doe to morrow. Miserable and, (though common to all)

inhuman *posture,* where I must practise my lying in the *grave,* by lying still, and not practise my *Resurrection,* by rising any more.

4. Medicusq; vocatur. *The Phisician is sent for.*

4. *Meditation.* It is too little to call *Man* a *little World;* Except *God,* Man is a *diminutive* to nothing. Man consistes of more pieces, more parts, then the world; then the world doeth, nay then the world is. And if those pieces were extended, and stretched out in Man, as they are in the world, Man would bee the *Gyant,* and the Worlde the *Dwarfe,* the World but the *Map,* and the Man the *World.* If all the *Veines* in our bodies, were extended to *Rivers,* and all the *Sinewes,* to *Vaines of Mines,* and all the *Muscles,* that lye upon one another, to *Hilles,* and all the *Bones* to *Quarries* of stones, and all the other pieces, to the proportion of those which correspond to them in the world, the *Aire* would be too litle for this *Orbe* of Man to move in, the firmament would bee but enough for this *Starre;* for, as the whole world hath nothing, to which something in man doth not answere, so hath man many pieces, of which the whol world hath no representation. Inlarge this Meditation upon this *great world, Man,* so farr, as to consider the immensitie of the creatures this world produces; our *creatures* are our *thoughts, creatures* that are borne *Gyants;* that reach from *East* to *West,* from *Earth* to *Heaven,* that doe not onely bestride all the *Sea,* and *Land,* but span the *Sunn* and *Firmament* at once; My thoughts reach all, comprehend all. Inexplicable mistery; I their *Creator* am in a close prison, in a sicke bed, any where, and any one of my *Creatures,* my *thoughts,* is with the *Sunne,* and beyond the *Sunne,* overtakes the *Sunne,* and overgoes the *Sunne* in one pace, one steppe, everywhere. And then as the other *world* produces *Serpents,* and *Vipers,* malignant, and venimous creatures, and *Wormes,* and *Caterpillars,* that endeavour to devoure that world which produces them, and *Monsters* compiled and complicated of divers parents, and kinds, so this world, our selves, produces all these in us, in producing *diseases,* and *sicknesses,* of all those sorts; venimous, and infectious diseases, feeding and consuming diseases, and manifold and entangled diseases, made up of many several ones. And can the other world name so many *venimous,* so many consuming,

so many monstrous creatures, as we can diseases, of all these kindes? O miserable abundance, O beggarly riches! how much doe wee lacke of having *remedies* for everie disease, when as yet we have not *names* for them? But wee have a *Hercules* against these *Gyants*, these *Monsters;* that is, the *Phisician;* hee musters up al the forces of the other world, to succour this; all Nature to relieve Man. We *have* the *Phisician,* but we *are not* the *Phisician.* Heere we shrinke in our proportion, sink in our dignitie, in respect of verie meane creatures, who are *Phisicians* to themselves. The *Hart* that is pursued and wounded, they say, knowes an Herbe, which being eaten, throwes off the arrow: A strange kind of *vomit.* The *dog* that pursues it, though hee bee subject to sicknes, even *proverbially,* knowes his *grasse* that recovers him. And it may be true, that the *Drugger* is as neere to *Man,* as to other *creatures,* it may be that obvious and present *Simples,* easie to bee had, would cure him; but the *Apothecary* is not so neere him, nor the *Phisician* so neere him, as they two are to other creatures; Man hath not that *innate instinct,* to apply these naturall medicines to his present danger, as those inferiour creatures have; he is not his owne *Apothecary,* his owne *Phisician,* as they are. Call back therefore thy Meditation again, and bring it downe; whats become of mans great extent and proportion, when himselfe shrinkes himselfe, and consumes himselfe to a handful of dust; whats become of his soaring thoughts, his compassing thoughts, when himselfe brings himselfe to the ignorance, to the thoughtlessnesse of the *Grave?* His *diseases* are his owne, but the *Phisician* is not; hee hath them at home, but hee must send for the *Phisician.*

10. Lentè et Serpenti satagunt occurrere Morbo. *They find the Disease to steale on insensibly, and endeavour to meet with it so.*

10. *Meditation.* This is *Natures nest of Boxes;* The Heavens containe the *Earth,* the *Earth,* Cities, *Cities,* Men. And all these are *Concentrique;* the common *center* to them all, is *decay, ruine;* only that is *Eccentrique,* which was never made; only that place, or garment rather, which we can *imagine,* but not *demonstrate,* That light, which is the very emanation of the light of *God,* in which the *Saints* shall dwell, with which the *Saints* shall be appareld, only that bends not to this *Center,* to *Ruine;* that which

was not made of *Nothing,* is not threatned with this annihilation.
All other things are; even *Angels,* even our *soules;* they move
upon the same *poles,* they bend to the same *Center;* and if they
were not made immortall by *preservation,* their *Nature* could not
keep them from sinking to this *center, Annihilation.* In all these
(the *frame of the heavens,* the *States upon earth,* and *Men in
them,* comprehend all) Those are the greatest mischifs, which
are least discerned; the most insensible in their *wayes* come to
bee the most sensible in their *ends.* The *Heavens* have had their
Dropsie, they drownd the world, and they shall have their *Fever,*
and burn the world. Of the *dropsie,* the flood, the world had a
foreknowledge 120 yeares before it came; and so some made provision against it, and were saved; the *fever* shall break out in an
instant, and consume all; The *dropsie* did no harm to the *heavens,* from whence it fell, it did not put out those *lights,* it did not
quench those *heates;* but the *fever,* the fire shall burne the *furnace* it selfe, annihilate those *heavens,* that breath it out; Though
the *Dog-Starre* have a pestilent breath, an infectious exhalation,
yet because we know when it wil rise, we clothe our selves, and
wee diet our selves, and we shadow our selves to a sufficient pre-
vention; but *Comets* and *blazing starres,* whose effects, or significations no man can interpret or frustrat, no man foresaw: no *Al-
manack* tells us, when a *blazing starre* will break out, the matter
is carried up in secret; no *Astrologer* tels us when the effects will
be accomplished, for thats a secret of a higher spheare, then the
other; and that which is most *secret,* is most *dangerous.* It is so
also here in the *societies* of men, in *States,* and *Commonwealths.*
Twentie *rebellious drums* make not so dangerous a noise, as a
few *whisperers,* and secret plotters in corners. The *Canon* doth
not so much hurt against a wal, as a *Myne* under the wall; nor a
thousand enemies that threaten, so much as a few that take an
oath to say *nothing. God* knew many heavy sins of the people, in
the wildernes and after, but still he charges them with that one,
with *Murmuring, murmuring* in their *hearts,* secret disobedi-
ences, secret repugnances against his declar'd wil; and these are
the most deadly, the most pernicious. And it is so to, with the
diseases of the *body;* and that is my case. The *pulse,* the *urine,*
the *sweat,* all have sworn to say nothing, to give no *Indication,*
of any dangerous *sicknesse.* My forces are not enfeebled, I find
no decay in my strength; my provisions are not cut off, I find no

abhorring in mine appetite; my counsels are not corrupted or infatuated, I find no false apprehensions, to work upon mine understanding; and yet they see, that invisibly, and I feele, that insensibly the *disease* prevailes. The *disease* hath established a *Kingdome*, an *Empire* in mee, and will have certaine *Arcana Imperii, secrets of State*, by which it will proceed, and not be bound to *declare* them. But yet against those secret conspiracies in the State, the *Magistrate* hath the *rack;* and against the insensible diseases, *Phisicians* have their *examiners;* and those these employ now.

16. Et properare meum clamant, è Turre propinqua,
Obstreperæ Campanæ aliorum in funere, funus.
From the Bells of the Church adjoyning, I am daily remembred
of my buriall in the funeralls of others.

16. *Meditation.* We have a *Convenient Author*, who writ a *Discourse of Bells,* when hee was prisoner in *Turky.* How would hee have enlarged himselfe if he had beene my *fellow-prisoner* in this *sicke bed,* so neere to that *Steeple,* which never ceases, no more than the *harmony of the spheres,* but is more heard. When the *Turkes* took *Constantinople,* they melted the *Bells* into *Ordnance;* I have heard both *Bells* and *Ordnance,* but never been so much affected with those, as with these *Bells.* I have a *lien* near a *Steeple,* in which there are said to be more than *thirty Bels;* And neere another, where there is one so bigge, as that the *Clapper* is said to weigh more than *six hundred pound,* yet never so affected as here. Here the *Bells* can scarse solemnise the funerall of any person, but that I knew him, or knew that he was my *Neighbour:* we dwelt in houses neere to one another before, but now hee is gone into that house, into which I must follow him. There is a way of correcting the *Children* of great persons, that other *Children* are corrected in their *behalfe,* and in their *names,* and this workes upon them, who indeed had more deserved it. And when these *Bells* tell me, that now one, and now another is buried, must not I acknowledge, that they have the *correction* due to me, and paid the *debt* that I owe? There is a story of a *Bell* in a *Monastery* which, when any of the house was sicke to death, rung alwaies *voluntarily,* and they knew the inevitablenesse of the danger by that. It rung once, when no man was sick; but the next day one of the house, fell from the *steeple,* and died,

and the *Bell* held the reputation of a *Prophet* still. If these *Bells* that warne to a *Funerall* now, were appropriated to none, may not I, by the houre of the *Funerall*, supply? How many men that stand at an *execution*, if they would aske, for what dies that man, should heare their owne faults condemned, and see themselves executed, by *Atturney*? We scarce heare of any man *preferred*, but wee thinke of our selves, that wee might very well have beene that *Man;* Why might not I have beene that *Man,* that is carried to his *grave* now? Could I fit my selfe, to *stand,* or *sit* in any mans *place,* and not to lie in any mans *grave?* I may lacke much of the *good parts* of the meanest, but I lacke nothing of the *mortality* of the weakest; They may have acquired better *abilities* than I, but I was borne to as many *infirmities* as they. To be an *Incumbent* by lying down in a *grave,* to be a *Doctor* by teaching *Mortification* by *Example,* by *dying,* though I may have *seniors,* others may be *elder* than I, yet I have proceeded apace in a good *University,* and gone a great way in a little time, by the furtherance of a vehement *Fever;* and whomsoever these *Bells* bring to the ground to day, if hee and I had beene compared yesterday, perchance I should have been thought likelier to come to this preferment, then, than he. *God* hath kept the power of *death* in his owne hands, lest any man should *bribe death.* If man knew the *gaine of death,* the *ease of death,* he would solicite, he would provoke *death* to assist him, by any hand, which he might use. But as when men see many of their owne professions preferd, it ministers a hope that that may light upon them; so when these hourely *Bells* tell me of so many *funerals* of men like me, it presents, if not a *desire* that it may, yet a *comfort* whensoever mine shall come.

17. Nunc lento sonitu dicunt, Morieris. *Now, this Bell tolling softly for another, saies to me, Thou must die.*

17. *Meditation.* Perchance hee for whom this *Bell* tolls, may be so ill, as that he knowes not it tolls for him; And perchance I may thinke my selfe so much better than I am, as that they who are about mee, and see my state, may have caused it to toll for mee, and I know not that. The *Church* is *Catholike, universall,* so are all her *Actions; All* that she does, belongs to *all.* When she *baptizes a child,* that action concernes mee; for that child is

thereby connected to that *Head* which is my *Head* too, and en-
graffed into that *body*, whereof I am a *member*. And when she
buries a Man, that action concernes me: All *mankinde* is of one
Author, and is one *volume;* when one Man dies, one *Chapter* is
not *torne* out of the *booke*, but *translated* into a better *language;*
and every *Chapter* must be so *translated; God* emploies several
translators; some peeces are translated by *age*, some by *sicknesse*,
some by *warre*, some by *justice;* but *Gods* hand is in every *translation;* and his hand shall binde up all our scattered leaves
againe, for that *Librarie* where every *booke* shall lie open to one
another: As therefore the *Bell* that rings to a *Sermon*, calls not
upon the *Preacher* onely, but upon the *Congregation* to come; so
this *Bell* calls us all: but how much more mee, who am brought
so neere the *doore* by this *sicknesse*. There was a *contention* as
farre as a *suite*, (in which both *pietie* and *dignitie*, *religion*, and
estimation, were mingled) which of the religious *Orders* should
ring to *praiers* first in the *Morning;* and it was *determined*, that
they should ring first that rose earliest. If we understand aright
the *dignitie* of this *Bell* that tolls for our *evening prayer*, wee
would bee glad to make it ours, by rising early, in that *application*, that it might bee ours, as wel as his, whose indeed it is. The
Bell doth toll for him that *thinkes* it doth; and though it *intermit*
againe, yet from that *minute*, that that occasion wrought upon
him, hee is united to *God*. Who casts not up his *Eie* to the *Sunne*
when it rises? but who takes off his *Eie* from a *Comet* when that
breakes out? Who bends not his *eare* to any *bell*, which upon any
occasion rings? but who can remove it from that *bell*, which is
passing a *peece of himselfe* out of this *world*? No man is an
Iland, intire of it selfe; every man is a peece of the *Continent*, a
part of the *maine;* if a *Clod* bee washed away by the *Sea, Europe*
is the lesse, as well as if a *Promontorie* were, as well as if a
Mannor of thy *friends* or of *thine owne* were; any mans *death*
diminishes *me*, because I am involved in *Mankinde;* And therefore never send to know for whom the *bell* tolls; It tolls for *thee*.
Neither can we call this a *begging* of *Miserie* or a *borrowing* of
Miserie, as though we were not miserable enough of our selves,
but must fetch in more from the next house, in taking upon us
the *Miserie* of our *Neighbours*. Truly it were an excusable *covetousnesse* if wee did; for *affliction* is a *treasure*, and scarce any
man hath *enough* of it. No man hath *affliction* enough that is

not matured, and ripened by it, and made fit for *God* by that *affliction*. If a man carry *treasure* in *bullion,* or in a *wedge* of *gold,* and have none coined into *currant Monies,* his *treasure* will not defray him as he travells. *Tribulation* is *Treasure* in the *nature* of it, but it is not *currant money* in the *use* of it, except wee get nearer and nearer our *home, Heaven,* by it. Another man may be *sicke* too, and sick to *death,* and this *affliction* may lie in his *bowels,* as *gold* in a *Mine,* and be of no use to him; but this *bell,* that tells me of his *affliction,* digs out, and applies that gold to *mee:* if by this consideration of anothers danger, I take mine owne into contemplation, and so secure my selfe, by making my recourse to my *God,* who is our onely securitie.

18. ——— At inde
Mortuus es, Sonitu celeri, pulsuque agitato.
The Bell rings out, and tells me in him, that I am dead.

18. Meditation. The *Bell* rings out; the *pulse* thereof is changed; the *tolling* was a *faint,* and *intermitting pulse,* upon one side; this *stronger,* and argues *more* and *better life.* His *soule* is gone out; and as a Man, who had a lease of 1000. *yeeres* after the expiration of a short one, or an inheritance after the *life* of a man in a *consumption,* he is now entred into the possession of his *better estate.* His *soule* is gone; *whither?* Who saw it *come in,* or who saw it *goe out? No body;* yet every body is sure, he *had one,* and *hath none.* If I will aske meere *Philosophers,* what the *soule* is, I shall finde amongst them, that will tell me, it is nothing, but the *temperament* and *harmony,* and *just and equall composition of the Elements in the body,* which produces all those *faculties* which we ascribe to the *soule;* and so, in it selfe is *nothing,* no *seperable substance,* that overlives the *body.* They see the *soule* is nothing else in other *Creatures,* and they affect an *impious humilitie,* to think *as low* of *Man.* But if my *soule* were no more than the soul of a *beast,* I could not thinke so; that *soule* that can *reflect* upon it selfe, *consider* it selfe, is *more* than so. If I will aske, not meere *Philosophers,* but *mixt men, Philosophicall Divines, how* the *soule,* being a *separate substance,* enters into *Man,* I shall finde some that will tell me, that it is by *generation,* and *procreation* from *parents,* because they thinke it hard, to charge the *soule* with the guiltiness of *originall* sinne, if the *soule* were infused into a *body,* in which it must necessarily grow *foule,* and contract *originall sinne,* whether it *will* or *no;* and I shall finde some that will tell mee, that it is by *immediate infusion from God,* because they think it hard, to maintaine an *immortality* in such a *soule,* as should be begotten, and derived with the *body* from *mortall parents.* If I will aske, not a *few men,* but almost *whole bodies, whole Churches,* what becomes of the *soules* of the *righteous,* at the *departing* thereof from the *body,* I shall bee told by some, *That they attend an expiation, a purification in a place of torment;* By some, that *they attend the fruition of the sight of God, in a place of rest; but yet, but of expectation;* By some, *that they passe to an immediate possession of the presence of God.* S. *Augustine* studied the *nature* of the *soule,* as much as any thing, but the *salvation of the soule;* and he sent an expresse *Messenger* to Saint *Hierome,* to consult of some things concerning the *soule:* But he satisfies himselfe with this: *Let the departure of my soule to salvation be evident to my faith, and I care the lesse, how darke the entrance of my soule, into my body, bee to my reason.* It is the *going out,* more than the *comming in,* that concernes us. This *soule,* this Bell tells me, is *gone out; Whither?* Who shall tell mee that? I know not *who it is;* much less *what he was;* The condition of the man, and the course of his life, which should tell mee *whither* hee is gone, I know not. I was not there in his *sicknesse,* nor at his *death;* I saw not his *way,* nor his *end,* nor can aske them, who did, thereby to *conclude,* or *argue,* whither he is gone. But yet I have one neerer mee than all these; mine owne *Charity;* I aske that; and that tels me, *He is gone to everlasting rest,* and *joy,* and *glory:* I owe him a good *opinion;* it is but *thankfull charity* in mee, because I received *benefit* and *instruction* from him when his *Bell* told: and I, being made the fitter to *pray,* by that disposition, wherein I was assisted by his occasion, did *pray* for him; and I *pray* not without *faith;* so I doe *charitably,* so I do *faithfully* beleeve, that that *soule* is gone to everlasting *rest,* and *joy,* and *glory.* But for the *body,* how poore a wretched thing is *that?* wee cannot expresse it *so fast,* as it growes *worse* and *worse.* That *body* which scarce *three minutes* since was such a *house,* as that that *soule,* which made but one step from thence to *Heaven,* was scarse thorowly content, to leave that for *Heaven:* that *body* hath lost the *name* of a *dwelling house,* because none dwells in it, and is making

haste to lose the name of a *body,* and dissolve to *putrefaction.*
Who would not bee affected, to see a cleere and sweet *River* in
the *Morning,* grow a *kennell* of muddy land water by *noone,* and
condemned to the saltnesse of the *Sea* by *night?* And how lame
a *picture,* how faint a *representation* is that, of the precipitation
of mans body to *dissolution? Now* all the parts built up, and knit
by a lovely *soule, now* but a *statue* of *clay,* and *now,* these limbs
melted off, as if that *clay* were but *snow;* and *now,* the whole
house is but a *handfull of sand,* so much *dust,* and but a *pecke* of
rubbidge, so much *bone.* If *he,* who, as this *Bell* tells mee, is gone
now, were some *excellent Artificer,* who comes to him for a
clocke, or for a *garment* now? or for *counsaile,* if hee were a
Lawyer? If a *Magistrate,* for *Justice?* Man, before hee hath his
immortall soule, hath a *soule* of *sense,* and a *soule* of *vegitation*
before that: This *immortall soule* did not forbid other *soules,* to
be in us before, but when this *soule* departs, it carries all with it;
no more *vegetation,* no more *sense:* such a *Mother in law* is the
Earth, in respect of our *naturall mother;* in her *wombe* we *grew;*
and when she was delivered of us, wee were planted in some
place, in some *calling* in the *world;* In the wombe of the *earth,*
wee *diminish,* and when shee is *deliverd* of us, our *grave opened*
for another, wee are not *transplanted,* but *transported,* our *dust*
blowne away with *prophane dust,* with *every wind.*

21. —— Atque annuit Ille,
Qui, per eos, clamat, Linquas jam, Lazare, lectum.
God prospers their practise, and he, by them,
calls Lazarus *out of his tombe, mee out of my bed.*

21. *Meditation.* If a man had beene left *alone* in this *world,* at
first, shall I thinke, that he would not have *fallen?* If there had
beene no *Woman,* would not man have served, to have beene his
own *Tempter?* When I see him now, subject to infinite weaknesses, fall into *infinite sinne,* without any *forraine tentations.*
shall I thinke, hee would have had *none,* if hee had beene *alone?*
God saw that Man needed a *Helper,* if hee should bee well; but to
make *Woman* ill, the *Devill* saw, that there needed no *third.*
When *God,* and *wee* were *alone,* in *Adam,* that was not enough;
when the *Devill* and wee were *alone,* in *Eve,* it was enough. O
what a *Giant* is *Man,* when he fights against himselfe, and what
a *Dwarfe* when hee *needs,* or *exercises* his owne assistance for

himselfe? I cannot *rise* out of my bed, till the *Physitian enable*
mee, nay I cannot tel, that I am able to rise, till *hee tell* me so. I
doe nothing, I *know* nothing of myselfe: how little, and how im-
potent a peece of the *world,* is any *Man* alone? and how much
lesse a peece of *himselfe* is that *Man?* So little, as that when it
falls out, (as it falls out in some cases) that more *misery,* and
more *oppression,* would be an *ease* to a *man,* he cannot give himselfe that *miserable addition,* of *more misery;* a *man* that is
pressed to death, and might be eased by more *weights,* cannot lay
those more *weights* upon himselfe: Hee can sinne *alone,* and
suffer *alone,* but not *repent,* not bee *absolved,* without *another.*
Another tels mee, I *may rise;* and I *doe* so. But is every *raising* a
preferment? or is every present *preferment* a *station?* I am read-
ier to fall to the *Earth,* now I am up, than I was when I *lay* in the
bed: *O perverse way, irregular motion* of *Man; even rising* it selfe
is the way to *Ruine.* How many *men* are raised, and then doe not
fill the place they are raised to? No *corner* of any place can bee
empty; there can be no *vacuity;* If that *Man* doe not fill the
place, *other men* will; complaints of his *insufficiency* will *fill* it;
Nay, such an abhorring is there in *Nature,* of *vacuity,* that if
there be but an *imagination* of not *filling,* in any *man,* that
which is but *imagination* neither, will *fill* it, that is, *rumor* and
voice, and it will be *given out,* (upon no ground, but *Imagination,* and no man knowes *whose imagination*) that hee is *corrupt*
in his place, or *insufficient* in his place, and another prepared to
succeed him in his place. A man *rises,* sometimes, and *stands*
not, because hee doth not, or is not beleeved to *fill* his place; and
sometimes he *stands* not, because hee *overfills* his place: Hee
may bring so much *vertue,* so much *Justice,* so much *integrity*
to the place, as shall *spoile* the place, *burthen* the place; his *integrity* may bee a *Libell* upon his *Predecessor,* and cast an *in-
famy* upon him, and a *burthen* upon his *successor,* to proceede
by *example,* and to bring the place itselfe to an *under-value,* and
the *market* to an *uncertainty.* I am *up,* and I seeme to *stand,* and
I goe *round;* and I am a new *Argument* of the *new Philosophie,*
That the *Earth* moves round; why may I not beleeve, that the
whole earth moves in a *round motion,* though that seeme to mee
to *stand,* when as I seeme to *stand* to my *Company,* and yet am
carried, in a giddy, and *circular motion,* as I *stand?* Man hath
no *center* but *misery; there* and onely *there,* hee is *fixt,* and sure

to finde himselfe. How little soever hee bee *raised*, he *moves*, and moves in a *circle*, giddily; and as in the *Heavens*, there are but a few *Circles*, that goe about the whole world, but many *Epicircles*, and other lesser *Circles*, but yet *Circles*, so of those men, which are *raised*, and put into *Circles*, few of them move from *place* to *place*, and passe through many and beneficiall places, but fall into little *Circles*, and, within a step or two, are at their *end*, and not so well, as they were in the *Center*, from which they were *raised*. Every thing serves to *exemplifie*, to *illustrate* mans *misery*. But I need goe no farther, than *my selfe*: for a long time, I was not able to *rise*; At last, I must bee *raised* by others; and now I am *up*, I am ready to sinke *lower* than before.

Sir Thomas Browne

Born in London in 1605, Sir Thomas Browne studied at Winchester from 1616 to 1623, Oxford from 1623 to 1629, and, from 1631 to 1634, continued his medical studies at Montpellier, Padua, and Leyden. In 1637 he settled at Norwich to practice medicine, married in 1641, and eventually had twelve children. In 1664 he testified at a trial of witches. He was knighted in 1671, and in 1682 died on his birthday. He published the authorized edition of Religio Medici *in 1643;* Pseudodoxia Epidemica *in 1646;* Hydriotaphia: Urn Burial *and* The Garden of Cyrus *in 1658. A Letter to a Friend was printed in 1690.*

FROM

Religio Medici:
THE FIRST PART

Section 1. For my Religion, though there be several Circumstances that might perswade the World I have none at all, as
the general scandal of my Profession, the natural course of my
Studies, the indifferency of my Behaviour and Discourse in matters of Religion, neither violently Defending one, nor with that
common ardour and contention Opposing another; yet, in de-
spight hereof, I dare, without usurpation assume the honourable Stile of a Christian. Not that I meerly owe this Title to the
Font, my Education, or Clime wherein I was born, as being bred
up either to confirm those Principles my Parents instilled into
my Understanding, or by a general consent proceed in the Religion of my Country: But having in my riper years and confirmed Judgment, seen and examined all, I find my self obliged
by the Principles of Grace, and the Law of mine own Reason,
to embrace no other Name but this: Neither doth herein my zeal
so far make me forget the general Charity I owe unto Humanity,
as rather to hate than pity *Turks, Infidels,* and (what is worse)
Jews; rather contenting my self to enjoy that happy Stile, than
maligning those who refuse so glorious a Title.

Section 2. But because the Name of a Christian is become too
general to express our Faith, there being a Geography of Religions as well as Lands, and every Clime distinguished not only

by their Laws and Limits, but circumscribed by their Doctrines and Rules of Faith; to be particular, I am of that Reformed new-cast Religion, wherein I dislike nothing but the Name; of the same belief our Saviour taught, the Apostles disseminated, the Fathers authorized, and the Martyrs confirmed, but by the sinister ends of Princes, the ambition and avarice of Prelates, and the fatal corruption of times, so decayed, impaired, and fallen from its native Beauty, that it required the careful and charitable hands of these times to restore it to its primitive Integrity. Now the accidental occasion whereupon, the slender means whereby the low and abject condition of the Person by whom so good a work was set on foot, which in our Adversaries beget contempt and scorn, fills me with wonder, and is the very same Objection the insolent Pagans first cast at Christ and his Disciples.

Section 3. Yet have I not so shaken hands with those desperate Resolutions, who had rather venture at large their decayed bottom, than bring her in to be new trimm'd in the Dock; who had rather promiscuously retain all, than abridge any, and obstinately be what they are, than what they have been, as to stand in Diameter[1] and Swords point with them: We have reformed from them, not against them; for omitting those Improperations, and Terms of Scurrility betwixt us, which only difference our Affections, and not our Cause, there is between us one common Name and Appellation, one Faith and necessary body of Principles common to us both; and therefore I am not scrupulous to converse and live with them, to enter their Churches in defect of ours, and either pray with them, or for them: I could never perceive any rational Consequence from those many Texts which prohibit the Children of *Israel* to pollute themselves with the Temples of the Heathens; we being all Christians, and not divided by such detested impieties as might prophane our Prayers, or the place wherein we make them; or that a resolved Conscience may not adore her Creator any where, especially in places devoted to his Service; where if their Devotions offend him, mine may please him; if theirs prophane it, mine may hallow it: Holy-water and Crucifix (dangerous to the common people) deceive not my judgment, nor abuse my devotion at all:

1 in Diameter: in opposition

I am, I confess, naturally inclined to that, which misguided Zeal terms Superstition: my common conversation I do acknowledge austere, my behaviour full of rigour, sometimes not without morosity; yet at my Devotion I love to use the civility of my knee, my hat, and hand, with all those outward and sensible motions which may express or promote my invisible Devotion. I should violate my own arm rather than a Church, nor willingly deface the name of Saint or Martyr. At the sight of a Cross or Crucifix I can dispense with my hat, but scarce with the thought or memory of my Saviour: I cannot laugh at, but rather pity, the fruitless journeys of Pilgrims, or contemn the miserable condition of Fryars; for though misplaced in Circumstances, there is something in it of Devotion. I could never hear the *Ave-Mary* Bell without an elevation; or think it a sufficient warrant, because they erred in one circumstance, for me to err in all, that is, in silence and dumb contempt; whilst, therefore, they directed their Devotions to Her, I offered mine to God, and rectified the Errors of their Prayers, by rightly ordering mine own: At a solemn Procession I have wept abundantly, while my consorts, blind with opposition and prejudice, have fallen into an excess of scorn and laughter: There are questionless both in *Greek, Roman,* and *African* Churches, Solemnities and Ceremonies, whereof the wiser Zeals do make a Christian use, and stand condemned by us, not as evil in themselves, but as allurements and baits of superstition to those vulgar heads that look asquint on the face of Truth, and those unstable Judgments that cannot resist in the narrow point and centre of Virtue without a reel or stagger to the Circumference.

Section 4. As there were many Reformers, so likewise many Reformations; every Country proceeding in a particular way and method, according as their national Interest, together with their Constitution and Clime inclined them; some angrily, and with extremity; others calmly, and with mediocrity,[2] not rending, but easily dividing the community, and leaving an honest possibility of a reconciliation; which though peaceable Spirits do desire, and may conceive that revolution of time and the mercies of God may effect, yet that judgment that shall consider the pres-

2 mediocrity: condition of being intermediate between two extremes

ent antipathies between the two extreams, their contrarieties in condition, affection, and opinion, may with the same hopes expect an union in the Poles of Heaven.

Section 5. But to difference my self nearer and draw into a lesser Circle: there is no Church whose every part so squares unto my Conscience; whose Articles, Constitutions, and Customs, seem so consonant unto reason, and as it were framed to my particular Devotion, as this whereof I hold my Belief, the Church of *England,* to whose Faith I am a sworn Subject; and therefore in a double Obligation subscribe unto her Articles, and endeavour to observe her Constitutions; whatsoever is beyond, as points indifferent, I observe according to the rules of my private reason, or the humour and fashion of my Devotion; neither believing this, because *Luther* affirmed it, or disproving that, because *Calvin* hath disavouched it. I condemn not all things in the Council of *Trent,* nor approve all in the Synod of *Dort.* In brief, where the Scripture is silent, the Church is my Text; where that speaks, 'tis but my Comment: where there is a joynt silence of both, I borrow not the rules of my Religion from *Rome* or *Geneva* but the dictates of my own reason. It is an unjust scandal of our adversaries, and a gross errour in our selves, to compute the Nativity of our Religion from Henry the Eighth, who though he rejected the Pope, refus'd not the faith of *Rome* and effected no more than what his own Predecessors desired and assayed in Ages past, and was conceived the State of *Venice* would have attempted in our days. It is as uncharitable a point in us to fall upon those popular scurrilities and opprobrious scoffs of the Bishop of *Rome,* to whom as a temporal Prince, we owe the duty of good language: I confess there is cause of passion between us; by his sentence I stand excommunicated, Heretick is the best language he affords me; yet can no ear witness, I ever returned him the name of Antichrist, Man of sin, or Whore of *Babylon.* It is the method of Charity to suffer without reaction: those usual Satyrs and invectives of the Pulpit may perchance produce a good effect on the vulgar, whose ears are opener to Rhetorick than Logick; yet do they in no wise confirm the faith of wiser Believers, who know that a good cause needs not to be patron'd by passion, but can sustain it self upon a temperate dispute.

. . .

Section 6. I could never divide my self from any man upon the difference of an opinion, or be angry with his judgment for not agreeing with me in that, from which perhaps within a few days I should dissent my self. I have no Genius to disputes in Religion, and have often thought it wisdom to decline them, especially upon a disadvantage, or when the cause of troth might suffer in the weakness of my patronage: Where we desire to be informed, 'tis good to contest with men above our selves; but to confirm and establish our opinions, 'tis best to argue with judgments below our own, that the frequent spoils and Victories over their reasons may settle in ourselves as esteem and confirmed Opinion of our own. Every man is not a proper Champion for Truth, nor fit to take up the Gauntlet in the cause of Verity: Many from the ignorance of these Maximes, and an inconsiderate Zeal unto Truth, have too rashly charged the Troops of Error, and remain as Trophies unto the enemies of Truth: A man may be in as just possession of Truth as of a City, and yet be forced to surrender; 'tis therefore far better to enjoy her with peace, than to hazzard her on a battle: if therefore there rise any doubts in my way, I do forget them, or at least defer them, till my better setled judgment, and more manly reason be able to resolve them, for I perceive every mans own reason is his best *Œdipus,* and will upon a reasonable truce, find a way to loose those bonds wherewith the subtleties of error have enchained our more flexible and tender judgments. In Philosophy, where Truth seems double-fac'd, there is no man more Paradoxical than my self; but in Divinity I love to keep the Road; and, though not in an implicite, yet an humble faith, follow the great wheel of the Church, by which I move, not reserving any proper Poles or motion from the Epicycle of my own brain; by this means I leave no gap for Heresie, Schismes, or Errors, of which at present I hope I shall not injure Truth to say I have no taint or tincture: I must confess my greener studies have been polluted with two or three, not any begotten in the latter Centuries, but old and obsolete, such as could never have been revived, but by such extravagant and irregular heads as mine: for indeed Heresies perish not with their Authors, but like the river Arethusa, though they lose their currents in one place, they rise up again in another: One *General* Council is not able to extirpate

one single Heresie; it may be cancell'd for the present, but revolution of time, and the like aspects from Heaven, will restore it,
when it will flourish till it be condemned again. For as though
there were a *Metempsuchosis* and the soul of one man passed
into another; Opinions do find after certain Revolutions, men
and minds like those that first begat them. To see our selves
again, we need not look for *Plato's* year[3]: every man is not only
himself; there hath been many *Diogenes* and as many *Timons,*
though but few of that name; men are liv'd over again, the
world is now as it was in Ages past; there was none then, but
there hath been some one since that Parallels him, and is, as it
were his revived self.

Section 7. Now the first of mine was that of the *Arabians.* That
the Souls of men perished with their Bodies, but should yet be
raised again at the last day: not that I did absolutely conceive
a mortality of the Soul; but if that were, which Faith, not Philosophy, hath yet thoroughly disproved, and that both entred the
grave together, yet I held the same conceit thereof that we all
do of the body, that it rise again. Surely it is but the merits of
our unworthy Natures, if we sleep in darkness until the last
Alarm. A serious reflex upon my own unworthiness did make
me backward from challenging this prerogative of my Soul; so
that I might enjoy my Saviour at the last, I could with patience
be nothing almost unto Eternity. The second was that of *Origen,*
That God would not persist in his vengeance for ever, but after
a definite time of his wrath, he would release the damned Souls
from torture: which error I fell into upon a serious contemplation of the great Attribute of God, his Mercy; and did a little
cherish it in my self, because I found therein no malice, and
a ready weight to sway me from the other extream of despair,
whereunto Melancholy and Contemplative Natures are too easily
disposed. A third there is which I did never positively maintain
or practise, but have often wished it had been consonant to
Truth, and not offensive to my Religion, and that is the Prayer
for the dead; whereunto I was inclin'd from some charitable in-
ducements, whereby I could scarce contain my Prayers for a
friend at the ringing of a Bell, or behold his Corps without an

3 Plato's year: a revolution of a thousand years when all things
return to their former place

Orison for his Soul: 'Twas a good way, methought, to be remembered by posterity, and far more noble than an History. These opinions I never maintained with pertinacy, or endeavoured to enveagle any man's belief unto mine, nor so much as ever revealed or disputed them with my dearest friends; by which means I neither propagated them in others, nor confirmed them in my self; but suffering them to flame upon their own substance, without addition of new fuel, they went out insensibly of themselves: therefore these Opinions, though condemned by lawful Councels, were not Heresies in me, but bare Errors, and single Lapses of my understanding without a joynt depravity of my will: Those have not onely depraved understandings, but diseased affections, which cannot enjoy a singularity without an Heresie, or be the Author of an Opinion without they be of a Sect also; this was the Villany of the first Schism of *Lucifer*, who was not content to err alone, but drew into his Faction many Legions, and upon this experience he tempted only *Eve*, as well understanding the Communicable nature of Sin, and that to deceive but one, was tacitely and upon consequence to delude them both.

Section 8. That Heresies should arise, we have the Prophesie of Christ; but that old ones should be abolished, we hold no prediction. That there must be Heresies, is true, not only in our Church, but also in any other: even in the doctrines heretical, there will be super-heresies; and Arians not only divided from their Church, but also among themselves: for heads that are disposed unto Schism and complexionally propense to innovation, are naturally indisposed for a community; nor will be ever confined unto the order or œconomy of one body; and therefore when they separate from others, they knit but loosely among themselves; nor contented with a general breach or dichotomy with their Church, do subdivide and mince themselves almost into Atoms. 'Tis true, that men of singular parts and humours have not been free from singular opinions and conceits in all Ages; retaining something, not only beside the opinion of his own Church or any other, but also any particular Author; which notwithstanding a sober Judgment may do without offence or heresie; for there is yet, after all the Decrees of Councils, and the niceties of Schools, many things untouch'd, unimagin'd, wherein the liberty of an honest reason may play and expatiate with security, and far without the circle of an Heresie.

Section 9. As for those wingy Mysteries in Divinity, and airy subtleties in Religion, which have unhing'd the brains of better heads, they never stretched the *Pia Mater*[4] of mine; methinks there be not impossibilities enough in Religion, for an active faith; the deepest Mysteries ours contains have not only been illustrated, but maintained by Syllogism, and the rule of Reason: I love to lose my self in a mystery, to pursue my Reason to an O *altitudo!* [5] 'Tis my solitary recreation to pose my apprehension with those involved Ænigmas and riddles of the Trinity, with Incarnation and Resurrection. I can answer all the Objections of Satan and my rebellious reason, with that odd resolution I learned of *Tertullian, Certum est quia impossibile est.*[6] I desire to exercise my faith in the difficultest point; for to credit ordinary and visible objects, is not faith, but perswasion. Some believe the better for seeing Christ's Sepulchre; and, when they have seen the Red Sea, doubt not of the Miracle. Now contrarily, I bless my self, and am thankful that I lived not in the days of Miracles, that I never saw Christ nor his Disciples; I would not have been one of those *Israelites* that pass'd the Red Sea, nor one of Christ's patients on whom he wrought his wonders; then had my faith been thrust upon me; nor should I enjoy that greater blessing pronounced to all that believe and saw not. 'Tis an easie and necessary belief, to credit what our eye and sense hath examined: I believe he was dead and buried, and rose again; and desire to see him in his glory, rather than to contemplate him in his Cenotaphe, or Sepulchre. Nor is this much to believe; as we have reason, we owe this faith unto History: they only had the advantage of a bold and noble Faith, who lived before his coming, who upon obscure prophesies and mystical

. . . . .

4 *Pia Mater:* innermost membrane enclosing the brain
5 *O altitudo:* from the Vulgate translation of Romans xi:33: "O the depth of the riches both of the wisdom and knowledge of God! how unsearchable are his judgments, and his ways past finding out!"
6 *Certum . . . est:* It is certain because it is impossible

Types could raise a belief, and expect apparent impossibilities.
Section 10. 'Tis true, there is an edge in all firm belief, and with
an easie Metaphor we may say the Sword of Faith; but in these
obscurities I rather use it in the adjunct the Apostle gives it, a
Buckler; under which I conceive a wary combatant may lye in-
vulnerable. Since I was of understanding to know we knew
nothing, my reason hath been more pliable to the will of Faith;
I am now content to understand a mystery without a rigid definition, in an easie and Platonick description. That allegorical
description of *Hermes,* pleaseth me beyond all the Metaphysical
definitions of Divines; where I cannot satisfy my reason, I love
to humour my fancy: I had as live you tell me that *anima est
angelus hominis, est Corpus Dei,* as *Entelechia; Lux est umbra
Dei,* as *actus perspicui;*[7] where there is an obscurity too deep for
our Reason, 'tis good to sit down with a description, periphrasis,
or adumbration; for by acquainting our Reason how unable it is
to display the visible and obvious effects of Nature, it becomes
more humble and submissive unto the subtleties of Faith; and
thus I teach my haggard [8] and unreclaimed Reason to stoop unto
the lure of Faith. I believe there was already a tree whose fruit
our unhappy Parents tasted, though in the same Chapter when
God forbids it, 'tis positively said, the plants of the field were
not yet grown; for God had not caus'd it to rain upon the earth.
I believe that the Serpent (if we shall literally understand it)
from his proper form and figure made his motion on his belly
before the curse. I find the tryal of the Pucellage[9] and virginity
of Women, which God ordained the *Jews* is very fallible. Experience and History informs me, that not onely many particular
Women, but likewise whole Nations, have escaped the curse of
Childbirth, which God seems to pronounce upon the whole Sex;
yet do I believe that all this is true, which indeed my Reason
would perswade me to be false; and this I think is no vulgar
part of Faith, to believe a thing not only above but contrary to
Reason, and against the Arguments of our proper Senses.

.   .   .

7 that *anima . . . perspicui:* that the soul is the angel of the
man, is the body of God, rather than that which naturally makes
the body move; that light is the shadow of God rather than that
it is visible movement
8 haggard: wild
9 Pucellage: maidenhood

Section 11. In my solitary and retired imagination, (*neque enim cum porticus, aut me lectulus accepit, desum mihi*)[1] I remember I am not alone, and therefore forget not to contemplate him and his Attributes who is ever with me, especially those two mighty ones, his Wisdom and Eternity: with the one I recreate, with the other I confound, my understanding: for who can speak of Eternity without a solœcism, or think thereof without an Extasie? Time we may comprehend: 'tis but five days elder then our selves, and hath the same Horoscope with the World; but to retire so far back as to apprehend a beginning, to give such an infinite start forwards as to conceive an end in an essence that we affirm hath neither the one nor the other, it puts my Reason to St. *Paul's* Sanctuary: my Philosophy dares not say the Angels can do it; God hath not made a Creature that can comprehend him; 'tis a privilege of his own nature: *I am that I am,* was his own definition unto *Moses;* and 'twas a short one, to confound mortality, that durst question God, or ask him what he was; indeed, he onely is; all others have and shall be: but in Eternity there is no distinction of Tenses; and therefore that terrible term *Predestination,* which hath troubled so many weak heads to conceive, and the wisest to explain, is in respect to God no prescious[2] determination of our Estates to come, but a definitive blast of his Will already fulfilled, and at the instant that he first decreed it; for to his Eternity, which is indivisible, and all together, the last Trump is already sounded, the reprobates in the flame, and the blessed in *Abraham's* bosome. St. *Peter* speaks modestly, when he saith, a thousand years to God are but as one day: for to speak like a Philosopher, those continued instances of time which flow into a thousand years, make not to him one moment; what to us is to come, to his Eternity is present, his whole duration being but one permanent point, without Succession, Parts, Flux, or Division.

Section 12. There is no Attribute that adds more difficulty to the mystery of the Trinity, where, though in a relative way of Father and Son, we must deny a priority. I wonder how Aristotle could conceive the World eternal, or how he could make good two Eternities: his similitude of a Triangle, comprehended in a

1 *neque . . . mihi:* not even when I am relaxing do I forget
2 prescious: prescient

square, doth somewhat illustrate the Trinity of our Souls, and that the Triple Unity of God; for there is in us not three, but a Trinity of Souls, because there is in us, if not three distinct Souls, yet differing faculties, that can and do subsist apart in different Subjects, and yet in us are so united as to make but one Soul and substance: if one Soul were so perfect as to inform three distinct Bodies, that were a petty Trinity: conceive, the distinct number of three, not divided nor separated by the Intellect, but actually comprehended in its Unity, and that is a perfect Trinity. I have often admired the mystical way of *Pythagoras* and the secret Magick of numbers. Beware of Philosophy, is a precept not to be received in too large a sense; for in this Mass of Nature there is a set of things that carry in their Front, though not in Capital Letters, yet in Stenography, and short Characters, something of Divinity, which to wiser Reasons serve as Luminaries in the Abyss of Knowledge, and to judicious beliefs, as Scales and Roundles to mount the Pinacles and highest pieces of Divinity. The severe Schools shall never laugh me out of the Philosophy of *Hermes,* that this visible World is but a Picture of the invisible, wherein, as in a Pourtraict, things are not truely, but in equivocal shapes, and as they counterfeit some more real substance in that invisible Fabrick.

Section 13. That other Attribute wherewith I recreate my devotion, is his Wisdom, in which, I am happy; and for the contemplation of this only, do not repent me that I was bred in the way of Study: The advantage I have of the vulgar, with the content and happiness I conceive therein, is an ample recompence for all my endeavours, in what part of knowledge soever. Wisdom is his most beauteous Attribute, no man can attain unto it, yet *Solomon* pleased God when he desired it. He is wise, because he knows all things; and he knoweth all things, because he made them all: but his greatest knowledge is in comprehending that he made not, that is, himself. And this is also the greatest knowledge in man. For this do I honour my own profession, and embrace the Counsel even of the Devil himself: had he read such a Lecture in Paradise as he did at *Delphos,* we had better known our selves, nor had we stood in fear to know him. I know he is wise in all, wonderful in what we conceive, but far more in what we comprehend not; for we behold him but asquint,

upon reflex or shadow; our understanding is dimmer than *Moses*
Eye; we are ignorant of the back-parts or lower side of his Divinity; therefore to prie into the maze of his Counsels, is not
only folly in man, but presumption even in Angels; like us, they
are his Servants, not his Senators; he holds no Counsel, but that
mystical one of the Trinity, wherein, though there be three Persons, there is but one mind that decrees without Contradiction:
nor needs he any; his actions are not begot with deliberation,
his Wisdom naturally knows what's best; his intellect stands
ready fraught with the Superlative and purest *Ideas* of goodness; consultation and election, which are two motions in us,
make but one in him; his actions springing from his power at
the first touch of his will. These are Contemplations Metaphysical: my humble speculations have another Method, and are content to trace and discover those expressions he hath left in his
Creatures, and the obvious effects of Nature; there is no danger
to profound these mysteries, no *sanctum sanctorum*[3] in Philosophy: the World was made to be inhabited by Beasts; but studied and contemplated by Man: 'tis the Debt of our Reason we
owe unto God, and the homage we pay for not being Beasts;
without this, the World is still as though it had not been, or as
it was before the sixth day, when as yet there was not a Creature
that could conceive, or say there was a World. The Wisdom of
God receives small honour from those vulgar Heads that rudely
stare about, and with a gross rusticity admire his works; those
highly magnifie him, whose judicious inquiry into his Acts, and
deliberate research into his Creatures, return the duty of a devout and learned admiration.

Therefore,

Search while thou wilt, and let thy Reason go
To ransome Truth, even to th' Abyss below;
Rally the scattered Causes; and that line
Which Nature twists, be able to untwine:
It is thy Maker's will, for unto none,
But unto Reason can he e're be known.
The Devils do know thee, but those damn'd Meteors
Build not thy Glory, but confound thy Creatures.
Teach my indeavours so thy works to read,
That learning them in thee, I may proceed.

3 *sanctum sanctorum:* holy of holies

Give thou my reason that instructive flight,
Whose weary wings may on thy hands still light.
Teach me to soar aloft, yet ever so,
When neer the Sun, to stoop again below.
Thus shall my humble Feathers safely hover,
And, though near Earth, more than the Heavens discover.
And then at last, when homeward I shall drive
Rich with the Spoils of Nature to my Hive,
There will I sit like that industrious Flie,
Buzzing Thy praises, which shall never die,
Till Death abrupts them, and succeeding Glory
Bid me go on in a more lasting story.

And this is almost all wherein an humble Creature may endeavour to requite, and some way to retribute unto his Creator: for if not he that saith, *Lord, Lord,* but *he that doth the will of his Father, shall be saved;* certainly our wills must be our performances, and our intents make out our Actions; otherwise our pious labours shall find anxiety in our Graves, and our best endeavours not hope, but fear a resurrection.

Section 14. There is but one first cause, and four second causes of all things; some are without efficient, as God; others without matter, as Angels; some without form, as the first matter: but every Essence created or uncreated, hath its final cause, and some positive end both of its Essence and Operation; this is the cause I grope after in the works of Nature; on this hangs the Providence of God: to raise so beauteous a structure as the World and the Creatures thereof, was but his Art; but their sundry and divided operations, with their predestinated ends, are from the Treasure of his Wisdom. In the causes, nature and affections of the Eclipses of the Sun and Moon, there is most excellent speculation; but to profound farther, and to contemplate a reason why his Providence hath so disposed and ordered their motions in that vast circle, as to conjoyn and obscure each other, is a sweeter piece of Reason, and a diviner point of Philosophy; therefore sometimes, and in some things, there appears to me as much Divinity in *Galen* his books *De usu partium,* as in *Suarez'* Metaphysicks: Had *Aristotle* been as curious in the enquiry of this cause as he was of the other, he had not left behind him an imperfect piece of Philosophy, but an absolute tract of Divinity.

Section 15. Natura nihil agit frustra,[4] is the only indisputed Axiome in Philosophy; there are no *Grotesques* in Nature; not anything framed to fill up empty Cantons, and unnecessary spaces: in the most imperfect Creatures, and such as were not preserved in the Ark, but having their Seeds and Principles in the womb of Nature, are every where, where the power of the Sun is; in these is the Wisdom of his hand discovered: Out of this rank *Solomon* chose the object of his admiration; indeed what Reason may not go to School to the wisdom of Bees, Ants, and Spiders? what wise hand teacheth them to do what Reason cannot teach us? Ruder heads stand amazed at those prodigious pieces of Nature, Whales, Elephants, Dromidaries and Camels; these, I confess, are the Colossus and Majestick pieces of her hand: but in these narrow Engines there is more curious Mathematicks; and the civility of these little Citizens, more neatly sets forth the Wisdom of their Maker. Who admires not *Regio-Montanus* his Fly beyond his Eagle, or wonders not more at the operation of two Souls in those little Bodies, than but one in the Trunk of a Cedar? I could never content my contemplation with those general pieces of wonder, the Flux and Reflux of the Sea, the increase of *Nile*, the conversion of the Needle to the North; and have studied to match and parallel those in the more obvious and neglected pieces of Nature, which without further travel I can do in the Cosmography of my self; we carry with us the wonders we seek without us: There is all *Africa* and her prodigies in us; we are that bold and adventurous piece of Nature, which he that studies wisely learns in a *compendium*, what others labour at in a divided piece and endless volume.

Section 16. Thus there are two Books from whence I collect my Divinity; besides that written one of God, another of his servant Nature, that universal and publick Manuscript, that lies expans'd unto the Eyes of all, those that never saw him in the one, have discovered him in the other: this was the Scripture and Theology of the Heathens; the natural motion of the Sun made

4 *Natura . . . frustra:* nothing which nature does is useless

them more admire him, than its supernatural station did the Children of *Israel;* the ordinary effects of Nature wrought more admiration in them than in the other all his Miracles; surely the Heathens knew better how to joyn and read these mystical Letters than we Christians, who cast a more careless Eye on these common Hieroglyphicks, and disdain to suck Divinity from the flowers of Nature. Nor do I so forget God as to adore the name of Nature; which I define not, with the Schools, to be the principle of motion and rest, but that streight and regular line, that settled and constant course the Wisdom of God hath ordained the actions of his creatures, according to their several kinds. To make a revolution every day, is the Nature of the Sun, because of that necessary course which God hath ordained it, from which it cannot swerve but by a faculty from that voice which first did give it motion. Now this course of Nature God seldome alters or perverts, but like an excellent Artist hath so contrived his work, that with the self same instrument, without a new creation, he may effect his obscurest designs. Thus he sweetneth the Water with a Word, preserveth the Creatures in the Ark, which the blast of his mouth might have as easily created; for God is like a skilful Geometrician, who when more easily and with one stroak of his Compass he might describe or divide a right line, had yet rather do this in a circle or longer way; according to the constituted and fore-laid principles of his Art: yet this rule of his he doth sometimes pervert, to acquaint the World with his Prerogative, lest the arrogancy of our reason should question his power, and conclude he could not: and thus I call the effects of Nature the works of God, whose hand and instrument she only is; and therefore to ascribe his actions unto her, is to devolve the honour of the principal agent, upon the instrument; which if with reason we may do, then let our hammers rise up and boast they have built our houses, and our pens receive the honour of our writing. I hold there is a general beauty in the works of God, and therefore no deformity in any kind or species of creature whatsoever: I cannot tell by what Logick we call a *Toad,* a *Bear,* or an *Elephant* ugly; they being created in those outward shapes and figures which best express the actions of their inward forms And having past that general Visitation of God, who saw that all that he had made was good, that is, conformable to his Will, which abhors deformity, and is the rule of order and beauty; there is no deformity but in Monstrosity; wherein, notwithstanding, there is a kind of Beauty, Nature so ingeniously contriving the irregular parts, as they become sometimes more remarkable than the principal Fabrick. To speak yet more narrowly, there was never any thing ugly or mis-shapen, but the Chaos; wherein, notwithstanding, to speak strictly, there was no deformity, because no form, nor was it yet impregnate by the voice of God; Now Nature is not at variance with Art, nor Art with Nature; they being both servants of his Providence: Art is the perfection of Nature: were the World now as it was the sixth day, there were yet a Chaos: Nature hath made one World, and Art another. In brief, all things are artificial; for Nature is the Art of God.

Section 17. This is the ordinary and open way of his providence, which Art and Industry have in good part discovered, whose effects we may foretel without an Oracle: to foreshew these, is not Prophesie, but Prognostication. There is another way full of Meanders and Labyrinths, whereof the Devil and Spirits have no exact Ephemerides,[5] and that is a more particular and obscure method of his providence, directing the operations of individuals and single Essences: this we call Fortune, that serpentine and crooked line, whereby he draws those actions his Wisdom intends, in a more unknown and secret way: This cryptick and involved method of his Providence have I ever admired, nor can I relate the History of my life, the occurrences of my days, the escapes of dangers, and hits of chance, with a *Bezo las Manos*[6] to Fortune, or a bare Gramercy to my good Stars: *Abraham* might have thought the *Ram* in the thicket came thither by accident; humane reason would have said that meer chance conveyed *Moses* in the Ark to the sight of *Pharaoh's* Daughter: what a Labyrinth is there in the story of *Joseph*, able to convert a Stoick! Surely there are in every man's Life certain rubs, doublings, and wrenches, which pass a while under the effects of chance, but at the last well examined, prove the meer hand of God. 'Twas not dumb chance, that to discover the Fougade or Powder-plot, contrived a miscarriage in the Letter. I like the Victory of '88 the better for that one occurrence which

5 Ephemerides: almanacs
6 *Bezo las Manos:* kiss of the hands

our enemies imputed to our dishonour and the partiality of Fortune, to wit, the tempests and contrariety of Winds. King Philip
did not detract from the Nation, when he said, he sent his Armado to fight with men, and not to combate with the Winds.
Where there is a manifest disproportion between the powers
and forces of two several agents, upon a Maxime of reason we
may promise the Victory to the Superior; but when unexpected
accidents slip in, and unthought of occurrences intervene, these
must proceed from a power that owes no obedience to those
Axioms: where, as in the writing upon the wall, we may behold
the hand, but see not the spring that moves it. The success of
that petty Province of *Holland* (of which the Grand *Seignour*
proudly said, if they should trouble him as they did the *Span-
iard,* he would send his men with shovels and pick-axes, and
throw it into the Sea) I cannot altogether ascribe to the inge-
nuity and industry of the people, but the mercy of God, that
hath disposed them to such a thriving Genius; and to the will
of his Providence, that disposeth her favour to each Country in
their pre-ordinate season. All cannot be happy at once; for because the glory of one State depends upon the ruine of another,
there is a revolution and vicissitude of their greatness, and must
obey the swing of that wheel, not moved by Intelligences, but
by the hand of God, whereby all Estates arise to their *Zenith*
and Vertical points according to their predestinated periods. For
the lives, not only of men, but of Commonwealths, and the
whole World, run not upon an Helix[7] that still enlargeth; but
on a Circle, where arriving to their Meridian, they decline in
obscurity, and fall under the Horizon again.

Section 18. These must not therefore be named the effects of
Fortune, but in a relative way, and as we term the works of
Nature. It was the ignorance of man's reason that begat this
very name, and by a careless term miscalled the Providence of
God: for there is no liberty for causes to operate in a loose and
stragling way; nor any effect whatsoever, but hath its warrant
from some universal or superiour Cause. 'Tis not a ridiculous
devotion to say a prayer before a game at Tables; for even in
sortilegies[8] and matters of greatest uncertainty, there is a setled

7 Helix: coil, spiral
8 *sortilegies:* drawing or casting of lots

and pre-ordered course of effects. It is we that are blind, not Fortune: because our Eye is too dim to discover the mystery of her effects, we foolishly paint her blind, and hoodwink the Providence of the Almighty. I cannot justifie that contemptible Proverb, *That fools only are Fortunate;* or that insolent Paradox, *That a wise man is out of the reach of Fortune;* much less those opprobrious epithets of Poets, *Whore, Bawd,* and *Strumpet.* 'Tis, I confess, the common fate of men of singular gifts of mind, to be destitute of those of Fortune; which doth not any way deject the Spirit of wiser judgments, who throughly understand the justice of this proceeding; and being inrich'd with higher donatives, cast a more careless eye on these vulgar parts of felicity. It is a most unjust ambition to desire to engross the mercies of the Almighty, not to be content with the goods of mind, without a possession of those of body or Fortune: and it is an error worse than heresie, to adore these complemental and circumstantial pieces of felicity, and undervalue those perfections and essential points of happiness, wherein we resemble our Maker. To wiser desires it is satisfaction enough to deserve, though not to enjoy the favours of Fortune; let Providence provide for Fools: 'tis not partiality, but equity in God, who deals with us but as our natural Parents: those that are able of Body and Mind he leaves to their deserts; to those of weaker merits he imparts a larger portion, and pieces out the defect of one by the excess of the other. Thus have we no just quarrel with Nature, for leaving us naked; or to envy the Horns, Hoofs, Skins and Furs of other Creatures, being provided with Reason, that can supply them all. We need not labour with so many Arguments to confute Judicial Astrology; for if there be a truth therein, it doth not injure Divinity: if to be born under *Mercury* disposeth us to be witty, under *Jupiter* to be wealthy; I do not owe a Knee unto these, but unto that merciful Hand that hath ordered my indifferent and uncertain nativity unto such benevolous Aspects. Those that hold that all things are governed by Fortune, had not erred, had they not persisted there: The *Romans* that erected a Temple to Fortune, acknowledged therein, though in a blinder way, somewhat of Divinity; for, in a wise supputation[9] all things begin and end in the Almighty. There is a nearer way to Heaven than *Homer's* Chain; an easie Logic may conjoyn Heaven and

9 supputation: calculation, computation

Earth in one Argument, and with less than a *Sorites*[1] resolve all things into God. For though we christen effects by their most sensible and nearest Causes, yet is God the true and infallible Cause of all, whose concourse though it be general, yet doth it subdivide it self into the particular Actions of every thing, and is that Spirit, by which each singular Essence not only subsists, but performs its operation.

Section 19. The bad construction and perverse comment on these pair of second Causes, or visible hands of God, have perverted the Devotion of many unto Atheism; who forgetting the honest Advisoes of Faith, have listened unto the conspiracy of Passion and Reason. I have therefore always endeavoured to compose those Feuds and angry Dissentions between Affection, Faith and Reason: for there is in our Soul a kind of Triumvirate, or triple Government of three Competitors, which distract the Peace of this our Commonwealth, not less than did that other the State of *Rome*.

As Reason is a Rebel unto Faith, so Passion unto Reason: as the propositions of Faith seem absurd unto Reason, so the Theorems of Reason unto Passion, and both unto Reason; yet a moderate and peaceable discretion may so state and order the matter, that they may be all Kings, and yet make but one Monarchy, every one exercising his Soveraignty and Prerogative in a due time and place, according to the restraint and limit of circumstance. There is, as in Philosophy, so in Divinity, sturdy doubts and boisterous Objections, wherewith the unhappiness of our knowledge too nearly acquainteth us. More of these no man hath known than my self, which I confess I conquered, not in a martial posture, but on my Knees. For our endeavours are not only to combat with doubts, but always to dispute with the Devil: the villany of that Spirit takes a hint of Infidelity from our Studies, and, by demonstrating a naturality in one way, makes us mistrust a miracle in another. Thus, having perused the *Archidoxis*, and read the secret Sympathies of things, he would disswade my belief from the miracle of the Brazen Serpent, make me conceit that Image worked by Sympathy, and was but an *Ægyptian* trick to cure their Diseases without a miracle. Again, having seen some experiments of *Bitumen*, and having read far

1 *Sorites:* type of syllogism

more of *Naphtha,* he whispered to my curiosity the fire of the Altar might be natural; and bid me mistrust a miracle in *Elias,* when he entrenched the Altar round with Water: for that inflamable substance yields not easily unto Water, but flames in the Arms of its Antagonist. And thus would he inveagle my belief to think the combustion of *Sodom* might be natural, and that there was an Asphaltick and Bituminous nature in that Lake before the Fire of *Gomorrah.* I know that Manna is now plentifully gathered in *Calabria;* and *Josephus* tells me, in his days it was as plentiful in *Arabia;* the Devil therefore made the quære, Where was then the miracle in the days of *Moses;* the *Israelites* saw but that in his time, the Natives of those Countries behold in ours. Thus the Devil played at Chess with me, and yielding a Pawn, thought to gain a Queen of me, taking advantage of my honest endeavours; and whilst I laboured to raise the structure of my Reason, he strived to undermine the edifice of my Faith.

Section 20. Neither had these or any other ever such advantage of me, as to incline me to any point of Infidelity or desperate positions of Atheism; for I have been these many years of opinion there was never any. Those that held Religion was the difference of Man from Beasts, have spoken probably, and proceed upon a principle as inductive as the other. That doctrine of *Epicurus,* that denied the Providence of God, was no Atheism, but a magnificent and high strained conceit of his Majesty, which he deemed too sublime to mind the trivial Actions of those inferiour Creatures. That fatal Necessity of the Stoicks, is nothing but the immutable Law of his will. Those that heretofore denied the Divinity of the Holy Ghost, have been condemned, but as Hereticks; and those that now deny our Saviour, (though more than Hereticks) are not so much as Atheists: for though they deny two persons in the Trinity, they hold as we do, there is but one God.

That Villain and Secretary of Hell, that composed that miscreant piece *Of the Three Impostors,* though divided from all Religions, and was neither Jew, Turk, nor Christian, was not a positive Atheist. I confess every Country hath its *Machiavel,* every Age its *Lucian,* whereof common Heads must not hear, nor more advanced Judgments too rashly venture on: it is the

Rhetorick of Satan, and may pervert a loose or pre-judicate belief.

Section 21. I confess I have perused them all, and can discover nothing that may startle a discreet belief; yet are there heads carried off with the Wind and breath of such motives. I remember a Doctor in Physick of *Italy* who could not perfectly believe the immortality of the Soul, because *Galen* seemed to make a doubt thereof. With another I was familiarly acquainted in *France,* a Divine, and a man of singular parts, that on the same point was so plunged and gravelled with three lines of *Seneca,* that all our Antidotes, drawn from both Scripture and Philosophy, could not expel the poyson of his errour. There are a set of Heads, that can credit the relations of Mariners, yet question the Testimonies of St. *Paul;* and peremptorily maintain the traditions of *Ælian* or *Pliny,* yet in Histories of Scripture raise Queries and Objections, believing no more than they can parallel in humane Authors. I confess there are in Scripture Stories that do exceed the Fables of Poets, and to a captious Reader sound like *Garagantua* or *Bevis:* Search all the Legends of times past, and the fabulous conceits of these present, and 'twill be hard to find one that deserves to carry the Buckler unto *Sampson;* yet is all this of an easie possibility, if we conceive a divine concourse, or an influence from the little Finger of the Almighty. It is impossible that either in the discourse of man, or in the infallible Voice of God, to the weakness of our apprehensions, there should not appear irregularities, contradictions, and antinomies: my self could shew a Catalogue of doubts, never yet imagined nor questioned, as I know, which are not resolved at the first hearing; not fantastick Queries or Objections of Air; for I cannot hear of Atoms in Divinity. I can read the History of the Pigeon that was sent out of the Ark, and returned no more, yet not question how she found out her Mate that was left behind: That *Lazarus* was raised from the dead, yet not demand where in the interim his Soul awaited; or raise a Lawcase, whether his Heir might lawfully detain his inheritance bequeathed unto him by his death, and he, though restored to life, have no Plea or Title unto his former possessions. Whether *Eve* was framed out of the left side of *Adam,* I dispute not; because I stand not yet assured which is the right side of a man;

or whether there be any such distinction in Nature: that she was edified out of the Rib of *Adam*, I believe, yet raise no question who shall arise with that Rib at the Resurrection: Whether Adam was an Hermaphrodite, as the Rabbins contend upon the Letter of the Text, because it is contrary to reason, there should be an Hermaphrodite, before there was a Woman; or a composition of two Natures, before there was a second composed. Likewise, whether the World was created in Autumn, Summer, or the Spring, because it was created in them all; for whatsoever Sign the Sun possesseth, those four Seasons are actually existent: It is the Nature of this Luminary to distinguish the several Seasons of the year, all which it makes at one time in the whole Earth, and successively in any part thereof. There are a bundle of curiosities, not only in Philosophy, but in Divinity, proposed and discussed by men of most supposed abilities, which indeed are not worthy our vacant hours, much less our serious Studies: Pieces only fit to be placed in Pantagruel's Library, or bound up with *Tartaretus de modo Cacandi*.

Section 22. These are niceties that become not those that peruse so serious a Mystery: There are others more generally questioned and called to the Bar, yet methinks of an easie and possible truth.

'Tis ridiculous to put off, or drown the general Flood of *Noah,* in that particular inundation of *Deucalion:* that there was a Deluge once, seems not to me so great a Miracle, as that there is not one always. How all the kinds of Creatures, not only in their own bulks, but with a competency of food and sustenance, might be preserved in one Ark, and within the extent of three hundred Cubits, to a reason that rightly examines it, will appear very feasible. There is another secret not contained in the Scripture, which is more hard to comprehend, and put the honest Father to the refuge of a Miracle: and that is, not only how the distinct pieces of the World, and divided Islands should be first planted by men, but inhabited by Tigers, Panthers, and Bears. How *America* abounded with Beasts of prey and noxious Animals, yet contained not in it that necessary Creature, a Horse, is very strange. By what passage those, not only Birds, but dangerous and unwelcome Beasts came over: How there be Creatures there, (which are not found in this Triple Continent;) all which must needs be strange unto us, that hold but one Ark, and that the Creatures began their progress from the Mountains of *Ararat:* They who to salve this would make the Deluge particular, proceed upon a principle that I can no way grant; not only upon the negative of holy Scriptures, but of mine own Reason, whereby I can make it probable, that the World was as well peopled in the time of *Noah,* as in ours; and fifteen hundred years to people the World, as full a time for them, as four thousand years since have been to us. There are other assertions and common Tenents drawn from Scripture, and generally believed as Scripture, whereunto notwithstanding, I would never betray the liberty of my Reason. 'Tis a Paradox to me, that *Methusalem* was the longest liv'd of all the Children of *Adam* and no man will be able to prove it; when, from the process of the Text, I can manifest it may be otherwise. That *Judas* perished by hanging himself, there is no certainty in Scripture: though in one place it seems to affirm it, and by a doubtful word hath given occasion to translate it; yet in another place, in a more punctual description, it makes it improbable, and seems to overthrow it. That our Fathers, after the Flood, erected the Tower of *Babel,* to preserve themselves against a second Deluge, is generally opinioned and believed, yet is there another intention of theirs expressed in Scripture: Besides, it is improbable from the circumstance of the place, that is, a plain in the Land of *Shinar:* These are no points of Faith, and therefore may admit a free dispute. There are yet others, and those familiarly concluded from the Text, wherein (under favour) I see no consequence the Church of *Rome* confidently proves the opinion of Tutelary Angels, from that Answer when Peter knockt at the Door, *'Tis not he, but his Angel;* that is, might some say, his Messenger, or some body from him; for so the Original signifies; and is as likely to be the doubtful Families meaning. This exposition I once suggested to a young Divine, that answered upon this point; to which I remember the *Franciscan* Opponent replyed no more, but That it was a new, and no authentick interpretation.

Section 23. These are but the conclusions and fallible discourses of man upon the Word of God, for such I do believe the holy Scriptures; yet were it of man, I could not chuse but say, it was the singularest, and superlative piece that hath been extant since the Creation: were I a Pagan, I should not refrain the Lecture of it; and cannot but commend the judgment of *Ptolomy,* that thought not his Library compleat without it. The Alcoran of the *Turks* (I speak without prejudice) is an ill composed Piece, containing in it vain and ridiculous Errors in Philosophy, impossibilities, fictions, and vanities beyond laughter, maintained by evident and open Sophisms, the Policy of Ignorance, deposition of Universities, and banishment of Learning; that hath gotten Foot by Arms and violence: this without a blow hath disseminated it self through the whole Earth. It is not unremarkable what *Philo* first observed, that the Law of *Moses* continued two thousand years without the least alteration; whereas, we see the Laws of other Commonweals do alter with occasions; and even those, that pretended their Original from some Divinity, to have vanished without trace or memory. I believe besides *Zoroaster,* there were divers that writ before *Moses* who, notwithstanding, have suffered the common fate of time. Men's Works have an age like themselves; and though they out-live their Authors, yet have they a stint and period to their duration: This only is a work too hard for the teeth of time, and cannot perish but in the general Flames, when all things shall confess their Ashes.

Section 24. I have heard some with deep sighs lament the lost lines of *Cicero;* others with as many groans deplore the combustion of the Library of *Alexandria:* for my own part, I think there be too many in the World, and could with patience behold the urn and ashes of the *Vatican,* could I, with a few others, recover the perished leaves of *Solomon.* I would not omit a Copy of *Enoch's* Pillars, had they many nearer Authors than *Josephus,* or did not relish somewhat of the Fable. Some men have written more than others have spoken; *Pineda* quotes more Authors in one work, than are necessary in a whole World. Of those three great inventions in *Germany,* there are two which are not without their incommodities, and 'tis disputable whether they exceed not their use and commodities. 'Tis not a melancholy *Utinam*[2] of my own, but the desires of better heads, that there were a general Synod; not to unite the incompatible difference of Religion, but

2 *Utinam:* earnest wish, fervent desire

for the benefit of learning, to reduce it as it lay at first, in a few, and solid Authors; and to condemn to the fire those swarms & millions of *Rhapsodies* begotten only to distract and abuse the weaker judgements of Scholars, and to *maintain the trade and mystery of Typographers.*

Section 25. I cannot but wonder with what exception the *Samaritans* could confine their belief to the *Pentateuch,* or five Books of *Moses.* I am ashamed at the Rabbinical Interpretation of the Jews, upon the old Testament, as much as their defection from the New. And truly it is beyond wonder, how that contemptible and degenerate issue of *Jacob,* once so devoted to Ethnick Superstition, and so easily seduced to the Idolatry of their Neighbours, should now in such an obstinate and peremptory belief adhere unto their own Doctrine, expect impossibilities, and in the face and eye of the Church, persist without the least hope of Conversion. This is a vice in them, that were a vertue in us; for obstinacy in a bad Cause, is but constancy in a good. And herein I must accuse those of my own Religion; for there is not any of such a fugitive Faith, such an unstable belief, as a Christian; none that do so oft transform themselves, not unto several shapes of Christianity and of the same Species, but unto more unnatural and contrary Forms, of Jew and Mahometan; that from the name of Saviour, can condescend to the bare term of Prophet; and from an old belief that he is come, fall to a new expectation of his coming. It is the promise of Christ to make us all one Flock; but how and when this Union shall be, is as obscure to me as the last day. Of course four Members of Religion we hold a slender proportion; there are, I confess, some new additions, yet small to those which accrew to our Adversaries, and those only drawn from the revolt of Pagans, men but of negative Impieties, and such as deny Christ, but because they never heard of him: but the Religion of the Jew is expresly against the Christian, and the Mahometan against both. For the Turk, in the bulk he now stands, he is beyond all hope of conversion: if he fall asunder, there may be conceived hopes, but not without strong improbabilities. The Jew is obstinate in all fortunes; the persecution of fifteen hundred years hath but confirmed them in their Errour: they have already endured whatsoever may be inflicted, and have suffered in a bad cause, even to the condemnation of their enemies. Persecution is a bad and indirect way to plant Religion; it hath been the unhappy method of angry Devotions, not only to confirm honest Religion, but wicked Heresies, and extravagant Opinions. It was the first stone and Basis of our Faith, none can more justly boast of Persecutions, and glory in the number and valour of Martyrs; For, to speak properly, those are true and almost only examples of fortitude: Those that are fetch'd from the field, or drawn from the actions of the Camp, are not oft-times so truely precedents of valour as audacity, and at the best attain but to some bastard piece of fortitude: If we shall strictly examine the circumstances and requisites which *Aristotle* requires to true and perfect valour, we shall find the name only in his Master, *Alexander,* and as little in that Roman Worthy, *Julius Cæsar;* and if any, in that easie and active way, have done so nobly as to deserve that name, yet in the passive and more terrible piece these have surpassed, and in a more heroical way may claim the honour of that Title. 'Tis not in the power of every honest Faith to proceed thus far, or pass to Heaven through the flames; every one hath it not in that full measure, nor in so audacious and resolute a temper, as to endure those terrible tests and trials; who notwithstanding in a peaceable way do truely adore their Saviour, and have (no doubt) a Faith acceptable in the eyes of God.

Section 26. Now, as all that dye in the War are not termed Souldiers; so neither can I properly term all those that suffer in matters of Religion, Martyrs. The Council of *Constance* condemns *John Huss* for an Heretick; the Stories of his own Party stile him a Martyr: He must needs offend the Divinity of both, that says he was neither the one nor the other: There are many (questionless) canonized on earth, that shall never be Saints in Heaven; and have their names in Histories and Martyrologies, who in the eyes of God are not so perfect Martyrs as was that wise Heathen *Socrates,* that suffered on a fundamental point of Religion, the Unity of God. I have often pitied the miserable Bishop that suffered in the cause of *Antipodes,* yet cannot chuse but accuse him of as much madness, for exposing his living on such a trifle; as those of ignorance and folly, that condemned him. I think my conscience will not give me the lye, if I say there are not many extant that in a noble way fear the face of death less than my self; yet from the moral duty I owe to the Commandment of God, and the natural respects that I tender unto the conservation of my essence and being, I would not perish upon a Ceremony, Politick points, or indifferency: nor is my belief of that untractible temper, as not to bow at their obstacles, or connive at matters wherein there are not manifest impieties: The leaven therefore and ferment of all, not only civil but Religious actions, is Wisdom; without which, to commit our selves to the flames, is Homicide, and (I fear) but to pass through one fire into another.

Section 27. That Miracles are ceased, I can neither prove, nor absolutely deny, much less define the time and period of their cessation: that they survived Christ, is manifest upon the Record of Scripture: that they out-lived the Apostles also, and were revived at the Conversion of Nations, many years after, we cannot deny, if we shall not question those Writers whose testimonies we do not controvert, in points that make for our own opinions; therefore that may have some truth in it that is reported by the Jesuites of their Miracles in the *Indies;* I could wish it were true, or had any other testimony than their own Pens. They may easily believe those Miracles abroad, who daily conceive a greater at home, the transmutation of those visible elements into the body and blood of our Saviour: for the conversion of Water into Wine, which he wrought in *Cana,* or what the Devil would have had him done in the Wilderness, of Stones into Bread, compared to this, will scarce deserve the name of a Miracle. Though indeed to speak properly, there is not one Miracle greater than another, they being the extraordinary effects of the Hand of God, to which all things are of an equal facility; and to create the World as easie as one single Creature. For this is also a Miracle, not onely to produce effects against, or above Nature, but before Nature; and to create Nature as great a Miracle, as to contradict or transcend her. We do too narrowly define the Power of God, restraining it to our capacities. I hold that God can do all things; how he should work contradictions I do not understand, yet dare not therefore deny. I cannot see why the Angel of God should question *Esdras* to recal the time past, if it were beyond his own power; or that God should pose mortality in that which he was not able to perform himself. I will not say God cannot, but he will not perform many things, which we plainly affirm he cannot: this I am sure is the mannerliest proposition, wherein, notwithstanding, I hold no Paradox. For strictly his power is the same with his will, and they both with all the rest do make but one God.

Section 28. Therefore that Miracles have been, I do believe; that they may yet be wrought by the living, I do not deny: but have no confidence in those which are fathered on the dead; and this hath ever made me suspect the efficacy of reliques, to examine the bones, question the habits and appurtenances of Saints, and even of Christ himself. I cannot conceive why the Cross that *Helena* found, and whereon Christ himself dyed, should have power to restore others unto life: I excuse not *Constantine* from a fall off his Horse, or a mischief from his enemies, upon the wearing those nails on his bridle, which our Saviour bore upon the Cross in his hands. I compute among *Piæ fraudes,*[3] nor many degrees before consecrated Swords and Roses, that which *Baldwyn,* King of *Jerusalem,* return'd the *Genovese* for their cost and pains in his War, to wit, the ashes of *John* the Baptist. Those that hold the sanctity of their souls doth leave behind a tincture and sacred faculty on their bodies, speak naturally of Miracles, and do not salve the doubt. Now one reason I tender so little Devotion unto Reliques is, I think, the slender and doubtful respect I have always held unto Antiquities: for that indeed which I admire, is far before Antiquity, that is, Eternity; and that is God himself; who though he be styled the ancient of days, cannot receive the adjunct of Antiquity, who was before the World, and shall be after it, yet is not older than it; for in his years there is no Climacter;[4] his duration is Eternity, and far more venerable than Antiquity.

Section 29. But above all things I wonder how the curiosity of wiser heads could pass that great and indisputable Miracle, the cessation of Oracles; and in what swoun their Reasons lay, to content themselves, and sit down with such a far-fetch'd and ridiculous reason as *Plutarch* alleadgeth for it. The Jews that can believe the supernatural Solstice of the Sun in the days of *Joshua,* have yet the impudence to deny the Eclipse, which every

3 *Piæ fraudes:* pious frauds
4 Climacter: critical period

Pagan confessed, at his death: but for this, it is evident beyond all contradiction, the Devil himself confessed it. Certainly it is not a warrantable curiosity, to examine the verity of Scripture by the concordance of humane history, or seek to confirm the Chronicle of *Hester* or *Daniel,* by the authority of *Megasthenes* or *Herodotus.* I confess I have had an unhappy curiosity this way, till I laughed my self out of it with a piece of *Justine,* where he delivers that the Children of *Israel* for being scabbed were banished out of *Egypt.* And truely since I have understood the occurrences of the World, and know in what counterfeit shapes, and deceitful vizards times present represent on the stage things past; I do believe them little more then things to come. Some have been of my opinion, and endeavoured to write the History of their own lives; wherein *Moses* hath outgone them all, and left not onely the story of his life, but, as some will have it, of his death also.

Section 30. It is a riddle to me, how this story of Oracles hath not worm'd out of the World that doubtful conceit of Spirits and Witches; how so many learned heads should so far forget their Metaphysicks, and destroy the ladder and scale of creatures, as to question the existence of Spirits: for my part, I have ever believed, and do now know, that there are Witches: they that doubt of these do not onely deny them, but spirits; and are obliquely and upon consequence a sort not of Infidels, but Atheists. Those that to confute their incredulity desire to see apparitions, shall questionless never behold any, nor have the power to be so much as Witches: the Devil hath them already in a heresie as capital as Witchcraft; and to appear to them, were but to convert them. Of all the delusions wherewith he deceives mortality, there is not any that puzzleth me more than the Legerdemain of *Changelings;* I do not credit those transformations of reasonable creatures into beasts, or that the Devil hath a power to transpeciate[5] a man into a Horse, who tempted Christ (as a trial of his Divinity) to convert but stones into bread. I could believe that Spirits use with man the act of carnality, and that in both sexes; I conceive they may assume, steal, or contrive a body, wherein there may be action enough to content decrepit lust, or passion to satisfie more active veneries; yet in both, without a possibility of

5 transpeciate: change into a different form

generation: and therefore that opinion that Antichrist should be born of the Tribe of *Dan,* by conjunction with the Devil, is ridiculous, and a conceit fitter for a Rabbin than a Christian. I hold that the Devil doth really possess some men, the spirit of Melancholly others, the spirit of Delusion others; that as the Devil is concealed and denyed by some, so God and good Angels are pretended by others whereof the late detection of the Maid of *Germany* hath left a pregnant example.

Section 31. Again, I believe that all that use sorceries, incantations and spells, are not Witches, or, as we term them, Magicians; I conceive there is a traditional Magick, not learned immediately from the Devil, but at second hand from his Scholars, who, having once the secret betrayed, are able, and do emperically practise without his advice, they both proceeding upon the principles of Nature; where actives, aptly conjoyned to disposed passives, will under any Master produce their effects. Thus I think at first a part of Philosophy was Witchcraft; which being afterward derived to one another, proved but Philosophy, and was indeed no more but the honest effects of Nature: What, invented by us is Philosophy, learned from him is Magick. We do surely owe the discovery of many secrets to the discovery of good and bad Angels. I could never pass that sentence of *Paracelsus,* without an asterisk, or annotation; *Ascendens, constellatum multa revelat, quærentibus magnalia naturæ,* i.e. *opera Dei.*[6] I do think that many mysteries ascribed to our own inventions, have been the courteous revelations of Spirits; for those noble essences in Heaven bear a friendly regard unto their fellow Nature on Earth; and therefore believe that those many prodigies and ominous prognosticks, which fore-run the ruines of States, Princes, and private persons, are the charitable premonitions of good Angels, which more careless enquiries term but the effects of chance and nature.

Section 32. Now besides these particular and divided Spirits, there may be (for ought I know) an universal and common Spirit to the whole World. It was the opinion of *Plato,* and it is

6 *Ascendens . . . Dei:* a constellation as it rises discloses many things to those who investigate the mighty works of nature, i.e., works of God

yet of the *Hermetical* Philosophers: if there be a common nature that unites and tyes the scattered and divided individuals into one species, why may there not be one that unites them all? However, I am sure there is a common Spirit that plays within us, yet makes no part in us; and that is the Spirit of God, the fire and scintillation of that noble and mighty Essence, which is the life and radical heat of spirits, and those essences that know not the vertue of the Sun, a fire quite contrary to the fire of Hell: This is that gentle heat that brooded on the waters, and in six days hatched the World; this is that irradiation that dispels the mists of Hell, the clouds of horrour, fear, sorrow, despair; and preserves the region of the mind in serenity: whatsoever feels not the warm gale and gentle ventilation of this Spirit, (though I feel his pulse) I dare not say he lives; for truely without this, to me there is no heat under the Tropick; nor any light, though I dwelt in the body of the Sun.

> As when the labouring Sun hath wrought his track
> Up to the top of lofty Cancer's back,[7]
> The ycie Ocean cracks, the frozen pole
> Thaws with the heat of the Celestial coale;
> So when Thy absent beams begin t' impart
> Again a Solstice on my frozen heart,
> My winter's ov'r; my drooping spirits sing,
> And every part revives into a Spring.
> But if thy quickning beams a while decline,
> And with their light bless not this Orb of mine,
> A chilly frost surpriseth every member,
> And in the midst of June I feel December.
> O how this earthly temper doth debase
> The noble Soul, in this her humble place
> Whose wingy nature ever doth aspire
> To reach that place whence first it took its fire.
> These flames I feel, which in my heart do dwell
> Are not thy beams, but take their fire from Hell
> O quench them all, and let thy light divine
> Be as the Sun to this poor Orb of mine;
> And to thy sacred Spirit convert those fires,
> Whose earthly fumes choak my devout aspires.

7 Cancer's back: zodiacal sign of the Crab

Section 33. Therefore for Spirits, I am so far from denying their existence, that I could easily believe, that not onely whole Countries, but particular persons, have their Tutelary and Guardian Angels: It is not a new opinion of the Church of *Rome*, but an old one of *Pythagoras* and *Plato;* there is no heresie in it, and if not manifestly defin'd in Scripture, yet is it an opinion of a good and wholesome use in the course and actions of man's life, and would serve as an *Hypothesis* to salve many doubts, whereof common Philosophy affordeth no solution. Now if you demand my opinion and Metaphysicks of their natures, I confess them very shallow, most of them in a negative way, like that of God; or in a comparative, between our selves and fellow-creatures; for there is in this Universe a Stair, or manifest Scale of creatures, rising not disorderly, or in confusion, but with a comely method and proportion. Between creatures of meer existence and things of life, there is a large disproportion of nature; between plans and animals or creatures of sense, a wider difference; between them and man, a far greater: and if the proportion hold on, between Man and Angels there should be yet a greater. We do not comprehend their natures, who retain the first definition of *Porphyry,* and distinguish them from our selves by immortality; for before his Fall, 'tis thought, Man also was Immortal; yet must we needs affirm that he had a different essence from the Angels; having therefore no certain knowledge of their Natures, 'tis no bad method of the Schools, whatsoever perfection we find obscurely in our selves, in a more compleat and absolute way to ascribe unto them. I believe they have an extemporary knowledge, and upon the first motion of their reason do what we cannot without study or deliberation; that they know things by their forms, and define by specifical difference what we describe by accidents and properties; and therefore probabilities to us may be demonstrations unto them: that they have knowledge not onely of the specifical, but numerical forms of individuals, and understand by what reserved difference each single *Hypostasis,* (besides the relation to its species) becomes its numerical self. That as the Soul hath a power to move the body it informs, so there's a faculty to move any, though inform none; ours upon restraint of time, place, and distance; but that invisible hand that conveyed *Habakkuk* to the Lyon's Den, or *Philip* to *Azotus*, infringeth this rule, and hath a secret conveyance, wherewith mortality is not acquainted: if they have that intuitive knowledge, whereby as in reflexion they behold the thoughts of one another, I cannot peremptorily deny but they know a great part of ours. They that to refute the Invocation of Saints, have denied that they have any knowledge of our affairs below, have proceeded too far, and must pardon my opinion, till I can throughly answer that piece of Scripture, *At the conversion of a sinner the Angels in Heaven rejoyce*. I cannot, with those in that great Father, securely interpret the work of the first day, *Fiat lux*,[8] to the creation of Angels, though I confess there is not any creature that hath so neer a glympse of their nature, as light in the Sun and Elements. We stile it a bare accident; but where it subsists alone, 'tis a spiritual Substance, and may be an Angel: in brief, conceive light invisible, and that is a Spirit.

Section 34. These are certainly the Magisterial and masterpieces of the Creator, the Flower, or (as we may say) the best part of nothing, actually existing, what we are but in hopes and probability; we are onely that amphibious piece between a corporal and spiritual Essence, that middle form that links those two together, and makes good the Method of God and Nature, that jumps not from extreams, but unites the incompatible distances by some middle and participating natures: that we are the breath and similitude of God, it is indisputable, and upon record of holy Scripture; but to call ourselves a Microcosm, or little World, I thought it onely a pleasant trope of Rhetorick, till my neer judgment and second thoughts told me there was a real truth therein: for first we are a rude mass, and in the rank of creatures, which onely are, and have a dull kind of being not yet priviledged with life, or preferred to sense or reason; next we live the life of Plants, the life of Animals, the life of Men, and at last the life of Spirits, running on in one mysterious nature those five kinds of existences, which comprehend the creatures not onely of the World, but of the Universe; thus is man that great and true *Amphibium*, whose nature is disposed to live not onely like other creatures in divers elements, but in divided and distinguished worlds: for though there be but one to sense, there are two to reason; the one visible, the other invisible, whereof Moses seems to have left description, and of the other so obscurely, that

8 *Fiat lux*: let there be light

some parts thereof are yet in controversie. And truely for the first chapters of *Genesis*, I must confess a great deal of obscurity; though Divines have to the power of humane reason endeavoured to make all go in a literal meaning, yet those allegorical inter- pretations are also probable, and perhaps the mystical method of *Moses* bred up in the Hieroglyphical Schools of the *Egyptians*.

Section 35. Now for that immaterial world, methinks we need not wander so far as beyond the first moveable; for even in this material Fabrick the spirits walk as freely exempt from the affec- tion of time, place, and motion, as beyond the extreamest circum- ference: do but extract from the corpulency of bodies, or resolve things beyond their first matter, and you discover the habitation of Angels, which if I call the ubiquitary,[9] and omnipresent es- sence of God, I hope I shall not offend Divinity: for before the Creation of the World God was really all things. For the Angels he created no new World, or determinate mansion, and therefore they are everywhere where is his Essence, and do live at a dis- tance even in himself. That God made all things for man, is in some sense true, yet not so far as to subordinate the Creation of those purer Creatures unto ours, though as ministring Spirits they do, and are willing to fulfil the will of God in these lower and sublunary affairs of man: God made all things for himself, and it is impossible he should make them for any other end than his own Glory; it is all he can receive, and all that is without himself: for, honour being an external adjunct, and in the hon- ourer rather than in the person honoured, it was necessary to make a Creature, from whom he might receive this homage, and that is, in the other world Angels, in this, Man; which when we neglect, we forget the very end of our Creation, and may justly provoke God, not onely to repent that he hath made the World, but that he hath sworn he would not destroy it. That there is but one World, is a conclusion of Faith. *Aristotle* with all his Philoso- phy hath not been able to prove it, and as weakly that the World was eternal; that dispute much troubled the Pen of the Philoso- phers, but *Moses* decided that question, and all is salved with the new term of a Creation, that is, a production of something out of nothing; and what is that? Whatsoever is opposite to something; or more exactly, that which is truely contrary unto God: for he

9 ubiquitary: ubiquitous

onely is, all others have an existence with dependency, and are
something but by a distinction; And herein is Divinity conform-
ant unto Philosophy, and generation not onely founded on contrarieties, but also creation; God being all things, is contrary unto
nothing, out of which were made all things, and so nothing became something, and Omneity informed *Nullity* into an Essence.

Section 36. The whole Creation is a Mystery, and particularly
that of Man; at the blast of his mouth were the rest of the Creatures made, and at his bare word they started out of nothing:
but in the frame of man (as the Text describes it) he played the
sensible operator, and seemed not so much to create, as make
him; when he had separated the materials of other creatures,
there consequently resulted a form and soul: but having raised
the walls of man, he was driven to a second and harder creation
of a substance like himself, an incorruptible and immortal Soul.
For these two affections we have the Philosophy and opinion of
the Heathens, the flat affirmative of *Plato,* and not a negative
from *Aristotle:* there is another scruple cast in by Divinity (concerning its production) much disputed in the *Germane* audito-
ries, and with that indifferency and equality of arguments, as
leave the controversie undetermined. I am not of *Paracelsus'*
mind, that boldly delivers a receipt to make a man without conjunction; yet cannot but wonder at the multitude of heads that
do deny traduction,[1] having no other argument to confirm their
belief, then that Rhetorical sentence, and *Antimetathesis*[2] of
Augustine, Creando infunditur, infundendo creatur:[3] either opinion will consist well enough with Religion; yet I should rather
incline to this, did not one objection haunt me, not wrung from
speculations and subtilties, but from common sense, and observation; not pickt from the leaves of any Author, but bred
amongst the weeds and tares of mine own brain: And this is a
conclusion from the equivocal and monstrous productions in the
copulation of Man with a Beast; for if the Soul of man be not
transmitted, and transfused in the seed of the Parents, why are
not those productions meerly beasts, but have also an impression
and tincture of reason in as high a measure, as it can evidence

---

1 traduction: transmission of soul to offspring by generation
2 *Antimetathesis:* inversion of the members of an antithesis
3 *Creando . . . creatur:* by the act of creating, grace is poured
on the world: the pouring of grace is itself a creative act

it self in those improper Organs? Nor truely can I peremptorily deny, that the Soul in this her sublunary estate, is wholly, and in all acceptions inorganical, but that for the performance of her ordinary actions, there is required not onely a symmetry and proper disposition of Organs, but a Crasis[4] and temper correspondent to its operations. Yet is not this mass of flesh and visible structure the instrument and proper corps of the Soul, but rather of Sense, and that the hand of Reason. In our study of Anatomy there is a mass of mysterious Philosophy, and such as reduced the very Heathens to Divinity; yet amongst all those rare discoveries and curious pieces I find in the Fabrick of man, I do not so much content my self, as in that I find not, there is no Organ or Instrument for the rational soul: for in the brain, which we term the seat of reason, there is not any thing of moment more than I can discover in the crany[5] of a beast: and this is a sensible and no inconsiderable argument of the inorganity of the Soul, at least in that sense we usually so conceive it. Thus we are men, and we know not how; there is something in us that can be without us, and will be after us, though it is strange that it hath no history, what it was before us, nor cannot tell how it entred in us.

Section 37. Now for these walls of flesh, wherein the Soul doth seem to be immured, before the Resurrection, it is nothing but an elemental composition, and a Fabrick that must fall to ashes. *All flesh is grass,* is not onely metaphorically, but litterally true; for all those creatures we behold, are but the herbs of the field, digested into flesh in them, or more remotely carnified in our selves. Nay further, we are what we all abhor, *Anthropophagi* and Cannibals, devourers not onely of men, but of our selves; and that not in an allegory, but a positive truth: for all this mass of flesh which we behold, came in at our mouths; this frame we look upon, hath been upon our trenchers; in brief, we have devour'd our selves. I cannot believe the wisdom of *Pythagoras* did ever positively, and in a literal sense affirm his *Metempsychosis,* or impossible transmigration of the Souls of men into beasts: of all Metamorphoses, or transmigrations, I believe only one, that is of *Lot's* wife; for that of *Nebuchodonosor* proceeded not so far;

4 Crasis: constitution
5 crany: cranium

in all others I conceive there is no further verity than is contained in their implicite sense and morality. I believe that the whole frame of a beast doth perish, and is left in the same state after death, as before it was materialled unto life; that the souls of men know neither contrary nor corruption; that they subsist beyond the body, and outlive death by the priviledge of their proper natures, and without a Miracle; that the Souls of the faithful, as they leave Earth, take possession of Heaven; that those apparitions and ghosts of departed persons are not the wandring souls of men, but the unquiet walks of Devils, prompting and suggesting us unto mischief, blood, and villany, instilling and stealing into our hearts; that the blessed Spirits are not at rest in their graves, but wander sollicitous of the affairs of the World; but that those phantasms appear often, and do frequent Cœmeteries, Charnel-houses and Churches, it is because those are the dormitories of the dead, where the Devil, like an insolent Champion beholds with pride the spoils and Trophies of his Victory over *Adam.*

Section 38. This is that dismal conquest we all deplore, that makes us so often cry, (O) *Adam, quid fecisti?* [6] I thank God I have not those strait ligaments, or narrow obligations to the World, as to dote on life, or be convulst and tremble at the name of death: Not that I am insensible of the dread and horrour thereof, or by raking into the bowels of the deceased, continual sight of Anatomies, Skeletons, or Cadaverous reliques, like Vespilloes, or Grave-makers, I am become stupid, or have forgot the apprehension of Mortality; but that marshalling all the horrours; and contemplating the extremities thereof, I find not any thing therein able to daunt the courage of a man, much less a well-resolved Christian. And therefore am not angry at the errour of our first Parents, or unwilling to bear a part of this common fate, and like the best of them to dye, that is, to cease to breathe, to take a farewel of the elements, to be a kind of nothing for a moment, to be within one instant of a spirit. When I take a full view and circle of my self, without this reasonable moderator, and equal piece of Justice, Death, I do conceive my self the miserablest person extant; were there not another life that I hope for, all the vanities of this World should not intreat a moments

6 *quid fecisti:* what hast thou done? (Gen. iii:13)

breath from me: could the Devil work my belief to imagine I could never dye, I would not outlive that very thought; I have so abject a conceit of this common way of existence, this retaining to the Sun and Elements, I cannot think this is to be a man, or to live according to the dignity of humanity: in exspectation of a better, I can with patience embrace this life, yet in my best meditations do often defie death: I honour any man that contemns it, nor can I highly love any that is afraid of it: this makes me naturally love a Souldier, and honour those tattered and contemptible Regiments, that will die at the command of a Sergeant. For a Pagan there may be some motives to be in love with life; but for a Christian to be amazed at death, I see not how he can escape this Dilemma, that he is too sensible of this life, or hopeless of the life to come.

Section 39. Some Divines count *Adam* 30 years old at his Creation, because they suppose him created in the perfect age and stature of man. And surely we are all out of the computation of our age, and every man is some months elder than he bethinks him; for we live, move, have a being, and are subject to the actions of the elements, and the malice of diseases, in that other World, the truest Microcosm, the Womb of our Mother. For besides that general and common existence we are conceived to hold in our Chaos, and whilst we sleep within the bosome of our causes, we enjoy a being and life in three distinct worlds, wherein we receive most manifest graduations: In that obscure World and womb of our mother, our time is short, computed by the Moon; yet longer then the days of many creatures that behold the Sun, our selves being not yet without life, sense, and reason; though for the manifestation of its actions, it awaits the opportunity of objects, and seems to live there but in its root and soul of vegetation; entring afterwards upon the scene of the World, we arise up and become another creature, performing the reasonable actions of man, and obscurely manifesting that part of Divinity in us; but not in complement and perfection till we have once more cast our secondine,[7] that is, this slough of flesh, and are delivered into the last world, that is, that ineffable place of *Paul,* that proper *ubi* of spirits. The smattering I have of the Philosophers Stone (which is something more then the perfect

7 secondine: afterbirth

exaltation of Gold) hath taught me a great deal of Divinity, and instructed my belief, how that immortal spirit and incorruptible substance of my Soul may lye obscure, and sleep a while within this house of flesh. Those strange and mystical transmigrations that I have observed in Silk-worms, turned my Philosophy into Divinity. There is in these works of nature, which seem to puzzle reason, something Divine, and hath more in it then the eye of a common spectator doth discover.

Section 40. I am naturally bashful, nor hath conversation, age or travel, been able to effront, or enharden me; yet I have one part of modesty which I have seldom discovered in another, that is, (to speak truely) I am not so much afraid of death, as ashamed thereof; 'tis the very disgrace and ignominy of our natures, that in a moment can so disfigure us, that our nearest friends, Wife and Children, stand afraid and start at us. The Birds and Beasts of the field, that before in a natural fear obeyed us, forgetting all allegiance begin to prey upon us. This very conceit hath in a tempest disposed and left me willing to be swallowed up in the abyss of waters; wherein I had perished unseen, unpityed, without wondering eyes, tears of pity, Lectures of mortality, and none had said, *Quantum mutatus ab illo!* [8] Not that I am ashamed of the Anatomy of my parts, or can accuse Nature for playing the bungler in any part of me, or my own vitious life for contracting any shameful disease upon me, whereby I might not call my self as wholesome a morsel for the worms as any.

Section 41. Some upon the courage of a fruitful issue, wherein, as in the truest Chronicle, they seem to outlive themselves, can with greater patience away with death. This conceit and counterfeit subsisting in our progenies, seems to be a meer fallacy, unworthy the desires of a man, that can but conceive a thought of the next World; who, in a nobler ambition, should desire to live in his substance in Heaven, rather than his name and shadow in the earth. And therefore at my death I mean to take a total adieu of the world, not caring for a Monument, History, or Epitaph, not so much as the memory of my name to be found any where but in the universal Register of God. I am not yet so Cynical, as

8 *Quantum . . . illo:* how much changed from his former self (*Aeneid* II, 274)

to approve the Testament of Diogenes, nor do I altogether allow that *Rodomontado* of Lucan,

—— *Cælo tegitur, qui non habet urnam.*

He that unburied lies wants not his Herse,
For unto him a Tomb's the Universe.

But commend in my calmer judgment, those ingenuous intentions that desire to sleep by the urns of their Fathers, and strive to go the neatest way unto corruption. I do not envy the temper of Crows and Daws, nor the numerous and weary days of our Fathers before the Flood. If there be any truth in Astrology, I may outlive a Jubilee; as yet I have not seen one revolution of *Saturn,* nor hath my pulse beat thirty years; and yet excepting one, have seen the Ashes, & left under ground all the Kings of *Europe;* have been contemporary to three Emperours, four Grand Signiours, and as many Popes. Methinks I have outlived my self, and begin to be weary of the Sun; I have shaken hands with delight: in my warm blood and Canicular[9] days, I perceive I do anticipate the vices of age; the World to me is but a dream or mock-show, and we all therein but Pantalones[1] and Anticks, to my severer contemplations.

Section 42. It is not, I confess, an unlawful Prayer to desire to surpass the days of our Saviour, or wish to outlive that age wherein he thought fittest to dye; yet if (as Divinity affirms) there shall be no gray hairs in Heaven, but all shall rise in the perfect state of men, we do but outlive those perfections in this World, to be recalled unto them by a greater Miracle in the next, and run on here but to be retrograde hereafter. Were there any hopes to outlive vice, or a point to be super-annuated from sin, it were worthy our knees to implore the days of *Methuselah.* But age doth not rectifie, but incurvate[2] our natures, turning bad dispositions into worser habits, and (like diseases) brings on incurable vices; for every day as we grow weaker in age, we grow stronger in sin, and the number of our days doth but make our sins innumerable. The same vice committed at sixteen, is not

9 Canicular: dog-days, preceding and following the rising of the dog-star
1 Pantalones: French for antics
2 incurvate: to bend or curve, especially inward

the same, though it agree in all other circumstances, as at forty, but swells and doubles from the circumstance of our ages, wherein, besides the constant and inexcusable habit of transgressing, the maturity of our judgment cuts off pretence unto excuse or pardon: every sin, the oftener it is committed, the more it acquireth in the quality of evil; as it succeeds in time, so it proceeds in degrees of badness; for as they proceed they ever multiply, and, like figures in Arithmetick, the last stands for more than all that went before it. And though I think no man can live well once, but he that could live twice, yet for my own part I would not live over my hours past, or begin again the thread of my days: not upon *Cicero's* ground, because I have lived them well, but for fear I should live them worse: I find my growing Judgment daily instructs me how to be better, but my untamed affections and confirmed vitiosity makes me daily do worse; I find in my confirmed age the same sins I discovered in my youth; I committed many then because I was a Child, and because I commit them still, I am yet an infant. Therefore I perceive a man may be twice a Child before the days of dotage, and stand in need of *Æson's* bath before threescore.

Section 43. And truely there goes a great deal of providence to produce a man's life unto threescore; there is more required than an able temper for those years; though the radical humour contain in it sufficient oyl for seventy, yet I perceive in some it gives no light past thirty: men assign not all the causes of long life, that write whole Books thereof. They that found themselves on the radical balsome, or vital sulphur of the parts, determine not why *Abel* lived not so long as *Adam*. There is therefore a secret glome[3] or bottome of our days; 'twas his wisdom to determine them, but his perpetual and waking providence that fulfils and accomplisheth them; wherein the spirits, our selves, and all the creatures of God in a secret and disputed way do execute his will. Let them not therefore complain of immaturity that die about thirty; they fall but like the whole World, whose solid and well-composed substance must not expect the duration and period of its constitution: when all things are completed in it, its age is accomplished; and the last and general fever may as naturally destroy it before six thousand, as me before forty; there is there-

3 glome: a ball or clue of yarn

fore some other hand that twines the thread of life than that of Nature: we are not onely ignorant in Antipathies and occult qualities; our ends are as obscure as our beginnings; the line of our days is drawn by night, and the various effects therein by a pensil that is invisible; wherein though we confess our ignorance, I am sure we do not err if we say it is the hand of God.

Section 44. I am much taken with two verses of *Lucan*, since I have been able not onely, as we do at School, to construe, but understand.

> *Victurosque Dei celant ut vivere durent,*
> *Felix esse mori.*

> *We're all deluded, vainly searching ways*
> *To make us happy by the length of days;*
> *For cunningly to make 's protract this breath,*
> *The Gods conceal the happiness of Death.*

There be many excellent strains in that Poet, wherewith his Stoical Genius hath liberally supplied him; and truely there are singular pieces in the Philosophy of Zeno, and doctrine of the Stoicks, which I perceive, delivered in a Pulpit, pass for current Divinity: yet herein are they in extreams, that can allow a man to be his own *Assassine*, and so highly extol the end and suicide of *Cato;* this is indeed not to fear death, but yet to be afraid of life. It is a brave act of valour to contemn death; but where life is more terrible than death, it is then the truest valour to dare to live; and herein Religion hath taught us a noble example: For all the valiant acts of *Curtius, Scevola,* or *Codrus,* do not parallel or match that one of *Job;* and sure there is no torture to the rack of a disease, nor any Ponyards in death it self, like those in the way or prologue to it. *Emori nolo, sed me esse mor tuum nihil curo;* I would not dye, but care not to be dead. Were I of *Cæsar's* Religion, I should be of his desires, and wish rather to go off at one blow, then to be sawed in pieces by the grating torture of a disease. Men that look no farther than their outsides, think health an appurtenance unto life, and quarrel with their constitutions for being sick; but I that have examined the parts of man, and know upon what tender filaments that Fabrick hangs, do wonder that we are not always so; and considering the thousand doors that lead to death, do thank my God that we can die but once.

'Tis not onely the mischief of diseases, and villany of poysons, that make an end of us; we vainly accuse the fury of Guns, and the new inventions of death; it is in the power of every hand to destroy us, and we are beholding unto everyone we meet, he doth not kill us. There is therefore but one comfort left, that though it be in the power of the weakest arm to take away life, it is not in the strongest to deprive us of death: God would not exempt himself from that, the misery of immortality in the flesh; he undertook not that was immortal. Certainly there is no happiness within this circle of flesh, nor is it in the Opticks of these eyes to behold felicity; the first day of our Jubilee is Death; the Devil hath therefore failed of his desires: we are happier with death than we should have been without it: there is no misery but in himself, where there is no end of misery; and so indeed in his own sense, the Stoick is in the right. He forgets that he can dye who complains of misery; we are in the power of no calamity while death is in our own.

Section 45. Now besides this literal and positive kind of death, there are others whereof Divines make mention, and those I think, not meerly Metaphorical, as mortification, dying unto sin and the World; therefore, I say, every man hath a double Horoscope, one of his humanity, his birth; another of his Christianity, his baptism; and from this do I compute or calculate my Nativity; not reckoning those *Horæ combusta*[4] and odd days, or esteeming my self any thing, before I was my Saviours, and inrolled in the Register of Christ: Whosoever enjoys not this life, I count him but an apparition, though he wear about him the sensible affections of flesh. In these moral acceptions, the way to be immortal is to dye daily; nor can I think I have the true Theory of death, when I contemplate a skull, or behold a Skeleton with those vulgar imaginations it casts upon us; I have therefore inlarged that common *Memento mori*,[5] into a more Christian memorandum, *Memento quatuor Novissima*,[6] those four inevitable points of us all, Death, Judgment, Heaven, and Hell. Neither did the contemplations of the Heathens rest in their graves, without further thought of *Rhadamanth*, or some judicial proceeding

4 *Horæ combusta:* the time when the moon is in conjunction and obscured by the sun
5 *Memento mori:* remember that you must die
6 *Memento . . . Novissima:* remember the four last things

after death, though in another way, and upon suggestion of their natural reasons. I cannot but marvail from what *Sibyl* or Oracle they stole the Prophesie of the worlds destruction by fire, or whence *Lucan* learned to say,

> *Communis mundo superest rogus, ossibus astra*
> *misturus.*
>
> *There yet remains to th' World one common Fire,*
> *Wherein our bones with stars shall make one Pyre.*

I believe the World grows near its end, yet is neither old nor decayed, nor shall ever perish upon the ruines of its own Principles. As the work of Creation was above nature, so is its adversary annihilation; without which the World hath not its end, but its mutation. Now what force should be able to consume it thus far, without the breath of God, which is the truest consuming flame, my Philosophy cannot inform me. Some believe there went not a minute to the Worlds creation, nor shall there go to its destruction; those six days so punctually described, make not to them one moment, but rather seem to manifest the method and Idea of the great work of the intellect of God, than the manner how he proceeded in its operation. I cannot dream that there should be at the last day any such Judicial proceeding, or calling to the Bar, as indeed the Scripture seems to imply, and the literal Commentators do conceive: for unspeakable mysteries in the Scriptures are often delivered in a vulgar and illustrative way; and being written unto man, are delivered, not as they truely are, but as they may be understood; wherein notwithstanding the different interpretations according to different capacities may stand firm with our devotion, nor be any way prejudicial to each single edification.

Section 46. Now to determine the day and year of this inevitable time, is not onely convincible and statute-madness, but also manifest impiety: How shall we interpret *Elias* 6,000 years, or imagine the secret communicated to a Rabbi, which God hath denyed unto his Angels? It had been an excellent Quære to have posed the Devil of *Delphos*, and must needs have forced him to some strange amphibology;[7] it hath not only mocked the predictions of sundry Astrologers in Ages past, but the prophesies of

7 amphibology: ambiguity

many melancholy heads in these present, who neither understanding reasonably things past or present, pretend a knowledge
of things to come; heads ordained onely to manifest the incredible effects of melancholy, and to fulfil old prophecies, rather than
be the authors of new. In those days there shall come Wars and
rumours of Wars, to me seems no prophecy, but a constant truth,
in all times verified since it was pronounced: There shall be
signs in the Moon and Stars; how comes he then like a Thief in
the night, when he gives an item of his coming? That common
sign drawn from the revelation of Antichrist, is as obscure as
any; in our common compute he hath been come these many
years; but for my own part, to speak freely, I am half of opinion
that Antichrist is the Philosophers stone in Divinity; for the discovery and invention thereof, though there be prescribed rules,
and probable inductions, yet hath hardly any man attained the
perfect discovery thereof. That general opinion that the World
grows near its end, hath possessed all ages past as neerly as
ours; I am afraid that the Souls that now depart, cannot escape
that lingring expostulation of the Saints under the Altar, *Quous-
que Domine? How long, O Lord?* and groan in the expectation of
that great Jubilee.

Section 47. This is the day that must make good that great attribute of God, his Justice; that must reconcile those unanswer-
able doubts that torment the wisest understandings, and reduce
those seeming inequalities, and respective distributions in this
world, to an equality and recompensive Justice in the next. This
is that one day, that shall include and comprehend all that went
before it; wherein, as in the last scene, all the Actors must enter,
to compleat and make up the Catastrophe of this great piece.
This is the day whose memory hath onely power to make us
honest in the dark, and to be vertuous without a witness. *Ipsa
sui pretium virtus sibi,* that Vertue is her own reward, is but a
cold principle, and not able to maintain our variable resolutions
in a constant and setled way of goodness. I have practised that
honest artifice of *Seneca,* and in my retired and solitary imaginations, to detain me from the foulness of vice, have fancied to my
self the presence of my dear and worthiest friends, before whom
I should lose my head, rather than be vitious; yet herein I found
that there was nought but moral honesty, and this was not to be

vertuous for his sake who must reward us at the last. I have tryed if I could reach that great resolution of his, to be honest without a thought of Heaven or Hell; and indeed I found upon a natural inclination, and inbred loyalty unto virtue, that I could serve her without a livery; yet not in that resolved and venerable way, but that the frailty of my nature, upon an easie temptation, might be induced to forget her. The life therefore and spirit of all our actions is the resurrection, and a stable apprehension that our ashes shall enjoy the fruit of our pious endeavours; without this, all Religion is a Fallacy, and those impieties of *Lucian, Euripides,* and *Julian,* are no blasphemies, but subtle verities, and Atheists have been the onely Philosophers.

Section 48. How shall the dead arise, is no question of my Faith; to believe only possibilities, is not Faith, but meer Philosophy. Many things are true in Divinity, which are neither inducible by reason, nor confirmable by sense; and many things in Philosophy confirmable by sense, yet not inducible by reason. Thus it is impossible by any solid or demonstrative reasons to perswade a man to believe the conversion of the Needle to the North; though this be possible and true, and easily credible, upon a single experiment unto the sense. I believe that our estranged and divided ashes shall unite again; that our separated dust after so many Pilgrimages and transformations into the parts of Minerals, Plants, Animals, Elements, shall at the Voice of God return into their primitive shapes, and joyn again to make up their primary and predestinate forms. As at the Creation there was a separation of that confused mass into its species; so at the destruction thereof there shall be a separation into its distinct individuals. As at the Creation of the World, all the distinct species that we behold, lay involved in one mass, till the fruitful Voice of God separated this united multitude into its several species; so at the last day, when those corrupted reliques shall be scattered in the Wilderness of forms, and seem to have forgot their proper habits, God by a powerful Voice shall command them back into their proper shapes, and call them out by their single individuals: Then shall appear the fertility of *Adam,* and the magick of that sperm that hath dilated into so many millions. I have often beheld as a miracle, that artificial resurrection and revivification of *Mercury,* how being mortified into a thousand shapes, it assumes again its own, and returns into its numerical self. Let us speak naturally, and like Philosophers, the forms of alterable bodies in these sensible corruptions perish not; nor as we imagine, wholly quit their mansions, but retire and contract themselves into their secret and unaccessible parts, where they may best protect themselves from the action of their Antagonist. A plant or vegetable consumed to ashes, by a contemplative and school-Philosopher seems utterly destroyed, and the form to have taken his leave for ever: But to a sensible Artist the forms are not perished, but withdrawn into their incombustible part, where they lie secure from the action of that devouring element. This is made good by experience, which can from the Ashes of a Plant revive the plant, and from its cinders recall it into its stalk and leaves again. What the Art of man can do in these inferiour pieces, what blasphemy is it to affirm the finger of God cannot do in these more perfect and sensible structures? This is that mystical Philosophy, from whence no true Scholar becomes an Atheist, but from the visible effects of nature grows up a real Divine, and beholds not in a dream, as *Ezekiel,* but in an ocular and visible object the types of his resurrection.

Section 49. Now, the necessary Mansions of our restored selves, are those two contrary and incompatible places we call Heaven and Hell; to define them, or strictly to determine what and where these are, surpasseth my Divinity. That elegant Apostle which seemed to have a glimpse of Heaven, hath left but a negative description thereof; *which neither eye hath seen, nor ear hath heard, nor can enter into the heart of man:* he was translated out of himself to behold it; but being returned into himself, could not express it. St. *John's* description by Emerals, Chrysolites, and precious Stones, is too weak to express the material Heaven we behold. Briefly therefore, where the Soul hath the full measure and complement of happiness; where the boundless appetite of that spirit remains compleatly satisfied, that it can neither desire addition nor alteration, that I think is truly Heaven: and this can onely be in the injoyment of that essence, whose infinite goodness is able to terminate the desires of it self, and the unsatiable wishes of ours; wherever God will thus manifest himself, there is Heaven though within the circle of this sensible world. Thus the Soul of man may be in Heaven any where, even within the limits of his own proper body; and when it ceaseth to live in the body, it may remain in its own soul, that is, its Creator. And thus we may say that *St. Paul,* whether in the body, or out of the body, was yet in Heaven. To place it in the Empyreal, or beyond the tenth sphear, is to forget the worlds destruction; for when this sensible world shall be destroyed, all shall then be here as it is now there, an Empyreal Heaven, a *quasi* vacuity; when to ask where Heaven is, is to demand where the Presence of God is, or where we have the glory of that happy vision. *Moses* that was bred up in all the learning of the *Egyptians,* committed a gross absurdity in Philosophy, when with these eyes of flesh he desired to see God, and petitioned his Maker, that is truth it self, to a contradiction. Those that imagine Heaven and Hell neighbours, and conceive a vicinity[8] between those two extreams, upon consequence of the Parable, where *Dives* discoursed with *Lazarus* in *Abraham's* bosome, do too grosly conceive of those glorified creatures, whose eyes shall easily out-see the Sun, and behold without a perspective the extreamest distances; for if there shall be in our glorified eyes, the faculty of sight and reception of objects, I could think the visible species there to be in as unlimitable a way as now the intellectual. I grant that two bodies placed beyond the tenth sphear, or in a vacuity, according to *Aristotle's* Philosophy, could not behold each other, because there wants a body or Medium to hand and transport the visible rays of the object unto the sense; but when there shall be a general defect of either Medium to convey, or light to prepare and dispose that Medium, and yet a perfect vision, we must suspend the rules of our Philosophy, and make all good by a more absolute piece of opticks.

Section 50. I cannot tell how to say that fire is the essence of Hell; I know not what to make of Purgatory, or conceive a flame that can either prey upon, or purifie the substance of a Soul: those flames of sulphur mention'd in the Scriptures, I take not to be understood of this present Hell, but of that to come, where fire shall make up the complement of our tortures, and have a body or subject wherein to manifest its tyranny. Some who have had the honour to be textuary[9] in Divinity, are of opinion

8 vicinity: proximity
9 textuary: learned in the text of the Bible

it shall be the same specifical fire with ours. This is hard to conceive, yet can I make good how even that may prey upon our bodies, and yet not consume us: for in this material World there are bodies that persist invincible in the powerfullest flames; and though by the action of fire they fall into ignition and liquidation, yet will they never suffer a destruction. I would gladly know how Moses with an actual fire calcin'd, or burnt the Golden Calf unto powder: for that mystical metal of Gold, whose solary and celestial nature I admire, exposed unto the violence of fire, grows onely hot and liquifies, but consumeth not: so when the consumable and volatile pieces of our bodies shall be refined into a more impregnable and fixed temper, like Gold, though they suffer from the action of flames, they shall never perish, but lye immortal in the arms of fire. And surely if this frame must suffer onely by the action of this element, there will many bodies escape; and not onely Heaven, but Earth will not be at an end, but rather a beginning. For at present it is not earth, but a composition of fire, water, earth and air; but at that time, spoiled of these ingredients, it shall appear in a substance more like it self, its ashes. Philosophers that opinioned the worlds destruction by fire, did never dream of annihilation, which is beyond the power of sublunary causes; for the last action of that element is but vitrification, or a reduction of a body into glass; and therefore some of our Chymicks facetiously affirm, that at the last fire all shall be christallized and reverberated into glass, which is the utmost action of that element. Nor need we fear this term annihilation or wonder that God will destroy the works of his Creation: for man subsisting, who is, and will then truely appear a Microcosm, the world cannot be said to be destroyed. For the eyes of God, and perhaps also of our glorified selves, shall as really behold and contemplate the World in its Epitome or contracted essence, as now it doth at large and in its dilated substance. In the seed of a Plant, to the eyes of God, and to the understanding of man, there exists, though in an invisible way, the perfect leaves, flowers and fruit thereof; (for things that are *in posse*[1] to the sense, are actually existent to the understanding). Thus God beholds all things, who contemplates as fully his works in their Epitome, as in their full volume; and beheld as amply the whole

---

1 *in posse:* the state of potential being

world in that little compendium of the sixth day, as in the scattered and dilated pieces of those five before.

Section 51. Men commonly set forth the torments of Hell by fire, and the extremity of corporal afflictions, and describe Hell in the same method that *Mahomet* doth Heaven. This indeed makes a noise, and drums in popular ears: but if this be the terrible piece thereof, it is not worthy to stand in diameter with Heaven, whose happiness consists in that part that is best able to comprehend it, that immortal essence, that translated divinity and colony of God, the Soul. Surely, though we place Hell under Earth, the Devil's walk and purlue is about it: men speak too popularly who place it in those flaming mountains, which to grosser apprehensions represent Hell. The heart of man is the place the Devils dwell in; I feel sometimes a Hell within my self; *Lucifer* keeps his Court in my breast; *Legion* is revived in me: There are as many Hells, as *Anaxagoras* conceited worlds: there was more than one Hell in *Magdalene,* when there were seven Devils; for every Devil is an Hell unto himself; he holds enough of torture in his own *ubi,* and needs not the misery of circumference to afflict him. And thus a distracted Conscience here, is a shadow or introduction unto Hell hereafter. Who can but pity the merciful intention of those hands that do destroy themselves? the Devil, were it in his power, would do the like; which being impossible, his miseries are endless, and he suffers most in that attribute wherein he is impassible, his immortality.

Section 52. I thank God that with joy I mention it, I was never afraid of Hell, nor never grew pale at the description of that place; I have so fixed my contemplations on Heaven, that I have almost forgot the Idea of Hell, and am afraid rather to lose the Joys of the one, than endure the misery of the other; to be deprived of them is a perfect Hell, and needs methinks no addition to compleat our afflictions; that terrible term hath never detained me from sin, nor do I owe any good action to the name thereof: I fear God, yet am not afraid of him; his Mercies make me ashamed of my sins, before his Judgments afraid thereof: these are the forced and secondary method of his wisdom, which he useth but as the last remedy, and upon provocation; a course rather to deter the wicked, than incite the virtuous to his wor-

ship. I can hardly think there was ever any scared into Heaven;
they go the fairest way to Heaven, that would serve God without
a Hell; other Mercenaries, that crouch into him in fear of Hell,
though they term themselves the servants, are indeed but the
slaves of the Almighty.

Section 53. And to be true, and speak my soul, when I survey
the occurrences of my life, and call into account the Finger of
God, I can perceive nothing but an abyss and mass of mercies,
either in general to mankind, or in particular to my self: and,
whether out of the prejudice of my affection, or an inverting
and partial conceit of his mercies, I know not; but those which
others term crosses, afflictions, judgments, misfortunes, to me
who inquire farther into them then their visible effects, they
both appear, and in event have ever proved the secret and dis-
sembled favours of his affection. It is a singular piece of Wisdom
to apprehend truly, and without passion, the Works of God; and
so well to distinguish his Justice from his Mercy, as not to mis-
call those noble Attributes: yet is it likewise an honest piece of
Logick, so to dispute and argue the proceedings of God, as to
distinguish even his judgments into mercies. For God is merciful unto all, because better to the worst, than the best deserve;
and to say he punisheth none in this World, though it be a Paradox, is no absurdity. To one that hath committed Murther, if
the Judge should only ordain a Fine, it were a madness to call
this a punishment, and to repine at the sentence, rather than
admire the clemency of the Judge. Thus our offences being mortal and deserving not onely Death, but Damnation; if the goodness of God be content to traverse and pass them over with a
loss, misfortune, or disease; what frensie were it to term this a
punishment, rather than an extremity of mercy; and to groan
under the rod of his Judgments, rather than admire the Scepter
of his Mercies? Therefore to adore, honour, and admire him,
is a debt of gratitude due from the obligation of our nature,
states, and conditions; and with these thoughts, he that knows
them best, will not deny that I adore him. That I obtain Heaven,
and the bliss thereof, is accidental, and not the intended work
of my devotion; it being a felicity I can neither think to deserve,
nor scarce in modesty to expect. For these two ends of us all,
either as rewards or punishments, are mercifully ordained and

disproportionably disposed unto our actions; the one being so far beyond our deserts, the other so infinitely below our demerits.

Section 54. There is no Salvation to those that believe not in Christ, that is, say some, since his Nativity, and, as Divinity affirmeth, before also; which makes me much apprehend the ends of those honest Worthies and Philosophers which dyed before his Incarnation. It is hard to place those Souls in Hell, whose worthy lives do teach us Virtue on Earth: methinks amongst those many subdivisions of Hell, there might have been one Limbo left for these. What a strange vision will it be to see their Poetical fictions converted into Verities, and their imagined and fancied Furies into real Devils? How strange to them will sound the History of *Adam*, when they shall suffer for him they never heard of? when they who derive their genealogy from the Gods, shall know they are the unhappy issue of sinful man? It is an insolent part of reason, to controvert the Works of God, or question the Justice of his proceedings. Could Humility teach others, as it hath instructed me, to contemplate the infinite and incomprehensible distance betwixt the Creator and the Creature; or did we seriously perpend[2] that on simile of St. *Paul, Shall the Vessel say to the Potter, Why hast thou made me thus?* it would prevent these arrogant disputes of reason, nor would we argue the definitive sentence of God, either to Heaven or Hell. Men that live according to the right rule and law of reason, live but in their own kind, as beasts do in theirs; who justly obey the prescript of their natures, and therefore cannot reasonably demand a reward of their actions, as onely obeying the natural dictates of their reason. It will therefore, and must at last appear, that all salvation is through Christ; which verity I fear these great examples of virtue must confirm, and make it good, how the perfectest actions of earth have no title or claim unto Heaven.

Section 55. Nor truely do I think the lives of these or of any other were ever correspondent, or in all points comfortable unto their doctrines. It is evident that *Aristotle* transgressed the rule of his own Ethicks: the Stoicks that condemn passion, and com-

2 perpend: consider

mand a man to laugh in *Phalaris* his Bull, could not endure
without a groan a fit of the Stone or Colick. The *Scepticks* that
affirmed they knew nothing, even in that opinion confute themselves, and thought they knew more than all the World beside.
Diogenes I hold to be the most vain glorious man of his time,
and more ambitious in refusing all Honours, than *Alexander* in
rejecting none. Vice and the Devil put a Fallacy upon our Reasons, and provoking us too hastily to run from it, entangle and
profound us deeper in it. The Duke of *Venice*, that weds himself
unto the Sea by a Ring of Gold, I will not argue of prodigality,
because it is a solemnity of good use and consequence in the
State: but the Philosopher that threw his money into the Sea
to avoid Avarice, was a notorious prodigal. There is no road or
ready way to virtue; it is not an easie point of art to disentangle
our selves from this riddle, or web of Sin: To perfect virtue, as
to Religion, there is required a *Panoplia*, or compleat armour;
that, whilst we lye at close ward against one Vice, we lye not
open to the venny[3] of another. And indeed wiser discretions
that have the thred of reason to conduct them, offend without
pardon; whereas under-heads may stumble without dishonour.
There go so many circumstances to piece up one good action,
that it is a lesson to be good, and we are forced to be virtuous
by the book. Again, the Practice of men holds not an equal pace,
yea, and often runs counter to their Theory: we naturally know
what is good, but naturally pursue what is evil: the Rhetorick
wherewith I perswade another, cannot perswade my self: there
is a depraved appetite in us, that will with patience hear the
learned instructions of Reason, but yet perform no farther than
agrees to its own irregular humour. In brief, we all are monsters, that is, a composition of Man and Beast; wherein we must
endeavour to be as the Poets fancy that wise man *Chiron*, that
is, to have the Region of Man above that of Beast, and Sense to
sit but at the feet of Reason. Lastly, I do desire with God that all,
but yet affirm with men, that few shall know Salvation; that the
bridge is narrow, the passage strait, unto life: yet those who
do confine the Church of God, either to particular Nations,
Churches, or Families, have made it far narrower than our
Saviour ever meant it.

3   venny: possibly dialect for bog, swamp (from fen)

Section 56. The vulgarity of those judgments that wrap the Church of God in *Strabo's* cloak, and restrain it unto *Europe,* seem to me as bad Geographers as *Alexander,* who thought he had Conquer'd all the World, when he had not subdued the half of any part thereof. For we cannot deny the Church of God both in *Asia* and *Africa,* if we do not forget the Peregrinations of the Apostles, the deaths of the Martyrs, the Sessions of many, and, even in our reformed judgment, lawful Councils, held in those parts in the minority and nonage of ours. Nor must a few differerences, more remarkable in the eyes of man, than perhaps in the judgment of God, excommunicate from Heaven one another, much less those Christians who are in a manner all Martyrs, maintaining their Faith, in the noble way of persecution, and serving God in the Fire, whereas we honour him but in the Sunshine. 'Tis true we all hold there is a number of Elect, and many to be saved; yet take our Opinions together, and from the confusion thereof there will be no such thing as salvation, nor shall any one be saved. For first, the Church of *Rome* condemneth us, we likewise them; the Sub-reformists and Sectaries sentence the Doctrine of our Church as damnable; the Atomist, or Familist, reprobates all these; and all these, them again. Thus, whilst the Mercies of God do promise us Heaven, our conceits and opinions exclude us from that place. There must be therefore more than one St. *Peter;* particular Churches and Sects usurp the gates of Heaven, and turn the key against each other: and thus we go to Heaven against each other's wills, conceits and opinions; and, with as much uncharity as ignorance, do err I fear in points not only of our own, but one anothers salvation.

Section 57. I believe many are saved, who to man seem reprobated; and many are reprobated, who in the opinion and sentence of man stand elected: there will appear at the Last day, strange and unexpected examples, both of his Justice and his Mercy; and therefore to define either, is folly in man, and insolency even in the Devils: those acute and subtil spirits in all their sagacity, can hardly divine who shall be saved; which if they could Prognostick, their labour were at an end; nor need they compass the earth seeking whom they may devour. Those who upon a rigid application of the Law, sentence *Solomon* unto damnation, condemn not onely him, but themselves, and the

whole World; for, by the Letter, and written Word of God, we
are without exception in the state of Death; but there is a prerogative of God, and an arbitrary pleasure above the Letter of
his own Law, by which alone we can pretend unto Salvation,
and through which *Solomon* might be as easily saved as those
who condemn him.

Section 58. The number of those who pretend unto Salvation,
and those infinite swarms who think to pass through the eye of
this Needle, have much amazed me. That name and compella-
tion of *little Flock*, doth not comfort, but deject, my Devotion,
especially when I reflect upon mine own unworthiness, wherein,
according to my humble apprehensions, I am below them all.
I believe there shall never be an Anarchy in Heaven, but as
there are Hierarchies amongst the Angels, so shall there be
degrees of priority amongst the Saints. Yet is it (I protest) beyond my ambition to aspire unto the first ranks; my desires
onely are, and I shall be happy therein, to be but the last man,
and bring up the Rere in Heaven.

Section 59. Again, I am confident, and fully perswaded, yet dare
not take my oath of my Salvation: I am as it were sure, and do
believe without all doubt, that there is such a City as *Constantinople;* yet for me to take my Oath thereon, were a kind of Per-
jury, because I hold no infallible warrant from my own sense
to confirm me in the certainty thereof: And truly, though many
pretend an absolute certainty of their Salvation, yet when an
humble Soul shall contemplate her own unworthiness, she shall
meet with many doubts, and suddenly find how little we stand
in need of the Precept of St. *Paul, Work out your salvation with
fear and trembling.* That which is the cause of my Election, I
hold to be the cause of my Salvation, which was the mercy and
beneplacit of God, before I was, or the foundation of the World.
Before Abraham was, I am, is the saying of Christ; yet is it true
in some sense, if I say it of my self; for I was not onely before
my self, but *Adam,* that is, in the Idea of God, and the decree
of that Synod held from all Eternity. And in this sense, I say,
the World was before the Creation, and at an end before it had
a beginning; and thus was I dead before I was alive; though my

grave be *England,* my dying place was Paradise; and *Eve* mis-carried of me before she conceiv'd of *Cain.*

Section 60. Insolent zeals, that do decry good Works, and rely onely upon Faith, take not away merit: for, depending upon the efficacy of their Faith, they enforce the condition of God, and in a more sophistical way do seem to challenge Heaven. It was decreed by God, that only those that lapt in the water like Dogs, should have the honour to destroy the *Midianites;* yet could none of those justly challenge, or imagine he deserved, that honour thereupon. I do not deny, but that true Faith, and such as God requires, is not onely a mark or token, but also a means, of our Salvation; but where to find this, is as obscure to me, as my last end. And if our Saviour could object unto his own Disciples and Favourites, a Faith, that, to the quantity of a grain of Mustard-seed, is able to remove Mountains; surely, that which we boast of, is not any thing, or at the most, but a remove from nothing. This is the Tenor of my belief; wherein, though there be many things singular, and to the humour of my irregular self; yet if they square not with maturer Judgments I disclaim them, and do no further favour them, than the learned and best judgments shall authorize them.

Jeremy Taylor

Jeremy Taylor was born in 1613 in Cambridge where he attended first the Perse School and then Gonville and Caius College from 1626 to 1635. He became a fellow of All Souls, Oxford, in 1636, and acted as rector at Uppingham from 1638 to 1642, during which period he married. In 1645 he was captured by parliamentary troops, having served as chaplain to the royal household. After his release, he retired to the protection of the Earl and Countess of Carbery at Golden Grove, but he was imprisoned again briefly in 1655. In 1658 he received a lectureship at Lisburn, Ireland, from Lord Conway, and two years later became Bishop of Down and Connor. He died and was buried in Dromore in 1667. Among his many works, he published The Liberty of Prophesying *in 1647;* The Great Exemplar *in 1649;* Holy Living *and* Holy Dying *in 1650/51; and* Unum Necessarium *in 1655.*

The Rule and Exercises of Holy Dying

CHAPTER I:

A GENERAL PREPARATION

TOWARDS A HOLY AND BLESSED DEATH:

by way of consideration

SECTION I:

CONSIDERATION OF THE VANITY AND SHORTNESS

OF MANS LIFE

A Man is a Bubble (said the Greek Proverb); which *Lucian* represents with advantages and its proper circumstances, to this purpose; saying, All the world is a Storm, and Men rise up in their several generations like Bubbles descending *à Jove pluvio*, from God and the dew of Heaven, from a tear and drop of rain, from Nature and Providence: and some of these instantly sink into the deluge of their first parent, and are hidden in a sheet of Water, having had no other businesse in the world but to be born that they might be able to die: others float up and down two or three turns, and suddenly disappear, and give their place to others: and they that live longest upon the face of the waters are in perpetual motion, restless and uneasy, and being crushed with the great drop of a cloud sink into flatness and a froth; the change not being great, it being hardly possible it should be more a nothing than it was before. So is every man: He is born in vanity and sin; he comes into the world like morning Mushromes, soon thrusting up their heads into the air, and convers-

ing with their kindred of the same production, and as soon they
turn into dust and forgetfulnesse; some of them without any
other interest in the affairs of the world, but that they made
their parents a little glad, and very sorrowful: others ride longer
in the storm; it may be until seven years of Vanity be expired,
and then peradventure the Sun shines hot upon their heads and
they fall into the shades below, into the cover of death and darkness of the grave to hide them. But if the bubble stands the
shock of a bigger drop, and outlives the chances of a childe, of
a careless Nurse, of drowning in a pail of water, of being over-
laid by a sleepy servant, or such little accidents, then the young
man dances like a bubble, empty and gay, and shines like a
Doves neck or the image of a rainbow, which hath no substance,
and whose very imagery and colours are phantastickal; and so
he dances out the gayety of his youth, and is all the while in a
storm, and endures, only because he is not knocked on the head
by a drop of bigger rain, or crushed by the pressure of a load
of indigested meat, or quenched by the disorder of an ill-placed
humor: and to preserve a man alive in the midst of so many
chances, and hostilities, is as great a miracle as to create him; to
preserve him from rushing into nothing, and at first to draw him
up from nothing were equally the issues of an Almighty power.
And therefore the wise men of the world have contended who
shall best fit mans condition with words signifying his vanity
and short abode. *Homer* calls a man a *leaf*, the smallest, the
weakest piece of a short liv'd unsteady plant. *Pindar* calls him
the dream of a shadow: Another, *the dream of the shadow of
smoak*. But S. *James* spake by a more excellent Spirit, saying,
Our life is but a vapour, viz., drawn from the earth by a celestial
influence: made of smoak, or the lighter parts of water, tossed
with every winde, moved by the motion of a superior body, without vertue in it self, lifted up on high, or left below, according
as it pleases the Sun its Foster-Father. But it is lighter yet. It is
but *appearing;* a phantastick vapor, an apparition, nothing
real: it is not so much as a mist, not the matter of a shower,
nor substantial enough to make a cloud; but it is like *Cas-
siopeia's* chair, or *Pelops* shoulder, or the circles of Heaven,
φαινόμενα,[1] for which you cannot have a word that can signify
a veryer nothing. And yet the expression is one degree more

---

1 φαινόμενα: appearances

made diminutive; *a vapour,* and phantastickal, or *a mere appearance,* and this but *for a little while* neither; the very dream, the phantasm disappears in a small time, *like the shadow that departeth,* or *like a tale that is told,* or *as a dream when one awaketh:* A man is so vain, so unfixed, so perishing a creature, that he cannot long last in the scene of fancy: a man goes off and is forgotten like the dream of a distracted person. The summe of all is this: *That thou art a man,* then whom there is not in the world any greater instance of heights and declensions, of lights and shadows, of misery and folly, of laughter and tears, of groans and death.

And because this consideration is of great usefulness and great necessity to many purposes of wisdom and the Spirit; all the succession of time, all the changes in nature, all the varieties of light and darknesse, the thousand thousands of accidents in the world, and every contingency to every man, and to every creature does preach our funeral Sermon, and calls us to look, and see, how the old Sexton *Time* throws up the earth, and digs a Grave where we must lay our sins, or our sorrows, and sowe our bodies, till they rise again in a fair, or in an intolerable eternity. Every revolution which the Sun makes about the world, divides between life and death; and death possesses both those portions by the next morrow; and we are dead to all those months which we have already lived, and we shall never live them over again: and still God makes little periods of our age. First we change our world, when we come from the womb to feel the warmth of the Sun: Then we sleep and enter into the image of death, in which state we are unconcerned in all the changes of the world; and if our Mothers, or our Nurses die, or a wild boar destroy our vineyards, or our King be sick, we regard it not, but, during that state, are as disinterest as if our eyes were closed with the clay that weeps in the bowels of the earth. At the end of seven years, our teeth fall and dye before us, representing a formal Prologue to the tragedy; and still every seven years it is oddes but we shall finish the last scene: and when Nature, or Chance, or Vice takes our body in pieces, weakening some parts, and loosing others, *we taste the grave* and the solemnities of our own Funerals, first, in those parts that ministred to Vice, and next in them that served for Ornament; and in a short time even they that served for necessity become uselesse, and intangled like the wheels of a broken clock. *Baldnesse* is but a dressing to our funerals, the proper ornament of mourning, and of a person entred very far into the regions and possession of Death: And we have many more of the same signification: Gray hairs, rotten teeth, dim eyes, trembling joynts, short breath, stiffe limbs, wrinkled skin, short memory, decayed appetite. Every dayes necessity calls for a reparation of that portion which Death fed on all night when we lay in his lap, and slept in his outer chambers: The very spirits of a man prey upon the daily portion of bread and flesh, and every meal is a rescue from one death, and lays up for another; and while we think a thought, we die; and the clock strikes, and reckons on our portion of Eternity; we form our words with the breath of our nostrils, we have the less to live upon for every word we speak.

Thus Nature calls us to meditate of death by those things which are the instruments of acting it; and God by all the variety of his Providence makes us see death every where, in all variety of circumstances, and dressed up for all the fancies, and the expectation of every single person. Nature hath given us one harvest every year, but death hath two: and the Spring and the Autumn send throngs of Men and Women to charnel-houses; and all the Summer long men are recovering from their evils of the Spring, till the Dog-days come, and then the Syrian star makes the Summer deadly; and the fruits of Autumn are laid up for all the years provision, and the man that gathers them eats and surfets, and dies and needs them not, and himself is laid up for Eternity; and he that escapes till Winter, only stays for another opportunity, which the distempers of that quarter minister to him with great variety. Thus death reigns in all the portions of our time. The Autumn with its fruits provides disorders for us: and the Winters cold turns them into sharp diseases, and the Spring brings flowers to strew our herse, and the Summer gives green turfe and brambles to binde upon our graves. Calentures,[2] and surfet, Cold, and Agues, are the four quarters of the year, and all minister to Death; and you can go no whither, but you tread upon a dead mans bones.

The wilde fellow in *Petronius* that escaped upon a broken table from the furies of a shipwrack, as he was sunning himself upon the rocky shore espied a man rolled upon his floating

2 Calentures: fevers

bed of waves, ballasted with sand in the folds of his garment, and carried by his civil enemy the sea towards the shore to find a grave: and it cast him into some sad thoughts; that peradventure this man's wife in some part of the Continent, safe and warme looks next moneth for the good mans return; or it may be his Son knows nothing of the Tempest; or his Father thinks of that affectionate kiss which still is warm upon the good old mans cheek ever since he took a kind farewel; and he weeps with joy to think how blessed he shall be when his beloved boy returns into the circle of his Fathers Arms. These are the thoughts of Mortals, this is the end and sum of all their designes: a dark night, and an ill Guide, a boysterous Sea, and a broken Cable, a hard rock, and a rough winde dash'd in pieces the fortune of a whole family, and they that shall weep loudest for the accident, are not yet entred into the storm, and yet have suffered shipwrack. Then looking upon the carkasse, he knew it, and found it to be the Master of the Ship, who the day before cast up the accounts of his patrimony and his trade, and named the day when he thought to be at home: See how the man swims who was so angry two days since; his passions are becalm'd with the storm, his accounts cast up, his cares at an end, his voyage done, and his gains are the strange events of death, which whither they be good or evil, the men that are alive seldom trouble themselves concerning the interest of the dead.

But seas alone do not break our vessel in pieces: Every-where we may be shipwracked. A valiant General, when he is to reap the harvest of his crowns and triumphs, fights unprosperously, or falls into a Feaver with joy and wine, and changes his Laurel into Cypress, his triumphal Chariot to an Hearse; dying the night before he was appointed to perish in the drunkennesse of his festival joyes. It was a sad arrest of the loosenesses and wilder feasts of the *French* Court, when their King (*Henry* II.) was killed really by the sportive image of a fight. And many brides have died under the hands of Paranymphs and Maidens dressing them for uneasy joy, the new and undiscerned chains of Marriage; according to the saying of *Bensirah* the wise Jew, *The Bride went into her chamber, and knew not what should befall her there.* Some have been paying their vows, and giving thanks for a prosperous return to their own house, and the roof hath descended upon their heads, and turned their loud religion into the deeper silence of a grave. And how many teeming Mothers have rejoyced over their swelling wombs, and pleased themselves in becoming the channels of blessing to a family; and the Midwife hath quickly bound their heads and feet, and carried them forth to burial? Or else the birth-day of an Heir hath seen the Coffin of the Father brought into the house, and the divided Mother hath been forced to travail twice, with a painful birth, and a sadder death.

There is no state, no accident no circumstance of our life, but it hath been sowred by some sad instance of a dying friend: a friendly meeting often ends in some sad mischance, and makes an eternal parting: and when the poet *Æschylus* was sitting under the walls of his house, an eagle hovering over his bald head, mistook it for a stone, and let fall his oyster, hoping there to break the shell, but pierced the poor mans skull.

Death meets us every-where, and is procured by every instrument, and in all chances, and enters in at many doors; by violence, and secret influence, by the aspect of a star, and the stink of a mist, by the emissions of a cloud, and the meeting of a vapor, by the fall of a chariot and the stumbling at a stone, by a full meal, or an empty stomach, by watching at the wine, or by watching at prayers, by the Sun or the Moon, by a heat or a cold, by sleeplesse nights or sleeping dayes; by water frozen into the hardnesse, and sharpnesse of a dagger, or water thawd into the floods of a river; by a hair, or a raisin, by violent motion, or sitting still, by severity, or dissolution, by Gods mercy or Gods anger, by every thing in Providence and every thing in manners, by every thing in nature and every thing in chance. *Eripitur persona, manet res:* we take pains to heap up things useful to our life, and get our death in the purchase; and the person is snatched away, and the goods remain: and all this is the law and constitution of nature, it is a punishment to our sins, the unalterable event of providence, and the decree of heaven. The chains that confine us to this condition are strong as destiny and immutable as the eternal laws of God.

I have conversed with some men who rejoyced in the death or calamity of others, and accounted it as a judgment upon them, for being on the other side, and against them in the contention; but within the revolution of a few moneths the same man met with a more uneasy and unhandsom death: which when I saw, I wept, and was afraid; for I knew that it must be so with all men, for we also shall die and end our quarrels and contentions by passing to a final sentence.

SECTION II:

THE CONSIDERATION REDUCED TO PRACTICE

It will be very material to our best and noblest purposes, if we represent this scene of change and sorrow a little more dressed up in Circumstances, for so we shall be more apt to practise those Rules, the doctrine of which is consequent to this Consideration. It is a mighty change that is made by the death of every person, and it is visible to us who are alive. Reckon but from the spritefulness of youth, and the fair cheeks and full eyes of childhood, from the vigorousness and strong flexure of the joynts of five-and-twenty, to the hollownesse and dead palenesse, to the loathsomenesse and horrour of a three days burial, and we shall perceive the distance to be very great, and very strange. But so have I seen a Rose newly springing from the clefts of its hood, and at first it was fair as the Morning, and full with the dew of Heaven, as a Lambs fleece; but when a ruder breath had forced open its virgin modesty, and dismantled its too youthful and unripe retirements, it began to put on darknesse, and to decline to softnesse, and the symptomes of a sickly age; it bowed the head, and broke its stalk, and at night having lost some of its leaves, and all its beauty, it fell into the portion of weeds and out-worn faces: The same is the portion of every man, and every woman; the heritage of worms and serpents, rottennesse and cold dishonour, and our beauty so changed, that our acquaintance quickly knew us not, and that change mingled with so much horrour, or else meets so with our fears and weak discoursings, that they who six hours ago tended upon us, either with charitable or ambitious services cannot without some regret stay in the room alone where the body lies stripped of its life and Honour. I have read of a fair young *German* Gentleman, who living, often refused to be pictured, but put off the importunity of his friends desire, by giving way that after a few dayes burial they might send a painter to his vault, and if they saw cause for it, draw the image *of his death unto life.* They did so, and found his face half eaten, and his midriffe and backbone full of serpents; and so he stands pictured among his

armed Ancestours. So does the fairest beauty change, and it will
be as bad with you and me; and then, what servants shall we
have to wait upon us in the grave, what friends to visit us, what
officious people to cleanse away the moist and unwholesom
cloud reflected upon our faces from the sides of the weeping
vaults, which are the longest weepers for our funeral.

This discourse will be useful, if we consider and practise by
the following Rules and Considerations respectively.

1. All the Rich and all the Covetous men in the world will
perceive, and all the world will perceive for them, that it is but
an ill recompence for all their cares, that by this time all that
shall be left will be this, that the Neighbours shall say he died
a rich man: and yet his wealth will not profit him in the grave,
but hugely swell the sad accounts of Doomsday; And he that
kills the Lords people with unjust or ambitious wars for an un-
rewarding interest, shall have this character, that he threw
away all the dayes of his life, that one year might be reckoned
with his Name, and computed by his reign, or consulship: and
many men by great labors and affronts, many indignities and
crimes, labour only for a pompous Epitaph, and a loud Title upon
their Marble; whilst those into whose possessions their heirs,
or kinred are entred, are forgotten, and lye unregarded as their
ashes, and without concernment or relation, as the turf upon
the face of their grave. A man may read a Sermon, the best and
most passionate that ever man preached, if he shall but enter
the Sepulchres of Kings. In the same Escurial where the *Spanish*
Princes live in greatnesse and power, and decree war or peace,
they have wisely placed a coemeterie where their ashes and their
glory shall sleep till time shall be no more: and where our Kings
have been crowned, their Ancestors lay interred, and they must
walk over their Grandsires head to take his Crown. There is an
acre sown with royal seed, the copy of the greatest change, from
rich to naked, from ceiled roofs to arched coffins, from *living
like Gods to die like Men*. There is enough to cool the flames of
lust, to abate the heights of pride, to appease the itch of covetous
desires, to sully and dash out the dissembling colours of a lust-
ful, artificial, and imaginary beauty. There the warlike and the
peaceful, the fortunate and the miserable, the beloved and the
despised Princes mingle their dust, and pay down their symbol

of Mortality, and tell all the world, that when we die, our ashes shall be equal to Kings, and our accounts easier, and our pains for our crowns shall be lesse. To my apprehension it is a sad record which is left by *Athenæus* concerning *Ninus* the great *Assyrian* Monarch, whose life and death is summed up in these words: *Ninus* the *Assyrian* had an ocean of gold, and other riches more than the sand in the *Caspian* sea; he never saw the stars, and perhaps he never desired it; he never stirred up the holy fire among the *Magi,* nor touched his God with the sacred rod according to the Laws; he never offered sacrifice, nor worshipped the Deity, nor administered justice, nor spake to his people, nor numbred them; but he was most valiant to eat and drink, and having mingled his wines he threw the rest upon the stones. This man is dead; Behold his Sepulchre, and now hear where *Ninus* is. Sometimes I was *Ninus,* and drew the breath of a living man, but now am nothing but clay. I have nothing but what I did eat, and what I served to myself in lust (that was and is all my portion); the wealth with which I was (esteemed) blessed, my enemies meeting together shall bear away, as the mad *Thyades* carry a raw Goat. I am gone to Hell, and when I went thither, I neither carried Gold, nor Horse, nor silver Chariot. I that wore a Miter, am now a little heap of dust. I know not any thing that can better represent the evil condition of a wicked Man, or a changing greatnesse, From the greatest secular dignity to dust and ashes, his nature bears him; and from thence to Hell his sins carry him, and there he shall be for ever under the dominion of chains and Devils, wrath and an intollerable calamity. This is the reward of an unsanctified condition, and a greatnesse ill gotten, or ill administred.

2. Let no man extend *his thoughts,* or let *his hopes* wander towards future and far-distant events and accidental contingencies. This day is mine and yours, but *ye know not what shall be on the morrow:* and every morning creeps out of a dark cloud, leaving behinde it an ignorance and silence deep as midnight, and undiscerned as are the Phantasms that make a Chrysome childe[3] to smile: so that we cannot discern what comes hereafter, unless we had a light from Heaven brighter than the vision of an Angel, even the Spirit of Prophecy. Without revela-

3 Chrysome childe: child in its christening cloth

tion we cannot tell whether we shall eat to-morrow, or whether
a Squinancy[4] shall choak us: and it is written in the unrevealed
folds of Divine Predestination, that many who are this day alive
shall to-morrow be laid upon the cold earth, and the women
shall weep over their shrowd, and dresse them for their funeral.
S. *James,* in his Epistle notes the folly of some men, his contemporaries, who were so impatient of the event of to-morrow,
or the accidents of next year, or the good or evils of old age, that
'they would consult Astrologers and Witches, Oracles and Devils
what should befall them the next Calends? [5] what should be the
event of such a voyage, what God had written in his book concerning the successe of battles, the Election of Emperors, the
Heir of Families, the price of Merchandise, the return of the
Tyrian fleet, the rate of *Sidonian* Carpets, and as they were
taught by the crafty and lying Demons, so they would expect
the issue; and oftentimes by disposing their affairs in order toward such events, really did produce some little accidents according to their expectation; and that made them trust the
Oracles in greater things, and in all. Against this, he opposes
his Counsel, that we should not search after forbidden records,
much lesse by uncertain significations: for whatsoever is disposed to happen by the order of natural causes, or civil counsels,
may be rescinded by a peculiar decree of providence, or be prevented by the death of the interested persons; who while their
hopes are full, and their causes conjoyned, and the work brought
forward, and the sickle put into the harvest, and the first-fruits
offered, and ready to be eaten, even then if they put forth their
hand to an event that stands but at the door, at that door their
body may be carried forth to burial, before the expectation shall
enter into fruition. When *Richilda* the widow of *Albert* Earl of
Ebersberg had feasted the Emperor *Henry* III., and petitioned
in behalf of her nephew *Welpho* for some lands formerly possessed by the Earl her husband; just as the Emperor held out
his hand to signifie his consent, the chamber-floor suddenly fell
under them, and *Richilda* falling upon the edge of a bathing
vessel, was bruised to death, and stayed not to see her Nephew
sleep in those lands which the Emperor was reaching forth to
her, and placed at the door of restitution.

4 Squinancy: quinsy, a disease of the throat
5 Calends: first day of any month

3. As our *hopes* must be confined, so must our *designs:* let us not project long designes; crafty plots, and diggings so deep that the intrigues of a designe shall never be unfolded till our Grand-children have forgotten our vertues or our vices. The work of our soul is cut short facile, sweet and plain, and fitted to the small portions of our shorter life: and as we must not trouble our inquiry, so neither must we intricate our labour and pur-poses with what we shall never enjoy. This rule does not forbid us to plant Orchards which shall feed our Nephews with their fruit; for by such provisions they do something towards an im-aginary immortality, and do charity to their Relatives: but such projects are reproved which discompose our present duty by long and future designes; such which by casting our labours to events at distance, make us lesse to remember our Death stand-ing at the door. It is fit for a Man to work for his dayes wages, or to contrive for the hire of a week, or to lay a train to make provisions for such a time as is within our eye, and in our duty, and within the usual periods of Mans life, for whatsoever is made necessary, is also made prudent; but while we plot and buisy ourselves in the toils of an ambitious war, or the levies of a great estate, Night enters in upon us, and tells all the world, how like fools we lived, and how deceived and miserably we dyed. *Seneca* tells of *Senecio Cornelius,* a man crafty in getting and tenacious in holding a great estate, and one who was as diligent in the care of his body, as of his money, curious of his health, as of his possessions; that he all day long attended upon his sick and dying friend; but when he went away was quickly comforted, supped merrily, went to bed cheerfully, and on a sudden being surprised by a Squinancy, scarce drew his breath until the Morning, but by that time dyed, being snatched from the torrent of his fortune, and the swelling tide of wealth, and a likely hope bigger than the necessities of ten men. This acci-dent was much noted then in *Rome,* because it happened in so great a fortune, and in the midst of wealthy designes; and pres-ently it made wise men to consider, how imprudent a person he is, who disposes of ten years to come, when he is not Lord of to-morrow.

4. Though we must not look so far off, and pry abroad, yet we must be busy near at hand; we must with all arts of the Spirit seize upon the present, because it passes from us while

we speak, and because in it all our certainty does consist. We must take our waters as out of a torrent and sudden shower which will quickly cease dropping from above, and quickly cease running in our channels here below. This instant will never return again, and yet it may be this instant will declare, or secure the fortune of a whole eternity. The old Greeks and Romans taught us the prudence of this rule: but Christianity teaches us the Religion of it. They so seized upon the present that they would lose nothing of the day's pleasure. *Let us eat and drink, for to-morrow we shall die;* that was their Philosophy; and at their solemn feasts they would talk of death to heighten the present drinking, and that they might warm their veins with a fuller chalice, as knowing the drink that was poured upon their graves would be cold and without relish. *Break the beds, drink your wine, crown your heads with Roses, and besmear your curled locks with Nard; for God bids you to remember death;* so the Epigrammatist speaks the sense of their drunken Principles. Something towards this signification is that of *Solomon, There is nothing better for a man than that he should eat and drink, and that he should make his soul enjoy good in his labour, for that is his portion, for who shall bring him to see that which shall be after him?* But although he concludes all this to be vanity, yet because it was the best thing that was then commonly known that they should seize upon the present with a temperate use of permitted pleasures, I had reason to say that Christianity taught us to turn this into Religion. For he that by a present and constant holiness secures the present, and makes it useful to his noblest purposes, he turns his condition into his best advantage, by making his unavoidable fate become his necessary religion.

To the purpose of this rule is that collect of *Tuscan* Hieroglyphics, which we have from *Gabriel Simeon.* 'Our life is very short, beauty is a cosenage, money is false and fugitive, Empire is odious and hated by them that have it not, and uneasy to them that have, Victory is always uncertain, and Peace most commonly is but a fraudulent bargain; Old age is miserable, death is the period, and is a happy one if it be not sowred by the sins of our life: but nothing continues but the effects of that wisdom which imploys the present time in the acts of a holy religion, and a peaceable conscience:' for they make us to live even beyond our funerals, embalmed in the spices and odours of a good name, and entombed in the grave of the Holy *Jesus* where we shall be dressed for a blessed resurrection to the state of Angels and beatified Spirits.

5. Since we stay not here, being people but of a dayes abode, and our age is like that of a fly, and contemporary with a gourd, we must look somewhere else for an abiding city, a place in another countrey to fix our house in, whose walls and foundation is God, where we must find rest, or else be restlesse for ever. For whatsoever ease we can have or fancy here is shortly to be changed into sadnesse, or tediousnesse: it goes away too soon like the periods of our life; or stays too long like the sorrows of a sinner: its own wearinesse or a contrary disturbance, is its load; or it is eased by its revolution into vanity and forgetfulness; and where either there is sorrow or an end of joy, there can be no true felicity: which because it must be had by some instrument, and in some period of our duration, we must carry up our affections to the mansions prepared for us above, where eternity is the measure, felicity is the state, Angels are the Company, the Lamb is the light, and God is the portion and inheritance.

SECTION III:

RULES AND SPIRITUAL ARTS OF LENGTHENING OUR DAYES,

AND TO TAKE OFF THE OBJECTION OF A SHORT LIFE

1. In the accounts of a mans life we do not reckon that portion of dayes in which we are shut up in the prison of the womb: we tell our years from the day of our birth: and the same reason that makes our reckoning to stay so long, says also that then it begins too soon. For then we are beholden to others to make the account for us: for we know not of a long time, whether we be alive or no, having but some little approaches and symptoms of a life. To feed, and sleep, and move a little, and imperfectly, is the state of an unborn childe; and when he is born, he does no more for a good while; and what is it that shall make him to be esteemed to live the life of a man? and when shall that account begin? For we should be loath to have the accounts of our age taken by the measures of a beast: and fools and distracted persons are reckoned as *civilly dead;* they are no parts of the Commonwealth, not subject to laws, but secured by them in Charity, and kept from violence as a man keeps his Ox: and a third part

of our life is spent, before we enter into a higher order, into the state of a man.

2. Neither must we think, that the life of a Man begins when he can feed himself or walk alone, when he can fight, or beget his like; for so he is contemporary with a camel, or a cow; but he is first a man, when he comes to a certain, steddy use of reason, according to his proportion; and when that is, all the world of men cannot tell precisely. Some are called *at age,* at fourteen, some at one and twenty, some never; but all men late enough; for the life of a man comes upon him slowly and insensibly. But as when the Sun approaches towards the gates of the morning, he first opens a little eye of Heaven, and sends away the spirits of darknesse, and gives light to a Cock, and calls up the Lark to Matins, and by and by gilds the fringes of a cloud, and peeps over the Eastern hills, thrusting out his golden horns, like those which decked the brows of *Moses* when he was forced to wear a vail, because himself had seen the face of God; and still while a man tells the story, the Sun gets up higher, till he shews a fair face and a full light, and then he shines one whole day, under a cloud often, and sometimes weeping great and little showers, and sets quickly: so is a mans reason and his life. He first begins to perceive himself to see or taste, making little reflections upon his actions of sense, and can discourse of flies and dogs, shells and play, horses and liberty; but when he is strong enough to enter into arts and little institutions, he is at first entertained with trifles and impertinent things not because he needs them, but because his understanding is no bigger; and little images of things are laid before him, like a cock-boat to a whale, only to play withal: but before a man comes to be wise he is half dead with gouts and consumptions, with catarrhes and aches, with sore eyes and a worn-out body: so that if we must not reckon the life of a man but by the accounts of his reason, he is long before his soul be dressed; and he is not to be called a man without a wise and an adorned soul, a soul at least furnished with what is necessary towards his well-being; but by that time his soul is thus furnished, his body is decayed; and then you can hardly reckon him to be alive, when his body is possessed by so many degrees of death.

3. But there is yet another arrest. At first he wants strength of body, and then he wants the use of reason; and when that is

come, it is ten to one, but he stops by the impediments of vice,
and wants the strengths of the *Spirit;* and we know that *Body*
and *Soul* and *Spirit* are the constituent parts of every Christian
man. And now let us consider what that thing is which we call
years of discretion? The young man is passed his Tutors, and
arrived at the bondage of a captive spirit; he is run from discipline, and is let loose to passion; the man by this time hath wit
enough to chuse his vice, to act his lust, to court his Mistresse,
to talk confidently, and ignorantly, and perpetually, to despise
his betters, to deny nothing to his appetite, to do things, that
when he is indeed a man he must for ever be ashamed of; for
this is all the discretion that most men shew in the first stage
of their Manhood; they can discern good from evil; and they
prove their skill by leaving all that is good, and wallowing in
the evils of folly, and an unbridled appetite. And by this time,
the young man hath contracted vitious habits, and is a beast in
manners, and therefore it will not be fitting to reckon the beginning of his life; he is a fool in his understanding, and that is
a sad death; and he is dead in trespasses and sins, and that is
a sadder: so that he hath no life but a natural, the life of a beast
or a tree; in all other capacities he is dead; he neither hath the
intellectual, nor the spiritual life, neither the life of a Man, nor
of a Christian; and this sad truth lasts too long. For old age
seizes upon most men while they still retain the minds of boyes
and vitious youths, doing actions from principles of great folly,
and a mighty ignorance, admiring things uselesse and hurtfull,
and filling up all the dimensions of their abode with businesses
of empty affairs, being at leisure to attend no vertue: they cannot pray, because they are busie, and because they are passionate: they cannot communicate, because they have quarrels and
intrigues of perplexed causes, complicated hostilities, and things
of the world; and therefore they cannot attend to the things of
God, little considering, that they must find a time to die in; when
death comes, they must be at leisure for that. Such men are like
sailers loosing from a port, and tost immediately with a perpetual tempest lasting till their cordage crack, and either they
sink, or return back again to the same place: they did not make
a voyage, though they were long at sea. The business and impertinent affairs of most men, steal all their time, and they are
restlesse in a foolish motion: but this is not the progress of a

Man; he is no further advanc'd in the course of a life, though
he reckon many years; for still his Soul is childish, and trifling
like an untaught boy.

If the parts of this sad complaint finde their remedy, we have
by the same instruments also cured the evils and the vanity of
a short life. Therefore,

1. Be infinitely curious you do not set back your life in the
accounts of God by the intermingling of criminal actions, or the
contracting vitious habits. There are some vices which carry a
sword in their hand and cut a man off before his time. There
is *a sword of the Lord,* and there is *a sword of a Man,* and there
is *a sword of the Devil.* Every vice of our own managing in the
matter of carnality, of lust, or rage, ambition or revenge is a
sword of Satan put into the hands of a man: These are the destroying Angels; sin is the *Apollyon,* the *Destroyer* that is gone
out, not *from the Lord,* but *from the Tempter;* and we hug the
poison, and twist willingly with the vipers, till they bring us
into the regions of an irrecoverable sorrow. We use to reckon
persons as good as dead, if they have lost their limbs and their
teeth, and are confined to a Hospital, and converse with none
but Surgeons and Physicians, Mourners and Divines, those *Pol-
linctores,* the Dressers of bodies and souls to Funeral: But it is
worse when the Soul, the principle of life is imployed wholly in
the offices of death: and that man was worse than dead of
whom *Seneca* tells, that being a rich fool, when he was lifted
up from the baths and set into a soft couch, asked his slaves,
An ego jam sedeo? Do I now sit? the beast was so drownd in
sensuality and the death of his soul, that whether he did sit or
no, he was to believe another. Idlenesse and every vice is as
much of death as a long disease is, or the expense of ten years:
and *she that lives in pleasures is dead while she liveth,* (saith
the Apostle), and it is the stile of the Spirit concerning wicked
persons, *They are dead in trespasses and sins.* For as every sen-
sual pleasure and every day of idleness and useless living lops
off a little branch from our short life; so every deadly sin and
every habitual vice does quite destroy us: but innocence leaves
us in our natural portions and perfect period; we lose nothing
of our life, if we lose nothing of our souls health; and therefore
he that would live a full age must avoid a sin, as he would decline the Regions of death and the dishonors of the grave.

2. If we would have our life lengthened, let us begin betimes to live in the accounts of reason and sober counsels, of Religion and the Spirit, and then we shall have no reason to complain that our abode on earth is so short: Many men find it long enough, and indeed it is so to all senses. But when we spend in waste, what God hath given us in plenty, when we sacrifice our youth to folly, our manhood to lust and rage, our old age to covetousnesse and irreligion, not beginning to live till we are to die, designing that time to Vertue which indeed is infirm to every thing and profitable to nothing, then we make our lives short, and lust runs away with all the vigorous and healthful part of it; and pride and animosity steal the manly portion, and craftiness and interest possess old age; *velut ex pleno et abundanti perdimus;* we spend as if we had too much time, and knew not what to do with it: We fear every thing like weak and silly mortals; and desire strangely, and greedily as if we were immortal: we complain our life is short, and yet we throw away much of it, and are weary of many of its parts; We complain the day is long, and the night is long and we want company, and seek out arts to drive the time away, and then weep because it is gone too soon. But so the treasure of the *Capitol* is but a small estate when *Cæsar* comes to finger it, and to pay with it all his Legions; and the Revenue of all *Egypt* and the Eastern provinces was but a little sum when they were to support the luxury of *Marc Antony,* and feed the riot of *Cleopatra:* But a thousand crowns is a vast proportion to be spent in the cottage of a frugal person, or to feed a Hermit. Just so is our life; it is too short to serve the ambition of a haughty Prince, or an usurping Rebel; too little time to purchase great wealth, to satisfie the pride of a vain-glorious fool, to trample upon all the enemies of our just or unjust interest; but for the obtaining vertue, for the purchase of sobriety and modesty, for the actions of Religion, God gave us time sufficient, if we make *the outgoings of the Morning and Evening,* that is, our infancy and old age, to be taken into the computations of a man. Which we may see in the following particulars.

1. If, our childhood, being first consecrated by a forward baptisme, it be seconded by a holy education, and a complying obedience; if our youth be chaste and temperate, modest and industrious, proceeding through a prudent and sober Manhood to a Religious Old age; then we have lived our whole duration, and

shall never die, but be changed in a just time to the preparations
of a better, and an immortal life.

2. If besides the ordinary returns of our prayers and periodical
and festival solemnities, and our seldom communions we would
allow to religion and the studies of wisdom, those great shares
that are trifled away upon vain sorrow, foolish mirth, troublesome ambition, buisy covetousnesse, watchful lust, and impertinent amours, and balls and revellings and banquets, all that
which was spent vitiously and all that time that lay fallow and
without imployment, our life would quickly amount to a great
sum. *Tostatus Abulensis* was a very painful person and a great
Cleak, and in the dayes of his Manhood he wrote so many books,
and they not ill ones, that the world computed a sheet for every
day of his life; I suppose they meant, after he came to the use of
reason and the state of a man: and *John Scotus* died about the
two and thirtieth year of his age; and yet, besides his publike
Disputations, his daily Lectures of Divinity in publick and private, the Books that he wrote being lately collected and printed
at Lyons, do equal the number of Volumes of any two the most
voluminous Fathers of the Latine Church. Every man is not en-
abled to such imployments, but every man is called and inabled
to the works of a sober and a religious life; and there are many
Saints of God that can reckon as many volumes of Religion and
mountains of Piety as those others did of good Books. *S. Ambrose*
(and I think, from his example, *S. Augustine*) divided every day
into three *tertias* of imployment: eight hours he spent in the
necessities of nature and recreation; eight hours in charity and
doing assistance to others, dispatching their businesses, reconcil-
ing their enmities, reproving their vices, correcting their errors,
instructing their ignorances, transacting the affairs of his Dio-
cesse, and the other eight hours he spent in study and prayer. If
we were thus minute and curious in the spending our time, it is
impossible but our life would seem very long. For so have I seen
an amorous person tell the minutes of his absence from his fancied joy; and while he told the sands of his Hour-glass, or the
throbs and little beatings of his Watch, by dividing an hour into
so many members, he spun out its length by number, and so
translated a day into the tediousness of a moneth. And if we tell
our days by Canonical hours of prayer, our weeks by a constant
revolution of Fasting-dayes or dayes of special Devotion, and

over all these draw a black Cypress, a veil of penitential sorrow, and severe mortification, we shall soon answer the calumny and objection of a short life. He that governs the day and divides the hours hastens from the eyes and observation of a merry sinner; but loves to stand still, and behold, and tell the sighs, and number the groans and sadly-delicious accents of a grieved penitent. It is a vast work that any man may do, if he never be idle; and it is a huge way that a man may go in vertue, if he never goes out of his way by a vitious habit, or a great crime; and he that perpetually reads good Books, if his parts be answerable, will have a huge stock of knowledge. It is so in all things else. Strive not to forget your time, and suffer none of it to pass undiscerned; and then measure your life, and tell me how you find the measure of its abode. However, *the time we live, is worth the money we pay for it:* and therefore it is not to be thrown away.

3. When vitious men are dying, and scar'd with the affrighting truths of an evil conscience, they would give all the world for a year, for a moneth; nay we read of some that called out with amazement *inducias usque ad mane, truce but till the morning:* and if that year or some few months were given, those men think they could do miracles in it. And let us a while suppose what *Dives* would have done if he had been loosed from the pains of Hell, and permitted to live on earth one year. Would all the pleasures of the world have kept him one hour from the Temple? would he not perpetually have been under the hands of Priests, or at the feet of the Doctors, or by *Moses* chair, or attending as near the Altar as he could get, or relieving poor *Lazarus*, or praying to God, and crucifying all his sin? I have read of a Melancholy person who saw Hell but in a dream or vision, and the amazement was such, that he would have chosen ten times to die, rather than to feel again so much of that horror: and such a person cannot be fancied but that he would spend a year in such holinesse, that the religion of a few moneths would equal the devotion of many years, even of a good man. Let us but compute the proportions. If we should spend all our years of reason so as such a person would spend that one, can it be thought that life would be short and trifling in which he had performed such a religion, served God with so much holinesse, mortified sin with so great a labour, purchased vertue at such a rate, and so rare an industry? It must needs be that such a man must dye when he

ought to die, and be like ripe and pleasant fruit falling from a fair tree and gathered into baskets for the planters use: He that hath done all his businesse, and is begotten to a glorious hope by the seed of an immortal Spirit, can never die too soon, nor live too long.

Xerxes wept sadly when he saw his army of 300,000 men, because he considered that within an hundred years all the youth of that army should be dust and ashes; and yet, as *Seneca* well observes of him, he was the man that should bring them to their graves, and he consumed all that army in two years, for whom he feared and wept the death after a hundred. Just so we do all. We complain that within thirty of fourty years, a little more, or a great deal lesse we shall descend again into the bowels of our Mother, and that our life is too short for any great imployment; and yet we throw away five and thirty yeers of our fourty, and the remaining five we divide between art and nature, civility and customs, necessity and convenience, prudent counsels and religion; but the portion of the last, is little and contemptible, and yet that little is all that we can prudently account of our lives: We bring that fate and that death near us, of whose approach we are so sadly apprehensive.

4. In taking the accounts of your life do not reckon by great distances, and by the periods of pleasure, or the satisfaction of your hopes, or the stating your desires: but let every intermedial day and hour passe with observation. He that reckons he hath lived but so many harvests, thinks they come not often enough, and that they go away too soon. Some lose the day with longing for the night, and the night in waiting for the day. Hope and phantastick expectations spend much of our lives; and while with passion we look for a coronation, or the death of an enemy, or a day of joy, passing from fancy to possession without any intermedial notices, we throw away a precious year, and use it but as the burden of our time, fit to be pared off and thrown away, that we may come at those little pleasures which first steal our hearts, and then steal our life.

5. A strict course of Piety is the way to prolong our lives in the natural sense, and to add good portions to the number of our years; and sin is sometimes by natural causality, very often by the anger of God, and the Divine judgment, a cause of sudden and untimely death. Concerning which I shall add nothing (to

what I have somewhere else said of this article) but only the observation of *Epiphanius;* that for 3332 years, even to the twentieth age, there was not one example of a Son that died before his Father, but the course of nature was kept, that he who was first-born in the descending line did first die (I speak of natural death, and therefore *Abel* cannot be opposed to this observation), till that *Terah* the Father of *Abraham* taught the People a new Religion, to make images of clay, and worship them; and concerning him it was first remarked, that *Haran died before his father Terah in the land of his Nativity:* God by an unheard-of judgment, and a rare accident punishing his newly-invented crime: by the untimely death of his Son.

6. But if I shall describe a living man; a man that hath that life that distinguishes him from a fool or a bird, that which gives him a capacity next to Angels; we shall find that even a good man lives not long, because it is long before he is born to this life, and longer yet before he hath a mans growth. 'He that can look upon Death, and see its face with the same countenance with which he hears its story; that can endure all the labours of his life with his Soul supporting his Body; that can equally despise Riches when he hath them, and when he hath them not; that is not sadder if they lye in his Neighbours trunks, nor more brag if they shine round about his own walls; he that is neither moved with good fortune coming to him, nor going from him; that can look upon another mans lands evenly and pleasedly as if they were his own, and yet look upon his own, and use them too, just as if they were another mans; that neither spends his goods prodigally and like a fool, nor yet keeps them avariciously and like a wretch; that weighs not benefits by weight and number, but by the mind and circumstances of him that gives them; that never thinks his charity expensive if a worthy person be the receiver; he that does nothing for opinion sake, but every thing for conscience, being as curious of his thoughts, as of his actings in Markets and Theatres, and is as much in awe of himself as of a whole assembly; he that knows God looks on, and contrives his secret affairs as in the presence of God and His holy angels; that eats and drinks because he needs it, not that he may serve a lust or load his belly; he that is bountifull and cheerfull to his friends, and charitable and apt to forgive his enemies; that loves his countrey

and obeys his Prince, and desires and endeavours nothing more than that he may do honour to God,' this person may reckon his life to be the life of a man, and compute his moneths, not by the course of the Sun, but the Zodiac and circle of his vertues: because these are such things which fools and children, and birds and beasts cannot have: These are therefore the actions of life, because they are the seeds of immortality. That day in which we have done some excellent thing, we may as truly reckon to be added to our life, as were the fifteen years to the days of *Hezekiah.*

John Milton

John Milton, born in London in 1608, attended St. Paul's School and,
from 1625 to 1632, Christ's College, Cambridge, from which he re-
ceived his B.A. and M.A. degrees. From 1632 to 1638 he continued
his studies privately in his father's house at Horton, and the follow-
ing year made a journey to Italy where he formed several literary
friendships. From 1641 he spent almost twenty years writing con-
troversial prose: the five anti-prelatical tracts in 1641 and 1642; the
four divorce tracts, Areopagitica, *and* Of Education *from 1643 to*
1645; the two Defenses of the English People *in 1651 and 1654; the*
Treatise of Civil Power *and* Likeliest Means to Remove Hirelings *in*
1659, and the Ready and Easy Way *in 1660. In 1649 he was ap-*
pointed Latin Secretary, continuing to serve even after he became
totally blind in 1652 until the Restoration, when he was deprived of
office, arrested, and released. He was married to Mary Powell in 1642
(died 1652), to Katharine Woodcock in 1656 (died 1658), and to
Elizabeth Minshull in 1663 who survived his death in 1674. His early
poems were published in 1645, Paradise Lost *in 1667,* Paradise Re-
gained *and* Samson Agonistes *in 1671. His last prose tract,* Of True
Religion, *was printed in 1673, but his theological treatise,* Of Christian Doctrine, *was never published during his lifetime.*

FROM

Of Reformation in England,

AND THE CAWSES THAT HITHERTO
HAVE HINDRED IT

. . . Thou therefore that sits't in light & glory unapprochable, *Parent* of *Angels* and *Men!* next thee I implore Omnipotent King, Redeemer of that lost remnant whose nature thou didst assume, ineffable and everlasting *Love!* And thou the third subsistence of Divine Infinitude, *illumining Spirit,* the joy and solace of created *Things!* one *Tri-personall* GODHEAD! looke upon this thy poore and almost spent, and expiring *Church,* leave her not thus a prey to these importunate *Wolves,* that wait and thinke long till they devoure thy tender *Flock,* these wilde *Boares* that have broke into thy *Vineyard,* and left the print of their polluting hoofs on the Soules of thy Servants. O let them not bring about their damned *designes* that stand now at the entrance of the bottom-lesse pit expecting the Watch-word to open and let out those dreadfull *Locusts* and *Scorpions,* to *re-involve* us in that pitchy *Cloud* of infernall darknes, where we shall never more see the *Sunne* of thy *Truth* againe, never hope for the cheerfull dawne, never more heare the *Bird* of *Morning* sing. Be mov'd with pitty at the afflicted state of this our shaken *Monarchy,* that now lies labouring under her throwes, and struggling against the grudges of more dreaded Calamities.

O thou that after the impetuous rage of five bloody Inunda-tions, and the succeeding Sword of intestine *Warre,* soaking the Land in her owne gore, didst pitty the sad and ceasles revolution of our swift and thick-comming sorrowes when wee were quite breathlesse, of thy *free grace* didst motion *Peace*, and termes of Cov'nant with us, & having first welnigh freed us from *Antichristian* thraldome, didst build up this *Britannick Empire* to a glorious and enviable heighth with all her Daughter Ilands about her, stay us in this felicitie, let not the obstinacy of our halfe Obedience and will-Worship bring forth that *Viper* of *Sedition*, that for these Fourescore Yeares hath been breeding to eat through the entrals of our *Peace;* but let her cast her Abortive Spawne without the danger of this travailling & throbbing *Kingdome.* That we may still remember in our *solemne Thanksgivings,* how for us the *Northren Ocean* even to the frozen *Thule* was scatter'd with the proud Ship-wracks of the *Spanish Armado,* and the very maw of Hell ransack't, and made to give up her conceal'd destruction, ere shee could vent it in that horrible and damned blast.

O how much more glorious will those former Deliverances appeare, when we shall know them not onely to have sav'd us from greatest miseries past, but to have reserv'd us for greatest happinesse to come. Hitherto thou hast freed us, and that not fully, from the unjust and Tyrannous Claime of thy Foes, now unite us intirely, and appropriate us to thy selfe, tie us everlastingly in willing Homage to the *Prerogative* of thy eternall Throne.

And now wee knowe, O thou our most certain hope and defence, that thine enemies have been consulting all the Sorceries of the *great Whore,* and have joyn'd their Plots with that sad Intelligencing Tyrant that mischiefes the World with his Mines of *Ophir,* and lies thirsting to revenge his Navall ruines that have larded our Seas; but let them all take Counsell together, and let it come to nought, let them Decree, and doe thou Cancell it, let them gather themselves, and bee scatter'd, let them embattell themselves and bee broken, let them imbattell, and be broken, for thou art with us.

Then amidst the *Hymns,* and *Halleluiahs* of *Saints* some one may perhaps bee heard offering at high *strains* in new and lofty *Measures* to sing and celebrate thy *divine Mercies,* and *marvelous Judgements* in this Land throughout all AGES; whereby this great and Warlike Nation instructed and inur'd to the fervent and continuall practice of *Truth* and *Righteousnesse,* and casting farre from her the *rags* of her old *vices* may presse on hard to that *high* and *happy* emulation to be found the *soberest, wisest,* and *most Christian People* at that day when thou the Eternall and shortly-expected King shalt open the Clouds to judge the severall Kingdomes of the World, and distributing *Nationall Honours* and *Rewards* to Religious and just *Common-wealths,* shalt put an end to all Earthly *Tyrannies,* proclaiming thy universal and milde *Monarchy* through Heaven and Earth. Where they undoubtedly that by their *Labours, Counsels,* and *Prayers* have been earnest for the *Common good* of *Religion* and their *Countrey,* shall receive, above the inferiour *Orders* of the *Blessed,* the *Regall* addition of *Principalities, Legions,* and *Thrones* into their glorious Titles, and in supereminence of *beatifick Vision* progressing the *datelesse* and *irrevoluble*[1] Circle of *Eternity* shall clasp inseparable Hands with *joy,* and *blisse* in over measure for ever.

But they contrary that by the impairing and diminution of the true *Faith,* the distresses and servitude of their *Countrey* aspire to high *Dignity, Rule* and *Promotion* here, after a shamefull end in this *Life* (which *God* grant them) shall be thrown downe eternally into the *darkest* and *deepest Gulfe* of HELL, where under the *despightfull controule,* the trample and spurne of all the other *Damned,* that in the anguish of their *Torture* shall have no other ease then to exercise a *Raving* and *Bestiall Tyranny* over them as their *Slaves* and *Negro's,* they shall remaine in that plight for ever, the *basest,* the *lowermost,* the *most dejected,* most *underfoot* and *downetrodden Vassals* of *Perdition.*

1 irrevoluble: of infinite circuit

FROM

Animadversions

UPON THE REMONSTRANTS DEFENCE,

AGAINST SMECTYMNUUS

Although it be a certaine truth that they who undertake a Religious Cause need not care to be Men-pleasers; yet because the satisfaction of tender and mild consciences is far different from that which is call'd Men-pleasing, to satisfie such, I shall adresse my selfe in few words to give notice before hand of something in this booke, which to some men perhaps may seeme offensive, that when I have render'd a lawfull reason of what is done, I may trust to have sav'd the labour of defending or excusing hereafter. Wee all know that in private and personall injuries, yea in publique sufferings for the cause of Christ, his rule and example teaches us to be so farre from a readinesse to speak evill, as not to answer the reviler in his language though never so much provok't. Yet in the detecting, and convincing of any notorious enimie to truth and his Countries peace, especially that is conceited to have a voluble and smart fluence of tongue, and in the vaine confidence of that, and out of a more tenacious cling to worldly respects, stands up for all the rest to justifie a long usurpation and convicted Pseudepiscopy of Prelates, with all their ceremonies, Liturgies, and tyrannies which God and man are now ready to explode and hisse out of the land, I suppose and more then suppose, it will be nothing disagreeing from Christian meeknesse to handle such a one in a rougher accent, and to send home his haughtinesse well bespurted with his owne holy-water. Nor to do thus are we unautoritied either from the morall precept of SALOMON *to answer him thereafter that prides him in his folly; nor from the example of Christ, and all his followers in all Ages, who in the refuting of those that resisted sound Doctrine, and by subtile dissimulations corrupted the minds of men, have wrought up their zealous souls into such vehemencies, as nothing could be more killingly spoken: for who can be a greater enemy to Mankind, who a more dangerous deceiver then he who defending a traditionall corruption uses no common Arts, but with a wily Stratagem of yeelding to the time a greater part of his cause, seeming to forgo all that mans invention hath done therein, and driven from much of his hold in Scripture, yet leaving it hanging by a twin'd threed, not from divine command but from Apostolicall prudence or assent, as if he had the surety of some rouling trench, creeps up by this meanes to his relinquish't fortresse of divine authority againe; and still hovering betweene the confines of that which hee dares not bee openly, and that which he will not be sincerely, traines on the easie Christian insensibly within the close ambushment of worst errors, and with a slye shuffle of counterfeit principles chopping and changing till hee have glean'd all the good ones out of their minds, leaves them at last, after a slight resemblance of sweeping and garnishing under the sevenfold possession of a desperate stupidity. And therefore they that love the soules of men, which is the dearest love, and stirs up the noblest jealousie, when they meet with such collusion, cannot be blam'd though they bee transported with the zeale of truth to a well heated fervencie; especially, seeing they which thus offend against the soules of their brethren, do it with delight to their great gaine, ease, and advancement in this world, but they that seeke to discover and oppose their false trade of deceiving, do it not without a sad and unwilling anger, not without many hazards, but without all private and personall spleene, and without any thought of earthly reward, when as this very course they take stopps their hopes of ascending above a lowly and unenviable pitch in this life. And although in the serious uncasing of a grand imposture (for to deale plainly with you Readers, Prelatry is no better) there be mixt here and there such a grim laughter, as may appeare at the same time in an austere visage, it cannot be taxt of levity or insolence: for even this veine of laughing (as I could produce out of grave Authors) hath oft-times a strong and sinewy force in teaching and confuting; nor can there be a more proper object of indignation and scorne together then a false Prophet taken in the greatest dearest and most dangerous cheat, the cheat of soules: in the disclosing whereof if it be harmfull to be*

angry, and withall to cast a lowring smile, when the properest
object calls for both, it will be long enough ere any be able to say
why those two most rationall faculties of humane intellect anger
and laughter were first seated in the brest of man. Thus much
(Readers) in favour of the softer spirited Christian, for other
exceptioners there was no thought taken. . . .

. . . *Answer.* It had beene happy for this land, if your priests
had beene but onely wooden, all *England* knowes they have been
to this Iland not wood, but wormewood, that have infected the
third part of our waters, like that Apostate starre in the Revelation; that many soules have di'd of their bitternesse; and if you
meane by wooden, illiterate, or contemptible, there was no want
of that sort among you, and their number increasing daily, as
their lazinesse, their Tavern-hunting, their neglect of all sound
literature, and their liking of doltish and monasticall Schoole-
men daily increast. What should I tell you how the Universities,
that men looke should be fountaines of learning and knowledge,
have been poyson'd and choak'd under your governance? and if
to be wooden be to be base, where could there be found among
all the reformed Churches, nay, in the Church of *Rome* it selfe a
baser brood of flattering and time-serving priests, according as
God pronounces by *Isaiah*, the Prophet that teacheth lies he is
the taile. As for your young schollers that petition for Bishopricks
and Deaneries to incourage them in their studies, and that many
Gentlemen else will not put their sons to learning, away with
such young mercenary stripplings and their Simoniacall fathers,
God has no neede of such, they have no part or lot in his Vineyard, they may as well sue for Nunneries, that they may have
some convenient stowage for their wither'd daughters, because
they cannot give them portions answerable to the pride and
vanity they have bred them in; this is the root of all our mis-
chiefe, that which they alleage for the incouragement of their
studies, should be cut away forthwith as the very bait of pride
and ambition, the very garbage that drawes together all the
fowles of prey and ravin in the land to come, and gorge upon the
Church; how can it be but ever unhappy to the Church of *Eng-*
land, while shee shall thinke to intice men to the pure service of
God by the same meanes that were us'd to tempt our Saviour to
the service of the devill, by laying before him honour and prefer-

ment. Fit professors indeed are they like to be, to teach others
that godlinesse with content is great gaine, whenas their godlinesse of teaching had not been but for worldly gaine. The
heathen Philosophers thought that vertue was for its owne sake
inestimable, and the greatest gaine of a teacher to make a soule
vertuous; so *Xenophon* writes of *Socrates* who never bargain'd
with any for teaching them; he fear'd not lest those who had
receiv'd so high a benefit from him, would not of their owne
free-will returne him all possible thankes. Was morall vertue so
lovely, and so alluring, and heathen men so enamour'd of her, as
to teach and study her with greatest neglect and contempt of
worldly profit and advancement; and is Christian piety so homely
and so unpleasant, and Christian men so cloy'd with her, as that
none will study and teach her, but for lucre and preferment! O
stale-growne piety! O Gospell rated as cheap as thy Master, at
thirty pence, and not worth the study, unlesse thou canst buy
those that will sell thee! O race of Capernaitans, senslesse of
divine doctrine, and capable onely of loaves and belly-cheere!
But they will grant, perhaps, piety may thrive, but learning will
decay: I would faine aske these men at whose hands they seeke
inferior things, as wealth, honour, their dainty fare, their lofty
houses? No doubt but they will soone answer, that all these
things they seeke at Gods hands. Doe they thinke then that all
these meaner and superfluous things come from God, & the divine
gift of learning from the den of *Plutus*, or the cave of *Mammon*?
Certainly never any cleare spirit nurst up from brighter influ-
ences with a soule inlarg'd to the dimensions of spacious art and
high knowledge ever enter'd there but with scorn, & thought it
ever foule disdain to make pelf or ambition the reward of his
studies, it being the greatest honor, the greatest fruit and proficiency of learned studies to despise these things. Not liberal science, but illiberal must that needs be that mounts in contemplation meerely for money. And what would it avail us to have a
hireling Clergy though never so learned? For such can have neither true wisdom nor grace, and then in vain do most trust in
learning, where these be wanting. If in lesse noble and almost
mechanik arts according to the difinitions of those Authors, he
is not esteem'd to deserve the name of a compleat Architect, an
excellent Painter, or the like, that beares not a generous mind
above the peasantly regard of wages, and hire; much more must

we thinke him a most imperfect, and incompleate Divine, who
is so farre from being a contemner of filthy lucre; that his whole
divinity is moulded and bred up in the beggarly, and brutish
hopes of a fat Prebendary, Deanery, or Bishoprick, which poore
and low pitch't desires, if they doe but mixe with those other
heavenly intentions that draw a man to this study, it is justly
expected that they should bring forth a baseborn issue of Divinity like that of those imperfect, and putrid creatures that receive
a crawling life from two most unlike procreants the Sun, and
mudde. And in matters of Religion, there is not any thing more
intollerable, then a learned foole, or a learned Hypocrite, the one
is ever coopt up at his empty speculations, a sot, an ideot for any
use that mankind can make of him, or else sowing the World
with nice, and idle questions and with much toyle, and difficulty
wading to his auditors up to the eyebrows in deep shallows that
wet not the instep: a plaine unlearned man that lives well by
that light which he has, is better, and wiser, and edifies others
more towards a godly and happy life then he: The other is still
using his sophisticated arts and bending all his studies how to
make his insatiate avarice, & ambition seem pious, and ortho-
doxall by painting his lewd and deceitfull principles with a
smooth, and glossy varnish in a doctrinall way to bring about his
wickedest purposes. In stead of the great harme therefore that
these men feare upon the dissolving of Prelates, what an ease,
and happinesse will it be to us, when tempting rewards are taken
away, that the cunningest and most dangerous mercenaries will
cease of themselves to frequent the fold, whom otherwise scarce
all the prayers of the faithfull could have kept back from devouring the flock? But a true Pastor of Christs sending hath this es-
peciall mark, that for greatest labours, and greatest merits in the
Church, he requires either nothing, if he could so subsist, or a
very common and reasonable supply of humane necessaries:
Wee cannot therefore doe better then to leave this care of ours
to God, he can easily send labourers into his Harvest, that shall
not cry, Give, give, but be contented with a moderate and be-
seeming allowance; nor will hee suffer true learning to be wanting, where true grace, and our obedience to him abounds: for if
he give us to know him aright, and to practice this our knowledge
in right establisht discipline, how much more will hee replenish
us with all abilities in tongues and arts, that may conduce to his

glory, and our good? He can stirre up rich Fathers to bestow ex-
quisite education upon their Children, and so dedicate them to
the service of the Gospell; he can make the sons of Nobles his
Ministers, and Princes to be his Nazarites; for certainely there
is no imployment more honourable, more worthy to take up a
great spirit, more requiring a generous and free nurture, then to
be the messenger, and Herald of heavenly truth from God to
man, and by the faithfull worke of holy doctrine, to procreate a
number of faithful men, making a kind of creation like to Gods,
by infusing his spirit and likenesse into them, to their salvation,
as God did into him; arising to what climat so ever he turne him,
like that Sun of righteousnesse that sent him, with healing in his
wings, and new light to break in upon the chill and gloomy
hearts of his hearers, raising out of darksome barrennesse a delicious, and fragrant Spring of saving knowledge, and good
workes. Can a man thus imployd, find himselfe discontented, or
dishonour'd for want of admittance to have a pragmaticall voyce
at Sessions, and Jayle deliveries? or because hee may not as a
Judge sit out the wrangling noyse of litigious Courts to shreeve
the purses of unconfessing and unmortify'd sinners, and not
their soules, or be discourag'd though men call him not Lord,
when as the due performance of his office would gaine him even
from Lords and Princes, the voluntary title of Father? would he
tugge for a Barony to sit and vote in Parliament, knowing that no
man can take from him the gift of wisedome, and sound doctrine
which leaves him free though not to be a member, yet a teacher,
and perswader of the Parliament? and in all wise apprehensions
the perswasive power in man to win others to goodnesse by instruction is greater, and more divine, then the compulsive power
to restraine men from being evill by terrour of the Law; and
therefore Christ left *Moses* to be the Law-giver, but himselfe
came down amongst us to bee a teacher, with which office his
heavenly wisedome was so well pleas'd, as that he was angry
with those that would have put a piece of temporall judicature
into his hands, disclaiming that he had any commission from
above for such matters.

Such a high calling therefore as this, sends not for those
drossy spirits that need the lure, and whistle of earthly preferment, like those animals that fetch, and carry for a morsell, no.
She can find such as therefore study her precepts, because

she teaches to despise preferment. And let not those wretched
Fathers thinke they shall impoverish the Church of willing, and
able supply, though they keep back their sordid sperm begotten
in the lustinesse of their avarice, and turne them to their
malting-kils, rather let them take heed what lessons they instill
into that lump of flesh which they are the cause of, lest, thinking
to offer him as a present to God, they dish him out for the Devill.
Let the novice learne first to renounce the world, and so give
himselfe to God, and not therefore give himselfe to God, that hee
may close the better with the World, like that false Shepheard
Palinode in the Eclogue of *May,* under whom the Poet lively per-
sonates our Prelates, whose whole life is a recantation of their
pastorall vow, and whose profession to forsake the World, as
they use the matter, boggs them deeper into the world: Those
our admired *Spencer* inveighs against, not without some presage
of these reforming times.

> *The time was once, and may again returne*
> *(For oft may happen that hath been beforn)*
> *When Shepheards had none inheritance*
> *Ne of land, nor fee in sufferance,*
> *But what might arise of the bare sheep,*
> *(Were it more or lesse) which they did keep.*
> *Well ywis was it with Shepheards tho.*
> *Naught having, naught feared they to forgoe*
> *For* Pan *himselfe was their inheritance*
> *And little them served for their maintenance,*
> *The Shepheards God so well them guided,*
> *That of naught they were unprovided*
> *Butter enough, honey, milk, and whay,*
> *And their flock fleeces them to array.*
> *But tract of Time, and long prosperity*
> *(That nurse of vice, this of insolency)*
> *Lulled the Shepheards in such security*
> *That not content with loyall obeysance*
> *Some gan to gape for greedy governance,*
> *And match themselves with mighty potentates*
> *Lovers of Lordships, and troublers of States.*
> *Tho gan Shepheards Swaines to looke aloft*
> *And leave to live hard, and learne to lig soft.*
> *Tho under colour of Shepheards some while*
> *There crept in wolves full of fraud and guile*

That often devoured their owne Sheep,
And often the Shepheard that did them keepe,
This was the first source of shepheards sorrow
That now nill be quit with bale, nor borrow.

By all this wee may conjecture, how little wee neede feare that the unguilding of our Prelates will prove the woodening of our Priests. In the meane while, let no man carry in his head either such narrow, or such evill eyes, as not to looke upon the Churches of *Belgia* and *Helvetia,* and that envied city *Geneva:* where in the Christian world doth learning more flourish than in these places? Not among your beloved Jesuits, nor their favourers, though you take all the Prelates into the number, and instance in what kinde of learning you please. And how in *England* all noble sciences attending upon the traine of Christian doctrine, may flourish more than ever; and how the able professors of every Art may with ample stipends be honestly provided; And finally, how there may be better care had that their hearers may benefit by them, and all this without the Prelates, the courses are so many and so easie, that I shall passe them over.

F R O M

The Reason of Church-government urg'd against Prelaty:

THE SECOND BOOK

How happy were it for this frail, and as it may be truly call'd, mortall life of man, since all earthly things which have the name of good and covenient in our daily use, are withall so cumbersome and full of trouble if knowledge yet which is the best and lightsomest possession of the mind, were as the common saying is, no burden, and that what it wanted of being a load to any part of the body, it did not with a heavie advantage overlay upon the spirit. For not to speak of that knowledge that rests in the contemplation of naturall causes and dimensions, which must needs be a lower wisdom, as the object is low, certain it is that he who hath obtain'd in more then the scantest measure to know any thing distinctly of God, and of his true worship, and what is infallibly good and happy in the state of mans life, what in it selfe evil and miserable, though vulgarly not so esteem'd, he that hath obtain'd to know this, the only high valuable wisdom indeed, remembring also that God even to a strictnesse requires the improvment of these his entrusted gifts, cannot but sustain a sorer burden of mind, and more pressing then any supportable toil, or waight, which the body can labour under; how and in what manner he shall dispose and employ those summes of knowledge and illumination, which God hath sent him into this world to trade with. And that which aggravats the burden more, is, that having receiv'd amongst his allotted parcels certain pretious truths of such an orient¹ lustre as no Diamond can equall, which never the lesse he has in charge to put off at any cheap rate, yea for nothing to them that will, the great Marchants of this world fearing that this cours would soon discover, and disgrace the fals glitter of their deceitfull wares wherewith they abuse the people, like poor Indians with beads and glasses, practize by all means how they may suppresse the venting of such rarities and such a cheapnes as would undoe them, and turn their trash upon their hands. Therefore by gratifying the corrupt desires of men in fleshly doctrines, they stirre them up to persecute with hatred and contempt all those that seek to bear themselves uprightly in this their spiritual factory: which they foreseeing, though they cannot but testify of Truth and the excellence of that heavenly traffick which they bring against what opposition, or danger soever, yet needs must it sit heavily upon their spirits, that being in Gods prime intention and their own, selected heralds of peace, and dispensers of treasure inestimable without price to them that have no pence, they finde in the discharge of their commission that they are made the greatest variance and offence, a very sword and fire both in house and City over the whole earth. This is that which the sad Prophet *Jeremiah* laments, *Wo is me my mother, that thou hast born me a man of strife, and contention.* And although divine inspiration must certainly have been sweet to those ancient profets, yet the irksomnesse of that truth which they brought was so unpleasant

---

¹ orient: shining, brilliant

to them, that every where they call it a burden. Yea that mysterious book of Revelation which the great Evangelist was bid to eat, as it had been some eye-brightning electuary[2] of knowledge, and foresight, though it were sweet in his mouth, and in the learning, it was bitter in his belly; bitter in the denouncing. Nor was this hid from the wise Poet *Sophocles,* who in that place of his Tragedy where *Tiresias* is call'd to resolve K. *Edipus* in a matter which he knew would be grievous, brings him in bemoaning his lot, that he knew more then other men. For surely to every good and peaceable man it must in nature needs be a hatefull thing to be the displeaser, and molester of thousands; much better would it like him doubtlesse to be the messenger of gladnes and contentment, which is his chief intended busines, to all mankind, but that they resist and oppose their own true happinesse. But when God commands to take the trumpet and blow a dolorous or a jarring blast, it lies not in mans will what he shall say or what he shall conceal. If he shall think to be silent, as *Jeremiah* did, because of the reproach and derision he met with daily, and *all his familiar friends watcht for his halting* to be reveng'd on him for speaking the truth, he would be forc't to confesse as he confest, *his word was in my heart as a burning fire shut up in my bones, I was weary with forbearing, and could not stay.* Which might teach these times not suddenly to condemn all things that are sharply spoken, or vehemently written, as proceeding out of stomach, virulence and ill nature, but to consider rather that if the Prelats have leav to say the worst that can be said, and doe the worst that can be don, while they strive to keep to themselves to their great pleasure and commodity those things which they ought to render up, no man can be justly offended with him that shall endeavour to impart and bestow without any gain to himselfe those sharp, but saving words which would be a terror, and a torment in him to keep back. For me I have determin'd to lay up as the best treasure, and solace of a good old age, if God voutsafe it me, the honest liberty of free speech from my youth, where I shall think it available in so dear a concernment as the Churches good. For if I be either by disposition, or what other cause too inquisitive, or suspitious of my self and mine own doings, who can help it? but this I foresee, that should the Church be brought under heavy oppression, and God

2 electuary: medicinal paste

have given me ability the while to reason against that man that should be the author of so foul a deed, or should she by blessing from above on the industry and courage of faithfull men change this her distracted estate into better daies without the lest furtherance or contribution of those few talents which God at that present had lent me, I foresee what stories I should heare within my selfe, all my life after, of discourage and reproach. Timorous and ingratefull, the Church of God is now again at the foot of her insulting enemies: and thou bewailst, what matters it for thee or thy bewailing? when time was, thou couldst not find a syllable of all that thou hadst read, or studied, to utter in her behalfe. Yet ease and leasure was given thee for thy retired thoughts out of the sweat of other men. Thou hadst the diligence, the parts, the language of a man, if a vain subject were to be adorn'd or beautifi'd, but when the cause of God and his Church was to be pleaded, for which purpose that tongue was given thee which thou hast, God listen'd if he could heare thy voice among his zealous servants, but thou wert domb as a beast; from hence forward be that which thine own brutish silence hath made thee. Or else I should have heard on the other eare, slothfull, and ever to be set light by, the Church hath now overcom her late distresses after the unwearied labours of many her true servants that stood up in her defence; thou also wouldst take upon thee to share amongst them of their joy: but wherefore thou? where canst thou shew any word or deed of thine which might have hasten'd her peace; what ever thou dost now talke, or write, or look is the almes of other mens active prudence and zeale. Dare not now to say, or doe any thing better then thy former sloth and infancy, or if thou darst, thou dost impudently to make a thrifty purchase of boldnesse to thy selfe out of the painfull merits of other men: what before was thy sin, is now thy duty to be, abject, and worthlesse. These and such like lessons as these, I know would have been my Matins duly, and my Even-song. But now by this litle diligence, mark what a privilege I have gain'd; with good men and Saints to clame my right of lamenting the tribulations of the Church, if she should suffer, when others that have ventur'd nothing for her sake, have not the honour to be admitted mourners. But if she lift up her drooping head and prosper, among those that have something more then wisht her welfare, I have my charter and freehold of rejoycing to me and my heires. Concerning therefore this wayward subject against prelaty, the touching whereof is so distastfull and disquietous to a number of men, as by what hath been said I may deserve of charitable readers to be credited, that neither envy nor gall hath enterd me upon this controversy, but the enforcement of conscience only, and a preventive fear least the omitting of this duty should be against me when I would store up to my self the good provision of peacefull hours, So lest it should be still imputed to me, as I have found it hath bin, that some self-pleasing humor of vain-glory hath incited me to contest with men of high estimation, now while green yeers are upon my head, from this needlesse surmisall I shall hope to disswade the intelligent and equal auditor, if I can but say succesfully that which in this exigent behoovs me, although I would be heard only, if it might be, by the elegant & learned reader, to whom principally for a while I shal beg leav I may addresse my selfe. To him it will be no new thing though I tell him that if I hunted after praise by the ostentation of wit and learning, I should not write thus out of mine own season, when I have neither yet compleated to my minde the full circle of my private studies, although I complain not of any insufficiency to the matter in hand, or were I ready to my wishes, it were a folly to commit any thing elaborately compos'd to the carelesse and interrupted listening of these tumultuous times. Next if I were wise only to mine own ends, I would certainly take such a subject as of it self might catch applause, whereas this hath all the disadvantages on the contrary, and such a subject as the publishing whereof might be delayd at pleasure, and time enough to pencill it over with all the curious touches of art, even to the perfection of a faultlesse picture, whenas in this argument the not deferring is of great moment to the good speeding, that if solidity have leisure to doe her office, art cannot have much. Lastly, I should not chuse this manner of writing wherein knowing my self inferior to my self, led by the genial power of nature to another task, I have the use, as I may account it, but of my left hand. And though I shall be foolish in saying more to this purpose, yet since it will be such a folly, as wisest men going about to commit, have only confest and so committed, I may trust with more reason, because with more folly to have courteous pardon. For although a Poet soaring in the high region of his fancies with his garland and singing robes about him might without apology speak more of himself then I mean to do, yet for me sitting here below in the cool element of prose, a mortall thing among many readers of no Empyreall [3] conceit, to venture and divulge unusual things of my selfe, I shall petition to the gentler sort, it may not be envy to me. I must say therefore that after I had from my first yeeres by the ceaselesse diligence and care of my father, whom God recompence, bin exercis'd to the tongues, and some sciences, as my age would suffer, by sundry masters and teachers both at home and at the schools, it was found that whether ought was impos'd me by them that had the overlooking, or betak'n to of mine own choise in English, or other tongue, prosing or versing, but chiefly this latter, the stile by certain vital signes it had, was likely to live. But this latelier in the privat Academies of *Italy,* whither I was favor'd to resort, perceiving that some trifles which I had in memory, compos'd at under twenty or thereabout (for the manner is that every one must give some proof of his wit and reading there) met with acceptance above what was lookt for, and other things which I had shifted in scarsity of books and conveniences to patch up amongst them, were receiv'd with written Encomiums, which the Italian is not forward to bestow on men of this side the *Alps,* I began thus farre to assent both to them and divers of my friends here at home, and not lesse to an inward prompting which now grew daily upon me, that by labour and intent study (which I take to be my portion in this life) joyn'd with the strong propensity of nature, I might perhaps leave something so written to aftertimes, as they should not willingly let it die. These thoughts at once possest me, and these other. That if I were certain to write as men buy Leases, for three lives and downward, there ought no regard be sooner had, then to Gods glory by the honour and instruction of my country. For which cause, and not only for that I knew it would be hard to arrive at the second rank among the Latines, I apply'd my selfe to that resolution which *Ariosto* follow'd against the perswasions of *Bembo,* to fix all the industry and art I could unite to the adorning of my native tongue; not to make verbal curiosities the end, that were a toylsom vanity, but to be an interpreter & relater of the best and sagest things among mine own Citizens throughout this Iland in the mother dialect. That what the greatest and

3 Empyreall: pertaining to the empyrean or highest heaven

choycest wits of *Athens, Rome,* or modern *Italy,* and those Hebrews of old did for their country, I in my proportion with this
over and above of being a Christian, might doe for mine: not
caring to be once nam'd abroad, though perhaps I could attaine
to that, but content with these British Ilands as my world, whose
fortune hath hitherto bin, that if the Athenians, as some say,
made their small deeds great and renowned by their eloquent
writers, *England* hath had her noble atchievments made small
by the unskilfull handling of monks and mechanicks.

Time servs not now, and perhaps I might seem too profuse to
give any certain account of what the mind at home in the spacious circuits of her musing hath liberty to propose to her self,
though of highest hope, and hardest attempting, whether that
Epick form whereof the two poems of *Homer,* and those other
two of *Virgil* and *Tasso* are a diffuse, and the book of *Job* a brief
model: or whether the rules of *Aristotle* herein are strictly to be
kept, or nature to be follow'd, which in them that know art, and
use judgement is no transgression, but an inriching of art. And
lastly what K. or Knight before the conquest might be chosen in
whom to lay the pattern of a Christian *Heroe.* And as *Tasso* gave
to a Prince of *Italy* his chois whether he would command him to
write of *Godfreys* expedition against the infidels, or *Belisarius*
against the Gothes, or *Charlemain* against the Lombards; if to
the instinct of nature and the imboldning of art ought may be
trusted, and that there be nothing advers in our climat, or the
fate of this age, it haply would be no rashnesse from an equal
diligence and inclination to present the like offer in our own
ancient stories. Or whether those Dramatick constitutions,
wherein *Sophocles* and *Euripides* raigne shall be found more
doctrinal and exemplary to a Nation, the Scripture also affords
us a divine pastoral Drama in the Song of *Salomon* consisting of
two persons and a double *Chorus,* as *Origen* rightly judges. And
the Apocalyps of Saint *John* is the majestick image of a high
and stately Tragedy, shutting up and intermingling her solemn
Scenes and Acts with a sevenfold *Chorus* of halleluja's and harp-
ing symphonies: and this my opinion the grave autority of
Pareus commenting that booke is sufficient to confirm. Or if
occasion shall lead to imitat those magnifick Odes and Hymns
wherein *Pindarus* and *Callimachus* are in most things worthy,
some others in their frame judicious, in their matter most an end

faulty: But those frequent songs throughout the law and prophets beyond all these, not in their divine argument alone, but in
the very critical art of composition may be easily made appear
over all the kinds of Lyrick poesy, to be incomparable. These
abilities, wheresoever they be found, are the inspired guift of
God rarely bestow'd, but yet to some (though most abuse) in
every Nation: and are of power beside the office of a pulpit, to
inbreed and cherish in a great people the seeds of vertu, and
publick civility, to allay the perturbations of the mind, and set
the affections in right tune, to celebrate in glorious and lofty
Hymns the throne and equipage of Gods Almightinesse, and
what he works, and what he suffers to be wrought with high
providence in his Church, to sing the victorious agonies of Martyrs and Saints, the deeds and triumphs of just and pious Nations doing valiantly through faith against the enemies of Christ,
to deplore the general relapses of Kingdoms and States from justice and Gods true worship. Lastly, whatsoever in religion is holy
and sublime, in vertu amiable, or grave, whatsoever hath passion
or admiration in all the changes of that which is call'd fortune
from without, or the wily suttleties and refluxes of mans thoughts
from within, all these things with a solid and treatable smooth-
nesse to paint out and describe. Teaching over the whole book of
sanctity and vertu through all the instances of example with
such delight to those especially of soft and delicious⁴ temper
who will not so much as look upon Truth herselfe, unlesse they
see her elegantly drest, that whereas the paths of honesty and
good life appear now rugged and difficult, though they be indeed
easy and pleasant, they would then appeare to all men both easy
and pleasant though they were rugged and difficult indeed. And
what a benefit this would be to our youth and gentry, may be
soon guest by what we know of the corruption and bane which
they suck in dayly from the writings and interludes of libidinous
and ignorant Poetasters, who having scars ever heard of that
which is the main consistence of a true poem, the choys of such
persons as they ought to introduce, and what is morall and
decent to each one, doe for the most part lap up vitious principles
in sweet pils to be swallow'd down, and make the tast of vertuous
documents harsh and sowr. But because the spirit of man cannot
demean it selfe lively in this body without some recreating inter-

4 delicious: dainty

mission of labour, and serious things, it were happy for the Common wealth, if our Magistrates, as in those famous governments of old, would take into their care, not only the deciding of our contentious Law cases and brauls, but the managing of our publick sports, and festival pastimes, that they might be, not such as were autoriz'd a while since, the provocations of drunkennesse and lust, but such as may inure and harden our bodies by martial exercises to all warlike skil and performance, and may civilize, adorn and make discreet our minds by the learned and affable meeting of frequent Academies, and the procurement of wise and artfull recitations sweetned with eloquent and gracefull inticements to the love and practice of justice, temperance and fortitude, instructing and bettering the Nation at all opportunities, that the call of wisdom and vertu may be heard every where, as *Salomon* saith, *She crieth without, she uttereth her voice in the streets, in the top of high places, in the chief concours, and in the openings of the Gates.* Whether this may not be not only in Pulpits, but after another persuasive method, at set and solemn Paneguries,[5] in Theaters, porches, or what other place, or way may win most upon the people to receiv at once both recreation, & instruction, let them in autority consult. The thing which I had to say, and those intentions which have liv'd within me ever since I could conceiv my self any thing worth to my Countrie, I return to crave excuse that urgent reason hath pluckt from me by an abortive and foredated discovery. And the accomplishment of them lies not but in a power above mans to promise; but that none hath by more studious ways endeavour'd, and with more unwearied spirit that none shall, that I dare almost averre of my self, as farre as life and free leasure will extend, and that the Land had once infranchis'd her self from this impertinent yoke of prelaty, under whose inquisitorius and tyrannical duncery no free and splendid wit can flourish. Neither doe I think it shame to covnant with any knowing reader, that for some few yeers yet I may go on trust with him toward the payment of what I am now indebted, as being a work not to be rays'd from the heat of youth, or the vapours of wine, like that which flows at wast from the pen of some vulgar Amorist, or the trencher fury of a riming parasite, nor to be obtain'd by the invocation of Dame Memory and her Siren daughters, but by devout prayer to that

5 Paneguries: religious festivals

eternall Spirit who can enrich with all utterance and knowledge, and sends out his Seraphim with the hallow'd fire of his Altar to touch and purify the lips of whom he pleases: to this must be added industrious and select reading, steddy observation, insight into all seemly and generous arts and affaires, till which in some measure be compast, at mine own peril and cost I refuse not to sustain this expectation from as many as are not loath to hazard so much credulity upon the best pledges that I can give them. Although it nothing content me to have disclos'd thus much before hand, but that I trust hereby to make it manifest with what small willingnesse I endure to interrupt the pursuit of no lesse hopes then these, and leave a calme and pleasing solitarynes fed with cherful and confident thoughts, to imbark in a troubl'd sea of noises and hoars disputes, put from beholding the bright countenance of truth in the quiet and still air of delightfull studies to come into the dim reflexion of hollow antiquities sold by the seeming bulk, and there be fain to club quotations with men whose learning and beleif lies in marginal stuffings, who when they have like good sumpters[6] laid ye down their hors load of citations and fathers at your dore, with a rapsody of who and who were Bishops here or there, ye may take off their pack-saddles, their days work is don, and episcopacy, as they think, stoutly vindicated. Let any gentle apprehension that can distinguish learned pains from unlearned drudgery, imagin what pleasure or profoundnesse can be in this, or what honour to deal against such adversaries. But were it the meanest under-service, if God by his Secretary conscience injoyn it, it were sad for me if I should draw back, for me especially, now when all men offer their aid to help ease and lighten the difficult labours of the Church, to whose service by the intentions of my parents and friends I was destin'd of a child, and in mine own resolutions, till comming to some maturity of yeers and perceaving what tyranny had invaded the Church, that he who would take Orders must subscribe slave, and take an oath withall, which unlesse he took with a conscience that would retch, he must either strait perjure, or split his faith, I thought it better to preferre a blamelesse silence before the sacred office of speaking bought, and begun with servitude and forswearing. Howsoever thus Church-outed by the Prelats, hence may appear the right I have to med-

6 sumpters: beasts of burden, pack-horses

dle in these matters, as before, the necessity and constraint appear'd.

F R O M

An Apology

AGAINST A PAMPHLET
CALL'D A MODEST CONFUTATION OF THE
ANIMADVERSIONS UPON THE REMONSTRANT
AGAINST SMECTYMNUUS

———————

. . . Yet I shall not decline the more for that, to speak my opinion in the controversie next mov'd. *Whether the people may be allow'd, for competent judges of a ministers ability.* For how else can be fulfill'd that which God hath promis'd, to power out such abundance of knowledge upon all sorts of men in the times of the Gospell? how should the people examine the doctrine which is taught them, as Christ and his Apostles continually bid them do? how should they *discerne and beware of false Prophets, and try every spirit,* if they must be thought unfit to judge of the ministers abilities: the Apostles ever labour'd to perswade the Christian flock that they *were call'd in Christ to all perfectnesse of spirituall knowledge, and full assurance of understanding in the mystery of God.* But the non-resident and plurality-gaping Prelats the gulphs and whirle pools of benefices, but the dry pits of all sound doctrine, that they may the better preach what they list to their sheep, are still possessing them that they are sheepe indeed, without judgement, without understanding, *the very beasts of Mount Sinai,* as this Confuter calls them; which words of theirs may serve to condemne them out of their owne mouths; and to shew the grosse contrarieties that are in their opinions. For while none thinke the people so void of knowledge as the Prelats think them, none are so backward and malignant as they to bestow knowledge upon them; both by suppressing the frequency of Sermons, and the printed explanations of the English Bible. No marvell if the people turne beasts, when their Teachers themselves as *Isaiah* calls them, *Are dumbe and greedy dogs that can never have anough, ignorant, blind, and cannot understand, who while they all look their own way every one for his gaine from his quarter,* how many parts of the land are fed with windy ceremonies instead of sincere milke; and while one Prelat enjoyes the nourishment and light of twenty Ministers, how many waste places are left as darke as *Galile of the Gentiles, sitting in the region and shadow of death;* without preaching Minister, without light. So little care they of beasts to make them men, that by their sorcerous doctrine of formalities they take the way to transforme them out of Christian men into *Judaizing* beasts. Had they but taught the land, or suffer'd it to be taught, as Christ would it should have bin, in all plenteous dispensation of the word, then the poore mechanick might have so accustom'd his eare to good teaching, as to have discern'd betweene faithfull teachers and false. But now with a most inhumane cruelty they who have put out the peoples eyes reproach them of their blindnesse. Just as the Pharisees their true Fathers were wont; who could not indure that the people should be thought competent judges of Christs doctrine, although we know they judg'd farre better then those great Rabbies. Yet *this people,* said they, *that knowes not the law is accurst.* We need not the autority of *Pliny* brought to tell us, the people cannot judge of a minister. Yet that hurts not. For as none can judge of a Painter, or Statuary but he who is an Artist, that is, either in the *Practick* or the *Theory,* which is often separated from the practick, and judges learnedly without it, so none can judge of a Christian teacher, but he who hath, either the practize, or the knowledge of Christian religion, though not so artfully digested in him. And who almost of the meanest Christians hath not heard the Scriptures often read from his childhood, besides so many Sermons and Lectures more in number then any student hath heard in Philosophy, whereby he may easily attaine to know when he is wisely taught and when weakly. Whereof three wayes I remember are set downe in Scripture. The one is to reade often that best of books written to this purpose, that not the wise only but the simple and ignorant may learne by them; the other way to know of a minister, is by the life he leads, whereof the meanest understanding may be apprehensive. The last way to judge aright in this point is when he who judges, lives a Christian life himselfe. Which of these three will the Confuter affirme to exceed the capacity of a plaine artizan? And what reason then is there left wherefore he should be deny'd his voice in the election of his minister, as not thought a competent discerner? It is but arrogance therefore, and the pride of a *metaphysicall* fume, to thinke that *the mutinous rabble* (for so he calls the Christian congregation) *would be so mistaken in a Clerk of the University* that were to be their minister. I doubt me those Clerks that think so, are more mistaken in themselves, and what with truanting and debaushery, what with false grounds and the weaknesse of naturall faculties in many of them (it being a maxim in some men to send the simplest of their sonnes thither) perhaps there would be found among them as many unsolid and corrupted judgements both in doctrine and life, as in any other two Corporations of like bignesse. This is undoubted that if any Carpenter, Smith, or Weaver, were such a bungler in his trade, as the greater number of them are in their profession, he would starve for any custome. And should he exercise his manifacture, as little as they do their talents, he would forget his art: and should he mistake his tools as they do theirs, he would marre all the worke he took in hand. How few among them that know to write, or speak in a pure stile, much lesse to distinguish the *idea's,* and various kinds of stile: in Latine barbarous, and oft not without *solecisms,* declaming in rugged and miscellaneous geare blown together by the foure winds, and in their choice preferring the gay ranknesse of *Apuleius, Arnobius,* or any moderne fustianist,[1] before the native *Latinisms* of *Cicero.* In the Greek tongue most of them unletter'd, or unenter'd to any sound proficiency in those *Attick* maisters of morall wisdome and eloquence. In the Hebrew text, which is so necessary to be understood except it be some few of them, their lips are utterly uncircumcis'd. No lesse are they out of the way in philosophy; pestring their heads with the saplesse dotages of old *Paris and Salamanca.* And that which is the main point, in their Sermons affecting the comments and postils[2] of Friers and Jesuits, but scorning and slighting the reformed writers. In so much that

1 fustianist: writer of fustian or bombast
2 postils: commentaries

the better sort among them will confesse it a rare matter to heare a true edifying Sermon in either of their great Churches; and that such as are most humm'd and applauded there, would scarce be suffer'd the second hearing in a grave congregation of pious Christians. Is there cause why these men should over-ween, and be so queasie of the rude multitude, lest their deepe worth should be undervalu'd for want of fit umpires? No my *matriculated confutant* there will not want in any congregation of this Island, that hath not beene altogether famisht, or wholly perverted with Prelatish leven, there will not want divers plaine and solid men, that have learnt by the experience of a good con-science, what it is to be well taught, who will soone look through and through both the lofty nakednesse of your *Latinizing* Bar-barian, and the finicall goosery of your neat Sermon-actor. And so I leave you and your fellow *starres*, as you terme them, *of either horizon*, meaning I suppose either *hemisphere*, unlesse you will be ridiculous in your astronomy. For the rationall hori-zon in heav'n is but one, and the sensible horizons in earth are innumerable; so that your allusion was as erroneous as your starres. But that you did well to prognosticat them all at lowest in the horizon, that is either seeming bigger then they are through the mist and vapour which they raise, or else sinking, and wasted to the snuffe in their westerne socket.

John Bunyan

*John Bunyan was born in Elstow, Bedfordshire, in 1628. From 1644
he fought in the Civil War, probably on the parliamentary side, and
four or five years later married for the first time. Having joined the
non-conformist congregation at Bedford in 1653, he moved there from
Elstow and began preaching in 1655, the year in which his wife died.
The next year he published his first work,* Some Gospel Truths
Opened, *against the Quakers, and a year later publicly assumed
the calling of preacher. In 1658 he was indicted at the assizes for
preaching at Eaton Socon, and in 1660 was committed to the county
jail where he remained (except for one interval in 1666) twelve
years, during which time he remarried. Released from prison in 1672,
he was granted a royal license to preach to his congregation at Bedford. In 1688 he died, while occupying the post of chaplain to Sir
John Shorter, Lord Mayor of London. Of his numerous works, the
most important are:* Grace Abounding *(1666);* The Pilgrim's Progress
I *(1678);* The Life and Death of Mr. Badman *(1680);* The Holy War
(1682); and The Pilgrim's Progress II *(1684).*

FROM

GRACE *Abounding*
to the Chief of Sinners:

OR, A BRIEF AND FAITHFUL RELATION
OF THE EXCEEDING MERCY OF GOD IN CHRIST,
TO HIS POOR SERVANT

JOHN BUNYAN

1. In this my relation of the merciful working of God upon my Soul, it will not be amiss, if in the first place, I do, in a few words, give you a hint of my pedegree, and manner of bringing up; that thereby the goodness and bounty of God towards me, may be the more advanced and magnified before the sons of men.

2. For my descent then, it was, as is well known by many, of a low and inconsiderable generation; my fathers house being of that rank that is meanest, and most despised of all the families in the Land. Wherefore I have not here, as others, to boast of Noble blood, or of a High-born state according to the flesh; though all things considered, I magnifie the Heavenly Majesty, for that by this door he brought me into this world, to partake of the Grace and Life that is in Christ by the Gospel.

3. But yet notwithstanding the meanness and inconsiderableness of my Parents, it pleased God to put it into their heart, to put me to School, to learn both to Read and Write; the which I also attained, according to the rate of other poor mens children, though to my shame I confess, I did soon loose that little I learned, even almost utterly, and that long before the Lord did work his gracious work of conversion upon my Soul.

4. As for my own natural life, for the time that I was without God in the world, it was indeed according to the course of this world, and the spirit that now worketh in the children of disobedience: Eph. 2. 2, 3. it was my delight to be taken captive by the Devil *at his will*, 2 Tim. 2. 26. being filled with all unrighteousness; the which did also so strongly work, and put forth itself, both in my heart and life, and that from a childe, that I had but few Equals, (especially considering my years, which were tender, being few) both for cursing, swearing, lying and blaspheming the holy Name of God.

5. Yea, so setled and rooted was I in these things, that they became as a second Nature to me; the which, as I also have with soberness considered since, did so offend the Lord, that even in my childhood he did scare and affright me with fearful dreams, and did terrifie me with dreadful visions. For often, after I had spent this and the other day in sin, I have in my bed been greatly afflicted, while asleep, with the apprehensions of Devils, and wicked spirits, who still, as I then thought, laboured to draw me away with them; of which I could never be rid.

6. Also I should at these years be greatly afflicted and troubled with the thoughts of the day of Judgment, and that both night and day, and should tremble at the thoughts of the fearful torments of Hell-fire; still fearing that it would be my lot to be found at last amongst those Devils and Hellish Fiends, who are there bound down with the chains and bonds of eternal darkness.

7. These things, I say, when I was but a childe, about nine or ten years old, did so distress my Soul, that then in the midst of my many sports and childish vanities, amidst my vain companions, I was often much cast down and afflicted in my mind therewith, yet could I not let go my sins: yea, I was so overcome with despair of Life and Heaven, that then I should often wish, either that there had been no Hell, or that I had been a Devil; supposing they were onely tormentors; that if it must needs be, that I indeed went thither, I might be rather a tormentor, then tormented my self.

8. A while after, these terrible dreams did leave me, which also I soon forgot; for my pleasures did quickly cut off the remembrance of them, as if they had never been: wherefore, with more greediness, according to the strength of Nature, I did still

let loose the reins to my lusts, and delighted in all transgression against the Law of God: so that until I came to the state of marriage, I was the very ringleader of all the Youth that kept me company, into all manner of vice and ungodliness.

9. Yea, such prevalency had the lusts and fruits of the flesh, in this poor Soul of mine, that had not a miracle of precious grace prevented, I had not onely perished by the stroke of eternal Justice, but had also laid my self open, even to the stroke of those Laws, which bring some to disgrace and open shame before the face of the world.

10. In these days, the thoughts of Religion was very grievous to me; I could neither endure it my self, nor that any other should; so that when I have but seen some read in those books that concerned Christian piety, it would be as it were a prison to me. *Then I said unto God, Depart from me, for I desire not the knowledge of thy ways,* Job. 21. 14, 15. I was now void of all good consideration; Heaven and Hell were both out of sight and minde; and as for Saving and Damning, they were least in my thoughts. *O Lord, thou knowest my life, and my ways were not hid from thee.*

11. Yet this I well remember, that though I could my self sin with the greatest delight and ease, and also take pleasure in the vileness of my companions; yet even then, if I have at any time seen wicked things by those who professed goodness, it would make my spirit tremble. As once above all the rest, when I was in my heighth of vanity, yet hearing one to swear that was reckoned for a religious man, it had so great a stroke upon my spirit, as it made my heart to ake.

12. But God did not utterly leave me, but followed me still, not now with convictions, but Judgements, yet such as were mixed with mercy. For once I fell into a crick of the Sea, and hardly escaped drowning: another time I fell out of a Boat into *Bedford*-River, but mercy yet preserved me alive: Besides, another time being in the field, with one of my companions, it chanced that an Adder passed over the High way, so I having a stick in mine hand, struck her over the back; and having stounded her, I forced open her mouth with my stick, and plucked her sting out with my fingers, by which act had not God been mercifull to me, I might by my desperateness have brought myself to mine end.

13. This also have I taken notice of with thanksgiving; when I was a Souldier, I with others were drawn out to go to such a place to besiege it; but when I was just ready to go, one of the company desired to go in my room, to which, when I had consented he took my place; and coming to the siege, as he stood Sentinel, he was shot into the head with a Musket bullet and died.

14. Here, as I said, were Judgements and Mercy, but neither of them did awaken my soul to Righteousness, wherefore I sinned still, and grew more and more rebellious against God, and careless of mine own Salvation.

15. Presently after this, I changed my condition into a married state, and my mercy was, to light upon a Wife whose Father was counted godly: this Woman and I, though we came togther as poor as poor might be, (not having so much household-stuff as a Dish or Spoon betwixt us both), yet this she had for her part, *The Plain Mans Path-way to Heaven*, and *The Practice of Piety*, which her Father had left her when he died. In these two Books I should sometimes read with her, wherein I also found some things that were somewhat pleasing to me: (but all this while I met with no conviction.) She also would be often telling of me what a godly man her Father was, and how he would reprove and correct Vice, both in his house, and amongst his neighbours; what a strict and holy life he lived in his day, both in word and deed.

16. Wherefore these books, with this relation, though they did not reach my heart to awaken it about my sad and sinful state, yet they did beget within me some desires to Religion: so that, because I knew no better, I fell in very eagerly with the Religion of the times, to wit, to go to Church twice a day, and that too with the foremost, and there should very devoutly both say and sing as others did; yet retaining my wicked life: but withal, I was so over-run with the spirit of superstition, that I adored, and that with great devotion, even all things, (both the High-place, Priest, Clerk, Vestments, Service, and what else) belonging to the Church; counting all things holy that were therein contained; and especially the Priest and Clerk most happy, and without doubt greatly blessed, because they were the Servants, as I then thought, of God, and were principal in the holy Temple, to do his work therein.

17. This conceit grew strong in little time upon my spirit, that had I but seen a Priest, (though never so sordid and debauched in his life) I should find my spirit fall under him, reverence him, and knit unto him; yea, I thought for the love I did bear unto them, (supposing they were the Ministers of God) I could have layn down at their feet, and have been trampled upon by them; their Name, their Garb, and Work, did so intoxicate and bewitch me.

18. After I had been thus for some considerable time, another thought came into my mind, and that was, Whether we were of the *Israelites,* or no: for finding in the Scriptures that they were once the peculiar People of God, thought I, if I were one of this race, my Soul must needs be happy. Now again I found within me a great longing to be resolved about this question, but could not tell how I should: at last, I asked my father of it, who told me, *No, we were not:* wherefore then I fell in my spirit, as to the hopes of that, and so remained.

19. But all this while, I was not sensible of the danger and evil of sin; I was kept from considering that sin would damn me, what Religion soever I followed, unless I was found in Christ: nay, I never thought of him, nor whether there was one or no. Thus man, while blind, doth wander, but wearieth himself with vanity: for he knoweth not the way to the City of God, *Eccles.* 10. 15.

20. But one day, (amongst all the Sermons our Parson made) his subject was, to treat of the Sabbath day, and of the evil of breaking that, either with labour, sports, or otherwise: (now I was, notwithstanding my Religion, one that took much delight in all manner of vice, and especially that was the Day that I did solace my self therewith.) Wherefore I fell in my conscience under his Sermon, thinking and believing that he made that Sermon on purpose to shew me my evil-doing; and at that time I felt what guilt was, though never before, that I can remember; but then I was for the present greatly loaden therewith, and so went home when the Sermon was ended, with a great burden upon my spirit.

21. This, for that instant, did benum the sinews of my best delights, and did imbitter my former pleasures to me: but behold, it lasted not; for before I had well dined, the trouble began to go off my minde, and my heart returned to its old course:

but Oh how glad was I, that this trouble was gone from me, and that the fire was put out, that I might sin again without controul! Wherefore, when I had satisfied nature with my food, I shook the Sermon out of my mind, and to my old custom of sports and gaming I returned with great delight.

2. But the same day, as I was in the midst of a game at Cat, and having struck it one blow from the hole; just as I was about to strike it the second time, a voice did suddenly dart from Heaven into my Soul, which said, *Wilt thou leave thy sins, and go to Heaven? or have thy sins, and go to Hell?* At this I was put to an exceeding maze; wherefore, leaving my Cat upon the ground, I looked up to Heaven, and was as if I had with the eyes of my understanding, seen the Lord Jesus looking down upon me, as being very hotly displeased with me, and as if he did severely threaten me with some grievous punishment for these, and other my ungodly practices.

23. I had no sooner thus conceived in my mind, but suddenly this conclusion was fastned on my spirit (for the former hint did set my sins again before my face) *That I had been a great and grievous Sinner, and that it was now too late for me to look after Heaven; for Christ would not forgive me, nor pardon my transgressions.* Then I fell to musing upon this also; and while I was thinking on it, and fearing lest it should be so, I felt my heart sink in despair, concluding it was too late; and therefore I resolved in my mind I would go on in sin: for thought I, if the case be thus, my state is surely miserable; miserable if I leave my sins; and but miserable if I follow them: I can but be damned; and if I must be so, I had as good be damned for many sins, as be damned for few.

24. Thus I stood in the midst of my play, before all that then were present; but yet I told them nothing: but, I say, I having made this conclusion, I returned desperately to my sport again; and I well remember, that presently this kind of despair did so possess my Soul, that I was perswaded I could never attain to other comfort then what I should get in sin; for Heaven was gone already, so that on that I must not think: wherefore I found within me a great desire to take my fill of sin, still studdying what sin was set to be committed, that I might taste the sweetness of it; and I made as much haste as I could to fill my belly with its delicates, lest I should die before I had my desire;

for that I feared greatly. In these things, I protest before *God,* I lye not, neither do I feign this sort of speech: these were really, strongly, and with all my heart, my desires; *the good Lord, whose mercy is unsearchable, forgive me my transgressions.*

25. (And I am very confident, that this temptation of the Devil is more than usual amongst poor creatures then many are aware of, even to over-run their spirits with a scurvie and seared frame of heart, and benumming of conscience: which frame, he stilly and slyly supplyeth with such despair, that though not much guilt attendeth the Soul, yet they continually have a secret conclusion within them, that there is no hopes for them; *for they have loved sins, therefor after them they will go,* Jer. 2. 25 & 18. 12.)

26. Now therefore I went on in sin with great greediness of mind, still grudging that I could not be so satisfied with it as I would: this did continue with me about a moneth, or more. But one day, as I was standing at a Neighbours Shop-window, and there cursing and swearing, and playing the Mad-man, after my wonted manner, there sate within the woman of the house, and heard me; who, though she was a very loose and ungodly Wretch, yet protested that I swore and cursed at that most fearful rate, that she was made to tremble to hear me; And told me further, *That I was the ungodliest Fellow for swearing that ever she heard in all her life; and that I, by thus doing, was able to spoile all the Youth in a whole Town, if they came but in my company.*

27. At this reproof I was silenced, and put to secret shame; and that too, as I thought, before the God of Heaven: wherefore, while I stood there, and hanging down my head, I wished with all my heart that I might be a little childe again, that my Father might learn me to speak without this wicked way of swearing: for, thought I, I am so accustomed to it, that it is but in vain for me to think of a reformation, for I thought it could never be.

28. But how it came to pass I know not, I did from this time forward so leave my swearing, that it was a great wonder to my self to observe it; and whereas before I knew not how to speak unless I put an Oath before, and another behind, to make my words have authority, now, I could, without it, speak better, and with more pleasantness than ever I could before: all this while

I knew not Jesus Christ, neither did I leave my sports and play.

29. But quickly after this, I fell in company with one poor man that made profession of Religion; who, as I then, thought, did talk pleasantly of the Scriptures, and of the matters of Religion: wherefore falling into some love and liking to what he said, I betook me to my Bible, and began to take great pleasure in reading, but especially with the historical part thereof: for, as for *Pauls* Epistles, and Scriptures of that nature, I could not away with them, being as yet but ignorant either of the corruptions of my nature, or of the want and worth of Jesus Christ to save me.

30. Wherefore I fell to some outward Reformation, both in my words and life, and did set the Commandments before me for my way to Heaven: which Commandments I also did strive to keep; and, as I thought, did keep them pretty well sometimes, and then I should have comfort; yet now and then should break one, and so afflict my Conscience; but then I should repent, and say I was sorry for it, and promise God to do better next time, and there get help again, for then I thought I pleased God as well as any man in *England*.

31. Thus I continued about a year, all which time our Neighbours did take me to be a very godly man, a new and religious man, and did marvel much to see such a great and famous alteration in my life and manners; and indeed so it was, though yet I knew not Christ, nor Grace, nor Faith, nor Hope; and truly as I have well seen since, had I then died, my state had been most fearful: well, this I say, continued about a twelve-month, or more.

32. But, I say, my Neighbours were amazed at this my great Conversion, from prodigious profaneness, to something like a moral life; and, truly, so they well might; for this my Conversion was as great, as for *Tom* of *Bethlem*[1] to become a sober man. Now, therefore, they began to praise, to commend, and to speak well of me, both to my face, and behind my back. Now, I was, as they said, become godly; now, I was become a right honest man. But Oh! when I understood that these were their words and opinions of me, it pleased me mighty well: For though, as yet, I was nothing but a poor painted Hypocrite, yet

---

1 *Tom* of *Bethlem* to become a sober man: a madman to become sane

I loved to be talked of as one that was truly Godly. I was proud of my Godliness; and, I did all I did, either to be seen of, or to be well spoken of, by men: well, this I say, continued for about a twelve-month or more.

33. Now you must know, that before this I had taken much delight in ringing, but my Conscience beginning to be tender, I thought that such a practice was but vain, and therefore forced my self to leave it, yet my mind hanckered, wherefore I should go to the Steeple house, and look on: though I durst not ring. But I thought this did not become Religion neither, yet I forced my self and would look on still; but quickly after, I began to think, How, if one of the Bells should fall: then I chose to stand under a main Beam that lay over thwart the Steeple from side to side, thinking there I might stand sure: But then I should think again, Should the Bell fall with a swing, it might first hit the Wall, and then rebounding upon me, might kill me for all this Beam; this made me stand in the Steeple door, and now thought I, I am safe enough, for if a Bell should then fall, I can slip out behind these thick Walls, and so be preserved notwithstanding.

34. So after this, I would yet go to see them ring, but would not go further than the Steeple door; but then it came into my head, how if the Steeple it self should fall, and this thought, (it may fall for ought I know) would when I stood and looked on, continually so shake my mind, that I durst not stand at the Steeple door any longer, but was forced to fly, for fear it should fall upon my head.

35. Another thing was my dancing, I was a full year before I could quite leave it; but all this while, when I thought I kept this or that Commandment, or did by word or deed any thing that I thought were good, I had great peace in my Conscience, and should think with my self, God cannot chuse but be now pleased with me, yea, to relate it in mine own way, I thought no man in *England* could please God better than I.

36. But poor Wretch as I was, I was all this while ignorant of Jesus Christ, and going about to establish my own righteousness, had perished therein, had not God in mercy shewed me more of my state by nature.

37. But upon a day, the good providence of God did cast me to *Bedford,* to work on my calling; and in one of the streets of

that town, I came where there was three or four poor women sitting at a door in the Sun, and talking about the things of God; and being now willing to hear them discourse, I drew near to hear what they said; for I was now a brisk talker also my self in the matters of Religion: but now I may say, *I heard, but I understood not;* for they were far above out of my reach, for their talk was about a new birth, the work of God on their hearts, also how they were convinced of their miserable state by nature: they talked how God had visited their souls with his love in the Lord Jesus, and with what words and promises they had been refreshed, comforted, and supported against the temptations of the Devil; moreover, they reasoned of the suggestions and temptations of Satan in particular, and told to each other by which they had been afflicted, and how they were borne up under his assaults: they also discoursed of their own wretchedness of heart, of their unbelief, and did contemn, slight, and abhor their own righteousness, as filthy, and insufficient to do them any good.

38. And me thought they spake as if joy did make them speak: they spake with such pleasantness of Scripture language, and with such appearance of grace in all they said, that they were to me as if they had found a new world, as if they were people that dwelt alone, and were not to be reckoned among their Neighbours, Num. 23.9.

39. At this I felt my own heart began to shake, as mistrusting my condition to be naught; for I saw that in all my thoughts about Religion and Salvation, the New birth did never enter into my mind, neither knew I the comfort of the Word and Promise, nor the deceitfulness and treachery of my own wicked heart. As for secret thoughts, I took no notice of them; neither did I understand what Satans temptations were, nor how they were to be withstood and resisted, *&c.*

FROM

The Pilgrim's Progress

FROM THIS WORLD TO THAT WHICH IS TO COME:

DELIVERED UNDER THE SIMILITUDE

OF A DREAM

As I walk'd through the wilderness of this world, I lighted on a certain place, where was a Denn; And I laid me down in that place to sleep: And as I slept I dreamed a Dream. I dreamed, and behold *I saw a Man cloathed with Raggs, standing in a certain place, with his face from his own House, a Book in his hand, and a great burden upon his Back.* I looked, and saw him open the Book, and Read therein; and he read, he wept and trembled: and not being able longer to contain, he brake out with a lamentable cry; saying, *what shall I do?*

In this plight therefore he went home, and refrained himself as long as he could, that his Wife and Children should not perceive his distress; but he could not be silent long, because that his trouble increased: wherefore at length he brake his mind to his Wife and Children; and thus he began to talk to them, *O my dear Wife*, said he, *and you the Children of my bowels, I your dear friend am in my self undone, by reason of a burden that lieth hard upon me: moreover, I am for certain informed, that this our City will be burned with fire from Heaven, in which fearful overthrow, both my self, with thee, my Wife, and you my sweet babes, shall miserably come to ruine; except (the which, yet I see not) some way of escape can be found, whereby we may be delivered.* At this his Relations were sore amazed; not for that they believed, that what he said to them was true, but because they thought, that some frenzy distemper had got into his head: therefore, it drawing towards night, and they hoping that sleep might settle his brains, with all hast they got him to

bed; but the night was as troublesome to him as the day: wherefore instead of sleeping, he spent it in sighs and tears. So when
the morning was come, they would know how he did; and he
told them worse and worse. He also set to talking to them again,
but they began to be hardened; they also thought to drive away
his distemper by harsh and surly carriages to him: sometimes
they would deride, sometimes they would chide, and sometimes
they would quite neglect him: wherefore he began to retire himself to his Chamber to pray for, and pity them; and also to con-
dole his own misery: he would also walk solitarily in the Fields,
sometimes reading, and sometimes praying: and thus for some
days he spent his time.

Now, I saw upon a time, when he was walking in the Fields,
that he was (as he was wont) reading in his Book, and greatly
distressed in his mind; and as he read, he burst out, as he had
done before, crying, *What shall I do to be saved?*

I saw also that he looked this way, and that way, as if he
would run; yet he stood still, because, as I perceived, he could
not tell which way to go. I looked then, and saw a man named
Evangelist coming to him, and asked, *Wherefore dost thou cry?*
He answered, Sir, I perceive, by the Book in my hand, that I am
Condemned to die, and after that to come to Judgment; and I
find that I am not willing to do the first, nor able to do the
second.

Then said *Evangelist,* Why not willing to die? since this life
is attended with so many evils? The Man answered, Because
I fear that this burden that is upon my back, will sink me lower
then the Grave; and I shall fall into *Tophet.* And Sir, if I be not
fit to go to Prison, I am not fit (I am sure) to go to Judgement,
and from thence to Execution; and the thoughts of these things
make me cry.

Then said *Evangelist,* If this be thy condition, why standest
thou still? He answered, Because I know not whither to go, Then
he gave him a *Parchment-Roll,* and there was written within,
Fly from the wrath to come.

The Man therefore Read it, and looking upon *Evangelist* very
carefully; said, Whither must I fly? Then said *Evangelist,* pointing with his finger over a very wide Field, Do you see yonder
Wicket-gate? The Man said, No. Then said the other, Do you see
yonder shining light? He said, I think I do. Then said *Evangelist,*

Keep that light in your eye, and go up directly thereto, so shalt thou see the Gate; at which when thou knockest, it shall be told thee what thou shalt do.

So I saw in my Dream, that the Man began to run; Now he had not run far from his own door, but his Wife and Children perceiving it, began to cry after him to return: but the Man put his fingers in his Ears, and ran on crying, Life, Life, Eternal Life: so he looked not behind him, but fled towards the middle of the Plain.

The Neighbors also came out to see him run, and as he ran, some mocked, others threatned; and some cried after him to return: Now among those that did so, there were two that were resolved to fetch him back by force. The name of the one was *Obstinate,* and the name of the other *Pliable.* Now by this time the Man was got a good distance from them; But however they were resolved to pursue him; which they did and in little time they over-took him. Then said the Man, Neighbours, *Wherefore are you come?* They said, To perswade you to go back with us; but he said, That can by no means be: You dwell, said he, in the City of *Destruction,* (the place also where I was born) I see it to be so; and dying there, sooner or later, you will sink lower then the Grave, into a place that burns with Fire and Brimstone: Be content good Neighbours, and go along with me.

What! said *Obstinate, and leave our Friends, and our Comforts behind us!*

Yes, said *Christian,* (for that was his name) because, that all, which you shall forsake, is not worthy to be compared with a little of that that I am seeking to enjoy, and if you will go along with me, and hold it, you shall fare as I my self; for there where I go, is enough, and to spare; Come away, and prove my words.

Obst. *What are the things you seek, since you leave all the world to find them?*

Chr. I seek an *Inheritance, incorruptible, undefiled, and that fadeth not away;* and it is laid up in Heaven, and fast there, to be bestowed at the time appointed, on them that diligently seek it. Read it so, if you will, in my Book.

Obst. *Tush,* said *Obstinate, away with your Book; will you go back with us, or no?*

Chr. No, not I, said the other; because I have laid my hand to the Plow.

Obst. *Come then, Neighbour* Pliable, *let us turn again, and go home without him; there is a company of these Craz'd-headed Coxcombs, that when they take a fancy by the end, are wiser in their own eyes then seven men that can render a reason.*

Pli. Then said *Pliable,* Don't revile; if what the good *Christian* says is true, the things he looks after are better then ours; my heart inclines to go with my Neighbour.

Obst. *What! more Fools still? be ruled by me and go back; who knows whither such a brain-sick fellow will lead you? go back, go back, and be wise.*

Chr. Come with me Neighbour *Pliable,* there are such things to be had which I spoke of, and many more Glories besides; If you believe not me, read here in this Book; and for the truth of what is exprest therein, behold, all is confirmed by the blood of him that made it.

Pli. *Well Neighbour* Obstinate (*said* Pliable) *I begin to come to a point; I intend to go along with this good man, and to cast in my lot with him: But my good Companion, do you know the way to this desired place?*

Chr. I am directed by a man whose name is *Evangelist,* to speed me to a little Gate that is before us, where we shall receive instruction about the way.

Pli. *Come then, good Neighbour, let us be going:* Then they went both together.

Obst. And I will go back to my place, said *Obstinate:* I will be no Companion of such mis-led fantastical Fellows.

Now I saw in my Dream, that when *Obstinate* was gon back, *Christian* and *Pliable* went talking over the Plain; and thus they began their discourse,

Chr. Come Neighbour *Pliable,* how do you do? I am glad you are perswaded to go along with me; and had even *Obstinate* himself, but felt what I have felt of the Powers, and Terrours of what is yet unseen, he would not thus lightly have given us the back.

Pli. *Come Neighbour* Christian, *since there is none but us two here, tell me now further, what the things are: and how to be enjoyed, whither we are going.*

Chr. I can better conceive of them with my Mind, then speak of them with my Tongue: But yet since you are desirous to know, I will read of them in my Book.

Pli. And do you think that the words of your Book are certainly true?

Chr. Yes verily, for it was made by him that cannot lye.

Pli. Well said; what things are they?

Chr. There is an endless Kingdom to be Inhabited, and everlasting life to be given us; that we may Inhabit that Kingdom for ever.

Pli. Well said, and what else?

Chr. There are Crowns of Glory to be given us; and Garments that will make us shine like the Sun in the Firmament of Heaven.

Pli. This is excellent; And what else?

Chr. There shall be no more crying, nor sorrow; For he that is owner of the place, will wipe all tears from our eyes.

Pli. And what company shall we have there?

Chr. There we shall be with *Seraphims,* and *Cherubins,* Creatures that will dazle your eyes to look on them: There also you shall meet with thousands, and ten thousands that have gone before us to that place; none of them are hurtful, but loving, and holy; every one walking in the sight of God; and standing in his presence with acceptance for ever: In a word, there we shall see the Elders with their Golden Crowns: There we shall see the Holy Virgins with their Golden Harps. There shall see Men that by the World were cut in pieces, burnt in flames, eaten of Beasts, drownded in the Seas, for the love that they bare to the Lord of the place; all well, and cloathed with Immortality, as with a Garment.

Pli. The hearing of this is enough to ravish ones heart; but are these things to be enjoyed? how shall we get to be Sharers hereof?

Chr. The Lord, the Governour of that Countrey, hath Recorded *that* in this Book: The substance of which is, If we be truly willing to have it, he will bestow it upon us freely.

Pli. Well, my good Companion, glad am I to hear of these things: Come on, let us mend our pace.

Chr. I cannot go so fast as I would, by reason of this burden that is upon my back.

Now I saw in my Dream, that just as they had ended this

talk, they drew near to a very *Miry Slough* that was in the midst of the Plain, and they being heedless, did both fall suddenly into the bogg. The name of the Slow was *Dispond*. Here therefore they wallowed for a time, being grieviously bedaubed with the dirt; And *Christian*, because of the burden that was on his back, began to sink in the Mire.

Pli. Then said Pliable, *Ah, Neighbour* Christian, *where are you now?*

Chr. Truly, said *Christian*, I do not know.

Pli. At that *Pliable* began to be offended; and angerly, said to his Fellow, *Is this the happiness you have told me all this while of? if we have such ill speed at our first setting out, What may we expect, 'twixt this and our Journeys end? May I get out again with my life, you shall possess the brave Country alone for me.* And with that he gave a desperate struggle or two, and got out of the Mire, on that side of the Slow which was next to his own House: So away he went, and *Christian* saw him no more.

Wherefore *Christian* was left to tumble in the Slow of *Dispond* alone; but still he endeavoured to struggle to that side of the Slow, that was still further from his own House, and next to the Wicket-gate; the which he did, but could not get out, because of the burden that was upon his back: But I beheld in my Dream, that a Man came to him, whose name was *Help*, and asked him, *What he did there?*

Chr. Sir, said *Christian*, I was bid go this way, by a Man called *Evangelist*, who directed me also to yonder Gate, that I might escape the wrath to come: And as I was going thither, I fell in here.

Help. *But why did you not look for the steps?*

Chr. Fear followed me so hard, that I fled the next way, and fell in.

Help. *Then*, said he, *Give me thy hand;* so he gave him his hand, and he drew him out, and set him upon sound ground, and bid him go on his way.

Then I stepped to him that pluckt him out, and said; Sir, Wherefore, since over this place is the way from the City of *Destruction*, to yonder *Gate*, is it, that *this* Plat is not mended, that poor Travellers might go thither with more security? And he said unto me, this *Miry slow*, is such a place as cannot be mended: It is the descent whither the scum and filth that attends conviction for sin doth continually run, and therefore is it called the *Slough of Dispond:* for still as the sinner is awakened about his lost condition, there ariseth in his soul many fears, and doubts, and discouraging apprehensions, which all of them get together, and settle in this place: And this is the reason of the badness of this ground.

It is not the pleasure of the King that this place should remain so bad; his Labourers also, have by the direction of His Majesties Surveyors, been for above this sixteen hundred years, imploy'd about this patch of ground, if perhaps it might have been mended: yea, and to my knowledge, said he, *Here* hath been swallowed up, at least, Twenty thousand Cart Loads; yea Millions of wholesom Instructions, that have at all seasons been brought from all places of the Kings Dominions; (and they that can tell, say, they are the best Materials to make good ground of the place,) If so be it might have been mended, but it is the *Slough of Dispond* still; and so will be, when they have done what they can.

True, there are by the direction of the Law-giver, certain good and substantiall steps, placed even through the very midst of this *Slough;* but at such time as this place doth much spue out its filth, as it doth against change of weather, these steps are hardly seen; or if they be, Men through the diziness of their Heads, step besides; and then they are bemired to purpose, notwithstanding the steps be there; but the ground is good when they are once got in at the Gate.

Now I saw in my Dream, that by this time *Pliable* was not home to his House again. So his Neighbours came to visit him; and some of them called him wise Man for coming back; and some called him Fool for hazarding himself with *Christian;* others again did mock at his Cowardliness; saying, Surely since you began to venture, I would not have been so base to have given out for a few difficulties. So *Pliable* sat sneaking among them. But at last he got more confidence, and then they all turned their tales, and began to deride poor *Christian* behind his back. And thus much concerning *Pliable.*

Now as Christian was walking solitary by himself, he espied one afar off, come crossing over the field to meet him; and their hap was to meet just as they were crossing the way of each other. The Gentleman's name was, Mr. *Worldly-Wiseman,* he dwelt in the Town of *Carnal-Policy*, a very great Town, and also hard by, from whence Christian came. This man then meeting with Christian, and having some inckling of him, for Christians setting forth from the City of *Destruction*, was much noised abroad, not only in the Town, where he dwelt, but also it began to be the *Town*-talk in some other places, Master *Worldly-Wiseman* therefore, having some guess of him, by beholding his laborious going, by observing his sighs and groans, and the like; began thus to enter into some talk with *Christian*.

Worl. *How now, good fellow, whither away after this burdened manner?*

Chr. A burdened manner indeed, as ever I think poor creature had. And whereas you ask me, *Whither away*, I tell you, Sir, I am going to yonder Wicket-gate before me; for there, as I am informed, I shall be put into a way to be rid of my heavy burden.

Worl. *Hast thou a Wife and Children?*

Chr. Yes, but I am so laden with this burden, that I cannot take that pleasure in them as formerly: methinks, I am as if I had none.

Worl. *Wilt thou hearken to me, if I give thee counsel?*

Chr. If it be good, I will; for I stand in need of good counsel.

Worl. *I would advise thee then, that thou with all speed get thy self rid of thy burden; for thou wilt never be settled in thy mind till then: nor canst thou enjoy the benefits of the blessing which God hath bestowed upon thee till then.*

Chr. That is that which I seek for, even to be rid of this heavy burden; but get it off my self I cannot: nor is there a man in our Country that can take it off my shoulders; therefore am I going this way, as I told you, that I may be rid of my burden.

Worl. *Who bid thee go this way to be rid of thy burden?*

Chr. A man that appeared to me to be a very great and honorable person; his name, as I remember is *Evangelist*.

Worl. *I beshrow[1] him for his counsel; there is not a more dangerous and troublesome way in the world, than is that unto which he hath directed thee; and that thou shalt find, if thou wilt be ruled by his counsel: Thou hast met with something (as I perceive) already; for I see the dirt of the* Slough of Dispond *is upon thee; but that Slough is the beginning of the sorrows that do attend those that go on in that way: hear me, I am older*

---

1 beshrow: curse

*than thou! thou art like to meet with the way which thou go-
est, Wearisomness, Painfulness, Hunger, Perils, Nakedness,
Sword, Lions, Dragons, Darkness; and in a word, death, and
what not? These things are certainly true, having been confirmed by many testimonies. And why should a man so carelessly
cast away himself, by giving heed to a stranger.*

Chr. Why, Sir, this burden upon my back is more terrible to
me than are all these things which you have mentioned: nay,
methinks I care not what I meet with in the way, so be I can
also meet with deliverance from my burden.

Worl. How camest thou by thy burden at first?

Chr. By reading this Book in my hand.

*Worl. I thought so; and it is happened unto thee as to other
weak men, who meddling with things too high for them, do suddenly fall into thy distractions; which distractions do not only
unman men, (as thine I perceive has done thee) but they run
them upon desperate ventures, to obtain they know not what.*

Chr. I know what I would obtain; it is ease for my heavy
burden.

*Worl. But why wilt thou seek for ease this way, seeing so
many dangers attend it, especially, since (hadst thou but patience to hear me) I could direct thee to the obtaining of what
thou desirest, without the dangers that thou in this way wilt run
thy self into: yea, and the remedy is at hand. Besides, I will add,
that instead of those dangers, thou shalt meet with much safety,
friendship, and content.*

Chr. Pray Sir open this secret to me.

Worl. Why in yonder Village, (the Village is named Morality)
there dwells a Gentleman, whose name is Legality, *a very judicious man (and a man of a very good name) that has skill to
help men off with such burdens as thine are, from their shoulders: yea, to my knowledge he hath done a great deal of good
this way: Ai, and besides, he hath skill to cure those that are
somewhat crazed in their wits with their burdens. To him, as I
said, thou mayest go, and be helped presently. His house is not
quite a mile from this place; and if he should not be at home
himself, he hath a pretty young man to his Son, whose name is*
Civility, *that can do it (to speak on) as well as the old Gentleman himself: There, I say, thou mayest be eased of thy burden,
and if thou art not minded to go back to thy former habitation,*

as indeed I would not wish thee, thou mayest send for thy wife
and Children to thee to this Village, where there are houses now
stand empty, one of which thou mayest have at reasonable rates:
Provision is there also cheap and good, and that which will make
thy life the more happy, is, to be sure there thou shalt live by
honest neighbors, in credit and good fashion.

Now was *Christian* somewhat at a stand, but presently he
concluded; if this be true which this Gentleman hath said, my
wisest course is to take his advice, and with that he thus farther spoke.

Chr. Sir, which is my way to this honest man's house?

Worl. Do you see yonder high hill?

Chr. Yes, very well.

Worl. By that *Hill* you must go, and the first house you come
at is his.

So *Christian* turned out of his way to go to Mr. *Legality's*
house for help: but behold, when he was got now hard by the
Hill, it seemed so high, and also that side of it that was next
the way side, did hang so much over, that Christian was afraid
to venture further, lest the *Hill* should fall on his head: wherefore there he stood still, and wotted not what to do. Also his
burden, *now,* seemed heavier to him, than while he was in his
way. There came also flashes of fire out of the Hill, that made
Christian afraid that he should be burned: here therefore he
swet, and did quake for fear. And now he began to be sorry that
he had taken Mr. *Worldly-Wisemans* counsel; and with that he
saw *Evangelist* coming to meet him; at the sight also of whom
he began to blush for shame. So *Evangelist* drew nearer, and
nearer, and coming up to him, he looked upon him with a severe
and dreadful countenance: and thus began to reason with
Christian.

Evan. What doest thou here? said he: at which word *Christian* knew not what to answer: wherefore, at present he stood
speechless before him. Then said *Evangelist* farther, *Art not*
thou the man that I found crying, without the walls of the City of
Destruction?

Chr. Yes, dear Sir, I am the man.

Evan. Did not I direct thee the way to the little Wicket-gate?

Chr. Yes, dear Sir said *Christian.*

Evan. How is it then that thou art so quickly turned aside, for thou art now out of the way?

Chr. I met with a Gentleman, so soon as I had got over the *Slough of Dispond*, who perswaded me, that I might in the *Village* before me, find a man that could take off my burden.

Evan. What was he?

Chr. He looked like a Gentleman, and talked much to me, and got me at last to yield; so I came hither: but when I beheld this Hill, and how it hangs over the way, I suddenly made a stand, lest it should fall on my head.

Evan. What said that Gentleman to you?

Chr. Why, he asked me whither I was going, and I told him.

Evan. And what said he then?

Chr. He asked me if I had a Family, and I told him: but, said I, I am so loaden with the burden that is on my back, that I cannot take pleasure in them as formerly.

Evan. And what said he then?

Chr. He bid me with speed get rid of my burden, and I told him 'twas ease that I sought: And said I, I am therefore going to yonder *Gate* to receive further direction how I may get to the place of deliverance. So he said that he would shew me a better way, and short, not so attended with difficulties, as the way, Sir, that you set me: which way, said he, will direct you to a Gentleman's house that hath skill to take off these burdens: So I believed him, and turned out of that way into this, if haply I might be soon eased of my burden: but when I came to this place, and beheld things as they are, I stopped for fear, (as I said) of danger: but I now know not what to do.

Evan. Then (said Evangelist) *stand still a little, that I may shew thee the words of God.* So he stood trembling. *Then* (said Evangelist) *See that ye refuse not him that speaketh; for if they escaped not who refused him that spake on Earth, much more shall not we escape, if we turn away from him that speaketh from Heaven. He said moreover, Now the just shall live by faith; but if any man draws back, my soul shall have no pleasure in him. He also did thus apply them, Thou art the man that art running into this misery, thou hast began to reject the counsel of the most high, and to draw back thy foot from the way of peace, even almost to the hazarding of thy perdition.*

Then *Christian* fell down at his foot as dead, crying, Woe is me, for I am undone: at the sight of which *Evangelist* caught him by the right hand, saying, All manner of sin and blasphemies shall be forgiven unto men; be not faithless, but believing; then did *Christian* again a little revive, and stood up trembling, as at first, before *Evangelist*.

Then *Evangelist* proceeded, saying, *Give more earnest heed to the things that I shall tell thee of.* I will now shew thee who it was that deluded thee, and who 'twas also to whom he sent thee. The man that met thee, is one *Worldly-Wiseman,* and rightly is he so called; partly, because he favoureth only the Doctrine of this World (therefore he always goes to the Town of *Morality* to Church) and partly because he loveth that Doctrine best, for it saveth him from the Cross; and because he is of this carnal temper, therefore he seeketh to prevent my ways, though right. Now there are three things in this mans counsel that thou must utterly abhor.

1. His turning thee out of the way.
2. His labouring to render the Cross odious to thee.
3. And his setting thy feet in that way that leadeth unto the administration of Death.

First, Thou must abhor his turning thee out of the way; yea, and thine own consenting thereto: because this is to reject the counsel of God, for the sake of the counsel of a *Worldly-Wiseman.* The Lord says, *Strive to enter in at the strait gate,* the gate to which I sent thee; *for strait is the gate that leadeth unto life, and few there be that find it.* From this little wicket-gate, and from the way thereto hath this wicked man turned thee, to the bringing of thee almost to destruction; hate therefore his turning thee out of the way, and abhor thy self for harkening to him.

Secondly, Thou must abhor his labouring to render the Cross odious unto thee; for thou art to *prefer it before the treasures in Egypt:* besides the King of glory hath told thee, that he that will save his life shall lose it: and *he that comes after him, and hates not his father and mother, and wife, and children, and brethren, and sisters; yea, and his own life also, he cannot be my Disciple.* I say therefore, for a man to labour to perswade thee, that that shall be thy death, without which the truth hath said, thou canst not have eternal life, this Doctrine thou must abhor.

Thirdly, thou must hate his setting of thy feet in the way that leadeth to the ministration of death. And for this thou must consider to whom he sent thee, and also how unable that person was to deliver thee from thy burden.

He to whom thou wast sent for ease, being by name *Legality*, is the Son of the Bond woman which now is, and is in bondage with her children, and is in a mystery this Mount *Sinai*, which thou hast feared will fall on thy head. Now if she with her children are in bondage, how canst thou expect by them to be made free? This *Legality* therefore is not able to set thee free from thy burden. No man was as yet ever rid of his burden by him, no, nor ever is like to be: ye cannot be justified by the Works of the Law; for by the deeds of the Law no man living can be rid of his burden: therefore Mr. *Worldly-Wiseman* is an alien, and Mr. *Legality* a cheat: and for his Son *Civility*, notwithstanding his simpering looks, he is but an hypocrite, and cannot help thee. Believe me, there is nothing in all this noise, that thou hast heard of this sottish man, but a design to beguile thee of thy Salvation, by turning thee from the way in which I had set thee. After this *Evangelist* called aloud to the Heavens for confirmation of what he had said; and with that there came words and fire out of the Mountain under which poor Christian stood, that made the hair of his flesh stand. The words were thus pronounced, *As many as are of the works of the Law, are under the curse; for it is written, Cursed is every one that continueth not in all things which are written in the Book of the Law to do them.*

Now *Christian* looked for nothing but death, and began to cry out lamentably, even cursing the time in which he met with Mr. *Worldly-Wiseman*, still calling himself a thousand fools for hearkening to his counsel: he also was greatly ashamed to think that this Gentlemans arguments, flowing only from the flesh, should have that prevalency with him as to cause him to forsake the right way. This done, he applied himself again to *Evangelist* in words and sense as follows.

Chr. Sir, what think you? is there hopes? may I now go back and go up to the *Wicket-gate*, shall I not be abandoned for this, and sent back from thence ashamed. I am sorry I have hearkened to this man's counsel, but may my sin be forgiven.

Evan. Then said *Evangelist* to him, Thy sin is very great, for by it thou hast committed two evils; thou hast forsaken the way that is good, to tread in forbidden paths: yet will the man at the

Gate receive thee, for he has *good will* for men; only, said he, take heed that thou turn not aside again, lest thou perish from the way when his wrath is kindled but a little. Then did *Christian* address himself to go back, and *Evangelist*, after he had kist him, gave him one smile, and bid him God speed; so he went on with hast, neither spake he to any man by the way; nor if any man asked him, would he vouchsafe them an answer. He went like one that was all the while treading on forbidden ground, and could by no means think himself safe, till again he was got into the way which he left to follow Mr. *Worldly-Wiseman's* counsel: so in process of time *Christian* got up to the Gate. Now over the Gate there was Written, *Knock and it shall be opened unto you.* He knocked therefore, more *then* once or twice, *saying,*

> *May I now enter here? will he within*
> *Open to sorry me, though I have bin*
> *An undeserving Rebel? then shall I,*
> *Not fail to Sing his lasting praise on high.*

At last there came a grave Person to the Gate: named *Good-will,* who asked, *Who was there? and whence he came? and what he would have?*

Chr. Here is a poor burdened sinner, I come from the City of *Destruction,* but am going to Mount *Zion,* that I may be delivered from the wrath to come; I would therefore, Sir, since I am informed that by this Gate is the way thither, know if you are *willing* to let me in.

Good-Will. I am *willing* with all my heart, said he; and with that he opened the Gate. . . .

.   .   .

. . . But now in this Valley of *Humiliation* poor *Christian* was hard put to it, for he had gone but a little way before he espied a foul *Fiend* coming over the field to meet him; his name is *Apollyon.* Then did *Christian* begin to be afraid, and to cast in his mind whether to go back, or to stand his ground. But he considered again, that he had no Armour for his back, and therefore thought that to turn the back to him, might give him greater advantage with ease to pierce him with his Darts; therefore he resolved to venture, and stand his ground. For thought he, had I no more in mine eye, then the saving of my life, 'twould be the best way to stand.

So he went on, and *Apollyon* met him; now the Monster was hidious to behold, he was cloathed with scales like a Fish (and they are his pride) he had Wings like a Dragon, feet like a Bear, and out of his belly came Fire and Smoak, and his mouth was as the mouth of a Lion. When he was come up to *Christian,* he beheld him with a disdainful countenance, and thus began to question with him.

Apol. Whence come you, and whither are you bound?

Chr. I come from the City of *Destruction,* which is the place of all evil, and am going to the City of *Zion.*

Apol. By this I perceive thou art one of my Subjects, for all that Countrey is mine; and I am the Prince and God of it. How is it then that thou hast ran away from thy King? Were it not that I hope thou maiest do me more service, I would strike thee now at one blow to the ground.

Chr. I was born indeed in your Dominions, but your service was hard, and your wages such as a man could not live on, *for the wages of Sin is death;* therefore when I was come to years, I did as other considerate persons do, look out, if perhaps I might mend my self.

Apol. There is no Prince that will thus lightly lose his Subjects; neither will I as yet lose thee. But since thou complainest of thy service and wages, be content to go back; what our Countrey will afford, I do here promise to give thee.

Chr. But I have let my self to another, even to the King of Princes, and how can I with fairness go back with thee?

Apol. Thou hast done in this, according to the Proverb, changed a bad for a worse: but it is ordinary for those that have professed themselves his Servants, after a while to give him the slip; and return again to me: do thou so too, and all shall be well.

Chr. I have given him my faith, and sworn my Allegiance to him; how then can I go back from this, and not be hanged as a Traitor?

Apol. Thou didest the same to me, and yet I am willing to pass by all, if now thou wilt yet turn again, and go back.

Chr. What I promised thee was in my none-age;[2] and besides, I count that the Prince under whose Banner now I stand, is able

2 none-age: minority

to absolve me; yea, and to pardon also what I did as to my com-
pliance with thee: and besides, (O thou destroying *Apollyon*) to
speak truth, I like his Service, his Wages, his Servants, his Government, his Company, and Countrey better then thine: and
therefore leave off to perswade me further, I am his Servant, and
I will follow him.

Apol. *Consider again when thou art in cool blood, what thou art
like to meet with in the way that thou goest. Thou knowest that
for the most part, his Servants come to an ill end, because they
are transgressors against me, and my ways: How many of them
have been put to shameful deaths! and besides, thou countest his
service better then mine, whereas he never came yet from the
place where he is, to deliver any that served him out of our
hands: but as for me, how many times, as all the World very
well knows, have I delivered, either by power or fraud, those that
have faithfully served me, from him and his, though taken by
them; and so I will deliver thee.*

Chr. His forbearing at present to deliver them, is on purpose
to try their love, whether they will cleave to him to the end: and
as for the ill end thou sayest they come to, that is most glorious
in their account: For, for present deliverance, they do not much
expect it; for they stay for their Glory, and then they shall have
it, when their Prince comes in his, and the Glory of the Angels.

Apol. *Thou hast already been unfaithful in thy service to him,
and how dost thou think to receive wages of him?*

Chr. Wherein, O *Apollyon*, have I been unfaithful to him;

Apol. *Thou didst faint at first setting out, when thou wast almost choked in the Gulf of Dispond. Thou didst attempt wrong
ways to be rid of thy burden, whereas thou shouldest have stayed
till thy Prince had taken it off. Thou didst sinfully sleep, and
loose thy choice thing: thou wast also almost perswaded to go
back, at the sight of the Lions; and when thou talkest of thy
Journey, and of what thou hast heard, and seen, thou art in-
wardly desirous of vain-glory in all that thou sayest or doest.*

Chr. All this is true, and much more, which thou hast left out;
but the Prince whom I serve and honour, is merciful, and ready
to forgive: but besides, these infirmities possessed me in thy
Countrey, for there I suckt them in, and I have groaned under
them, been sorry for them, and have obtained Pardon of my
Prince.

Apol. Then *Apollyon* broke out into a grievous rage, saying, *I am an enemy to this Prince: I hate his Person, his Laws, and People: I am come out on purpose to withstand thee.*

Chr. Apollyon, beware what you do, for I am in the Kings High-way, the way of Holiness, therefore take heed to your self.

Apol. Then *Apollyon* strodled quite over the whole breadth of the way, and said, I am void of fear in this matter, prepare thy self to dye, for I swear by my Infernal Den, that thou shalt go no further, here will I spill thy soul: and with that he threw a flaming Dart at his brest; but *Christian* had a Shield in his hand, with which he caught it, and so prevented the danger of that. Then did *Christian* draw, for he saw 'twas time to bestir him; and *Apollyon* as fast made at him, throwing Darts as thick as hail; by the which, notwithstanding all that *Christian* could do to avoid it, *Apollyon* wounded him in his *head,* his *hand* and *foot;* this made *Christian* give a little back: *Apollyon* therefore followed his work amain, and *Christian* again took courage, and resisted as manfully as he could. This sore Combat lasted for above half a day, even till *Christian* was almost quite spent. For you must know, that *Christian,* by reason of his wounds, must needs grow weaker and weaker.

Then *Apollyon* espying his opportunity, began to gather up close to *Christian,* and wrestling with him, gave him a dreadful fall; and with that *Christian's* Sword flew out of his hand. Then said *Apollyon, I am sure of thee now;* and with that, he had almost prest him to death; so that *Christian* began to despair of life. But as God would have it, while *Apollyon* was fetching of his last blow, thereby to make a full end of this good Man, *Christian* nimbly reached out his hand for his Sword, and caught it, saying, *Rejoyce not against me, O mine Enemy! when I fall, I shall arise;* and with that, gave him a deadly thrust, which made him give back, as one that had received his mortal wound: *Christian* perceiving that, made at him again, saying, *Nay, in all these things we are more then Conquerours, through him that loved us.* And with that, *Apollyon* spread forth his Dragons wings, and sped him away, that *Christian* saw him no more.

In this Combat no man can imagine, unless he had seen and heard as I did, what yelling, and hideous roaring *Apollyon* made all the time of the fight, he spake like a Dragon: and on the other side, what sighs and groans brast from *Christians* heart. I never saw him all the while give so much as one pleasant look, till he perceived he had wounded *Apollyon* with his two-edg'd Sword, then indeed he did smile, and look upward: but twas the dreadfullest sight that ever I saw.

So when the Battel was over, *Christian* said, I will here give thanks to him that hath delivered me out of the mouth of the Lion; to him that did help me against *Apollyon:* and so he did, saying,

> *Great* Beelzebub, *the Captain of this Fiend,*
> *Design'd my ruin; therefore to this end*
> *He sent him harnest out, and he with rage*
> *That hellish was, did fiercely me Ingage:*
> *But blessed* Michael *helped me, and I*
> *By dint of Sword did quickly make him flye;*
> *Therefore to him let me give lasting praise,*
> *And thank and bless his holy name always.*

Then there came to him an hand with some of the leaves of the Tree of Life, the which *Christian* took, and applyed to the wounds that he had received in the Battel, and was healed immediately. He also sat down in that place to eat Bread, and to drink of the Bottle that was given him a little before; so being refreshed, he addressed himself to his Journey, with his Sword drawn in his hand; for he said, I know not but some other enemy may be at hand. But he met with no other affront from *Apollyon,* quite through this Valley.

Now at the end of this Valley, was another, called the Valley of the *Shadow of Death,* and *Christian* must needs go through it, because the way to the Cœlestial City lay through the midst of it: Now this Valley is a very solitary place. The Prophet *Jeremiah* thus describes it, *A Wilderness, a Land of desarts, and of Pits, a Land of drought, and of the shadow of death, a Land that no Man* (but a Christian) *passeth through, and where no man dwelt.*

Now here *Christian* was worse put to it then in his fight with *Apollyon,* as by the sequel you shall see.

I saw then in my Dream, that when *Christian* was got to the Borders of the Shadow of Death, there met him two Men, Children of them that brought up an evil report of the good Land, making haste to go back: to whom *Christian* spake as follows.

Chr. *Whither are you going?*

Men. They said, Back, back; and would have you to do so too, if either life or peace is prized by you.

Chr. *Why? what's the matter? said* Christian?

Men. Matter! said they; we were going that way as you are going, and went as far as we durst; and indeed we were almost past coming back, for had we gone a little further, we had not been here to bring the news to thee.

Chr. *But what have you met with? said* Christian.

Men. Why we were almost in the Valley of the shadow of Death, but that by good hap we looked before us, and saw the danger before we came to it.

Chr. *But what have you seen? said* Christian.

Men. Seen! Why the Valley it self, which is as dark as pitch; we also saw there the Hobgoblins, Satyrs, and Dragons of the Pit: we heard also in that Valley a continual howling and yelling, as of a People under unutterable misery; who there sat bound in affliction and Irons: and over that Valley hangs the discouraging Clouds of confusion, death also doth always spread his wings over it: in a word, it is every whit dreadful, being utterly without Order.

Chr. *Then said* Christian, *I perceive not yet, by what you have said, but that this is my way to the desired Haven.*

Men. Be it thy way, we will not chuse it for ours; so they parted, and *Christian* went on his way, but still with his Sword drawn in his hand, for fear lest he should be assaulted.

I saw then in my Dream, so far as this Valley reached, there was on the right hand a very deep Ditch; that Ditch is it into which the blind have led the blind in all Ages, and have both there miserably perished. Again, behold on the left hand, there was a very dangerous Quagg, into which, if even a good Man falls, he can find no bottom for his foot to stand on: Into that Quagg *King* David *once did fall,* and had no doubt therein been smothered, had not He that is able, pluckt him out.

The path-way was here also exceeding narrow, and therefore good *Christian* was the more put to it; for when he sought in the dark to shun the ditch on the one hand, he was ready to tip over into the mire on the other; also when he sought to escape the mire, without great carefulness he would be ready to fall into the ditch. Thus he went on, and I heard him here sigh bitterly: for, besides the dangers mentioned above, the path way was here so dark, that oft times when he lift up his foot to set forward, he knew not where, or upon what he should set it next.

About the midst of this Valley, I perceived the mouth of Hell to be, and it stood also hard by the way side: Now thought *Christian*, what shall I do? And ever and anon the flame and smoke would come out in such abundance, with sparks and hideous noises, (things that cared not for *Christians* Sword, as did *Apollyon* before) that he was forced to put up his Sword, and betake himself to another weapon called *All-prayer:* so he cried in my hearing, *O Lord I beseech thee deliver my Soul.* Thus he went on a great while, yet still the flames would be reaching towards him: also he heard doleful voices, and rushings too and fro, so that sometimes he thought he should be torn in pieces, or trodden down like mire in the Streets. This frightful sight was seen, and these dreadful noises were heard by him for several miles together: and coming to a place, where he thought he heard a company of *Fiends* coming forward to meet him, he stopt; and began to muse what he had best to do. Somtimes he had half a thought to go back. Then again he thought he might be half way through the Valley; he remembered also how he had already vanquished many a danger: and that the danger of going back might be much more, then for to go forward; so he resolved to go on. Yet the *Fiends* seemed to come nearer and nearer, but when they were come even almost at him, he cried out with a most vehement voice, *I will walk in the strength of the Lord God;* so they gave back, and came no further.

One thing I would not let slip, I took notice that now poor *Christian* was so confounded, that he did not know his own voice: and thus I perceived it: Just when he was come over against the mouth of the burning Pit, one of the wicked ones got behind him, and stept up softly to him, and whisperingly suggested many grievous blasphemies to him, which he verily thought had proceeded from his own mind. This put *Christian* more to it than any thing that he met with before, even to think that he should now blaspheme him that he loved so much before; yet, could he have helped it, he would not have done it: but he had not the discretion neither to stop his ears, nor to know from whence those blasphemies came.

When *Christian* had travelled in this disconsolate condition some considerable time, he thought he heard the voice of a man, as going before him, saying, *Though I walk through the valley of the shaddow of death, I will fear none ill, for thou art with me.*

Then was he glad, and that for these reasons:

First, because he gathered from thence, that some who feared God were in this Valley as well as himself.

Secondly, For that he perceived, God was with them, though in that dark and dismal state; and why not, thought he, with me, though by reason of the impediment that attends this place, I cannot perceive it.

Thirdly, For that he hoped (could he over-take them) to have company by and by. So he went on, and called to him that was before, but he knew not what to answer; for that he also thought himself to be alone: And by and by, the day broke; then said *Christian, He hath turned the shadow of death into the morning.*

Now morning being come, he looked back, not of desire to return, but to see, by the light of the day, what hazards he had gone through in the dark. So he saw more perfectly the Ditch that was on the one hand, and the Quagg that was on the other; also how narrow the way was which lay betwixt them both; also now he saw the Hobgoblins, and Satyrs, and Dragons of the Pit, but all afar off; for after break of day, they came not nigh; yet they were discovered to him, according to that which is written, *He discovereth deep things out of darkness, and bringeth out to light the shadow of death.*

Now was *Christian* much affected with his deliverance from all the dangers of his solitary way, which dangers, though he feared them more before, yet he saw them more clearly now, because the light of the day made them conspicuous to him; and about this time the Sun was rising, and this was another mercy to *Christian:* for you must note, that tho the first part of the Valley of the shadow of Death was dangerous, yet this second part which he was yet to go, was, if possible, far more dangerous: for from the place where he now stood, even to the end of the Valley, the way was all along set so full of Snares, Traps, Gins,[3] and Nets here, and so full of Pits, Pitfalls, deep holes, and shelvings down there, that had it now been dark, as it was when he came the first part of the way, had he had a thousand

3 Gins: devices for trapping

souls, they had in reason been cast away; but, as I said, just now the Sun was rising. Then said he *His candle shineth on my head, and by his light I go through darkness.*

In this light therefore he came to the end of the Valley. Now I saw in my Dream, that at the end of this Valley lay blood, bones, ashes, and mangled bodies of men, even of Pilgrims that had gone this way formerly: And while I was musing what should be the reason, I espied a little before me a Cave, where two Giants, *Pope* and *Pagan,* dwelt in old time, by whose Power and Tyranny the Men whose bones, blood, ashes, &c. lay there, were cruelly put to death. But by this place *Christian* went without much danger, whereat I somewhat wondered; but I have learnt since, that *Pagan* has been dead many a day; and as for the other, though he be yet alive, he is by reason of age, and also of the many shrewd brushes that he met with in his younger dayes, grown so crazy and stiff in his joynts, that he can now do little more then sit in his Caves mouth, grinning at Pilgrims as they go by, and biting his nails, because he cannot come at them. . . .

.   .   .

. . . Oh said *Faithful* to his Brother, who comes yonder? Then *Christian* looked, and said, It is my good friend *Evangelist.* Ai, and my good friend too, said *Faithful;* for 'twas he that set me the way to the Gate. Now was *Evangelist* come up unto them, and thus saluted them.

Evan. Peace be with you, dearly beloved, and, peace be to your helpers.

Chr. *Welcome, welcome, my good* Evangelist, *the sight of thy countenance brings to my remembrance, thy ancient kindness, and unwearied laboring for my eternal good.*

Faith. *And, a thousand times welcome, said good* Faithful; *Thy company, O sweet* Evangelist, *how desirable is it to us, poor Pilgrims!*

Evan. Then, said *Evangelist,* How hath it fared with you, my friends, since the time of our last parting? *what* have you met with, and *how* have you behaved your selves?

Chr. *Then* Christian, *and* Faithful *told him of all things that had happened to them in the way; and* how, *and with* what *difficulty they had arrived to that place.*

Evan. Right glad am I, said *Evangelist;* not that you met with trials, but that you have been victors; and for that you have (notwithstanding many weaknesses,) continued in the way to this very day.

I say, right glad am I of this thing, and that for mine own sake and yours; I have sowed, and you have reaped, and the day is coming, when both he that sowed, and they that reaped shall rejoyce together; that is, if you hold out: for, in due time ye shall reap, if you faint not. The Crown is before you, and it is an incorruptible one; so run that you may obtain it. Some there be that set out for this Crown, and after they have gone far for it, another comes in, and takes it from them; hold fast therefore that you have, let no man take your Crown; you are not yet out of the gun-shot of the Devil: you have not resisted unto blood, striving against sin: let the Kingdom be always before you, and believe stedfastly concerning things that are invisible. Let nothing that is on this side the other world get within you; and above all, look well to your own hearts, and to the lusts thereof; for they are deceitful above all things, and desperately wicked: set your faces like a flint, you have all power in Heaven and Earth on your side.

Chr. *Then Christian thanked him for his exhortation, but told him withal, that they would have him speak farther to them for their help, the rest of the way; and the rather, for that they well knew that he was a Prophet, and could tell them of things that might happen unto them; and also how they might resist and overcome them. To which request* Faithful *also consented. So* Evangelist *began as followeth.*

Evan. My Sons, you have heard in the words of the truth of the Gospel, that you must through many tribulations enter into the Kingdom of Heaven. And again, that in every City, bonds and afflictions abide in you; and therefore you cannot expect that you should go long on your Pilgrimage without them, in some sort or other. You have found something of the truth of these testimonies upon you already, and more will immediately follow: for now, as you see, you are almost out of this Wilderness, and therefore you will soon come into a Town that you will by and by see before you: and in that Town you will be hardly beset with enemies, who will strain hard but they will kill you: and be you sure that one or both of you must seal the testimony which you hold, with blood: but be you faithful unto death, and the King will give you a Crown of life. He that shall die there, although his death will be unnatural, and his pain perhaps great, he will yet have the better of his fellow; not only because he will be arrived at the Cœlestial City soonest, but because he will escape many miseries that the other will meet with in the rest of his Journey. But when you are come to the Town, and shall find fulfilled what I have here related, then remember your friend and quit your selves like men; and commit the keeping of your souls to your God, as unto a faithful Creator.

Then I saw in my Dream, that when they were got out of the Wilderness, they presently saw a Town before them, and the name of that Town is *Vanity;* and at the Town there is a *Fair* kept called *Vanity-Fair:* It is kept all the year long, it beareth the name of *Vanity-Fair,* because the Town where tis kept, *is lighter then* Vanity; and also, because all that is there sold, or that cometh thither, is *Vanity.* As is the saying of the wise, *All that cometh is vanity.*

This Fair is no new erected business, but a thing of Ancient standing; I will shew you the original of it.

Almost five thousand years agone, there were Pilgrims walking to the Cœlestial City, as these two honest persons are; and *Beelzebub, Apollyon,* and *Legion,* with their Companions, perceiving by the path that the Pilgrims made, that their way to the City lay through *this Town* of *Vanity,* they contrived here to set up a Fair; a Fair wherein should be sold of *all sorts of Vanity,* and that it should last all the year long. Therefore at *this Fair* are all such Merchandize sold, as Houses, Lands, Trades, Places, Honours, Preferments, Titles, Countreys, Kingdoms, Lusts, Pleasures, and Delights of all sorts, as Whores, Bauds, Wives, Husbands, Children, Masters, Servants, Lives, Blood, Bodies, Souls, Silver, Gold, Pearls, Precious Stones, and what not.

And moreover, at this Fair there is at all times to be seen Juglings, Cheats, Games, Plays, Fools, Apes, Knaves, and Rogues, and that of all sorts.

Here are to be seen too, and that for nothing, Thefts, Murders, Adultries, False-swearers, and that of a blood-red colour.

And as in other Fairs of less moment, there are the several Rows and Streets under their proper names, where such and

such Wares are vended: So here likewise, you have the proper
Places, Rows, Streets, (*viz.* Countreys, and Kingdoms) where
the Wares of this Fair are soonest to be found: Here is the
Britain Row, the *French* Row, the *Italian* Row, the *Spanish* Row,
the *German* Row, where several sorts of Vanities are to be sold.
But as in other *fairs,* some one Commodity is as the chief of all
the *fair,* so the Ware of *Rome* and her Merchandize is greatly
promoted in *this fair:* Only our *English* Nation, with some
others, have taken a dislike thereat.

Now, as I said, the way to the Cœlestial City lyes just thorow
this Town, where this lusty Fair is kept; and he that will go to
the City, and yet not go thorow this Town, must needs *go out
of the World.* The Prince of Princes himself, when here, went
through *this Town* to his own Countrey, and that upon a *Fair-
day* too: Yea, and as I think it was *Beelzebub,* the chief Lord of
this *Fair,* that invited him to buy of his *Vanities;* yea, would
have made him Lord of the *Fair,* would he but have done him
Reverence as he went thorow the *Town.* Yea, because he was
such a person of Honour, *Beelzebub* had him from *Street* to
Street, and shewed him all the Kingdoms of the World in a little time, that he might, if possible alure that Blessed One, to
cheapen and *buy* some of his *Vanities.* But he had no mind to
the Merchandize, and therefore left the *Town;* without laying
out so much as one Farthing upon these *Vanities.* This *Fair*
therefore is an Ancient thing, of long standing, and a very great
Fair.

Now these Pilgrims, as I said, must needs go thorow this
Fair: Well, so they did; but behold, even as they entred into the
Fair, all the people in the *Fair* were moved, and the Town it self
as it were in a Hubbub about them; and that for several reasons: For,

First, The Pilgrims were cloathed with such kind of Raiment,
as was diverse from the Raiment of any that traded in that *fair.*
The people therefore of the *fair* made a great gazing upon them:
Some said they were Fools, some they were Bedlams, and some
they are Outlandish-men.

Secondly, And as they wondred at their Apparel, so they did
likewise at their Speech; for few could understand what they
said; they naturally spoke the Language of *Canaan;* But they
that kept the *fair,* were the men of this World: So that from one

end of the *fair* to the other, they seemed *Barbarians* each to the other.

Thirdly, But that which did not a little amuse the Merchandizers, was, that these Pilgrims set very light by all their Wares, they cared not so much as to look upon them: and if they called upon them to buy, they would put their fingers in their ears, and cry, *Turn away mine eyes from beholding vanity;* and look upwards, signifying that their Trade and Traffick was in Heaven.

One chanced mockingly, beholding the carriages of the men, to say unto them, What will ye buy? but they, looking gravely upon him, said, *We buy the Truth.* At that, there was an occasion taken to despise the men the more; some mocking, some taunting, some speaking reproachfully, and some calling upon others to smite them. At last things came to an hubbub, and great stir in the *fair;* insomuch that all order was confounded. Now was word presently brought to the *great one* of the *fair,* who quickly came down, and deputed some of his most trusty friends to take these men into examination, about whom the *fair* was almost overturned. So the men were brought to examination; and they that sat upon them, asked them whence they came, whither they went, and what they did there in such an unusual Garb? The men told them, that they were Pilgrims and Strangers in the world, and that they were going to their own Countrey, which was the Heavenly *Jerusalem;* and that they had given none occasion to the men of the Town, nor yet to the Merchandizers, thus to abuse them, and to let them in their Journey. Except it was, for that, when one asked them what they would buy, they said, they would *buy the Truth.* But they that were appointed to examine them, did not believe them to be any other then Bedlams and Mad, or else such as came to put all things into a confusion in the *fair.* Therefore they took them, and beat them, and besmeared them with dirt, and then put them into the Cage, that they might be made a Spectacle to all the men of the *fair.* There therefore they lay for some time, and were made the objects of any mans sport, or malice, or revenge. The great one of the *fair* laughing still at all that befel them. But the men being patient, and not rendering railing for railing, but contrarywise blessing, and giving good words for bad, and kindness for injuries done: Some men in the *fair* that were more observing, and less prejudiced then the rest, began to check and blame the baser sort for their continual abuses done by them to the men: They therefore in angry manner let fly at them again, counting them as bad as the men in the Cage, and telling them that they seemed confederates, and should be made partakers of their misfortunes. The other replied, That for ought they could see, the men were quiet, and sober, and intended no body any harm; and that there were many that Traded in their *fair*, that were more worthy to be put into the Cage, yea, and Pillory too, then were the men that they had abused. Thus, after divers words had passed on both sides, (the men behaving themselves all the while very wisely, and soberly before them) they fell to some Blows, among themselves, and did harm one to another. Then were these two poor men brought before their Examiners again, and there charged as being guilty of the late Hubbub that had been in the *fair*. So they beat them pitifully, and hanged Irons upon them, and led them in Chaines up and down the *fair*, for an example and a terror to others, lest any should further speak in their behalf, or joyn themselves unto them. But *Christian and Faithful* behaved themselves yet more wisely, and received the ignominy and shame that was cast upon them, with so much meekness and patience, that it won to their side (though but few in comparison of the rest) several of the men in the *fair*. This put the other party yet into a greater rage, insomuch that they concluded the death of these two men. Wherefore they threatned that the Cage, nor Irons, should serve their turn, but that they should die, for the abuse they had done, and for deluding the men of the *fair*.

Then were they remanded to the Cage again, until further order should be taken with them. So they put them in, and made their feet fast in the Stocks.

Here also they called again to mind what they had heard from their faithful friend *Evangelist,* and was the more confirmed in their way and sufferings, by what he told them would happen to them. They also now comforted each other, that whose lot it was to suffer, even he should have the best on't; therefore each man secretly wished that he might have that preferment: but committing themselves to the All-wise dispose of him that ruleth all things, with much content they abode in the condition in which they were, until they should be otherwise disposed of.

Then a convenient time being appointed, they brought them forth to their Tryal in order to their Condemnation. When the time was come, they were brought before their Enemies and arraigned; the Judges name was Lord *Hategood*. Their Indictment was one and the same in substance, though somewhat varying in form; the Contents whereof was this.

That they were enemies to, and disturbers of their Trade; that they had made Commotions and Divisions in the Town, and had won a party to their own most dangerous Opinions, in contempt of the Law of their Prince.

Then *Faithful* began to answer, That he had only set himself against that which had set it self against him that is higher then the highest. And, said he, As for disturbance, I make none, being my self a man of Peace; the Party that were won to us, were won, by beholding our Truth and Innocence, and they are only turned from the worse to the better. And as to the King you talk of; since he is *Beelzebub*, the Enemy of our Lord, I defie him and all his Angels.

Then Proclamation was made, that they that had ought to say for their Lord the King against the Prisoner at the Bar, should forthwith appear, and give in their evidence. So there came in three Witnesses, to wit, *Envy*, *Superstition*, and *Pickthank*. They was then asked, If they knew the Prisoner at the Bar? and what they had to say for their Lord the King against him.

Then stood forth *Envy*, and said to this effect; My Lord, I have known this man a long time, and will attest upon my Oath before this honourable Bench, That he is—

Judg. Hold, give him his Oath: So they sware him. Then he said, My Lord, this man, notwithstanding his plausible name, is one of the vilest men in our Countrey; He neither regardeth Prince nor People, Law nor Custom; but doth all that he can to possess all men with certain of his disloyal notions, which he in the general calls Principles of Faith and Holiness. And in particular, I heard him once my self affirm, *That Christianity, and the Customs of our Town of* Vanity, *were Diametrically opposite, and could not be reconciled.* By which saying, my Lord, he doth at once, not only condemn all our laudable doings, but us in the doing of them.

Judg. Then did the Judge say to him, Hast thou any more to say?

Envy. My Lord, I could say much more, only I would not be tedious to the Court. Yet if need be, when the other Gentlemen have given in their Evidence, rather then any thing shall be wanting that will dispatch him, I will enlarge my Testimony against him. So he was bid stand by. Then they called *Superstition,* and bid him look upon the Prisoner; they also asked, What he could say for their Lord the King against him? Then they sware him, so he began.

Super. My Lord, I have no great acquaintance with this man, nor do I desire to have further knowledge of him; However this I know, that he is a very pestilent fellow, from some discourse that the other day I had with him in this *Town;* for then talking with him, I heard him say, That our Religion was naught, and such by which a man could by no means please God: which sayings of his, my Lord, your Lordship very well knows, what necessarily thence will follow, *to wit,* That we still do worship in vain, are yet in our Sins, and finally shall be damned; and this is that which I have to say.

Then was *Pickthank* sworn, and bid say what he knew, in behalf of their Lord the King against the Prisoner at the Bar.

Pick. My Lord, and you Gentlemen all, This fellow I have known of a long time, and have heard him speak things that ought not to be spoke. For he hath railed on our noble Prince *Beelzebub,* and hath spoke contemptibly of his honourable Friends, whose names are the Lord *Old man,* the Lord *Carnal delight,* the Lord *Luxurious,* the Lord *Desire of Vain-glory,* my old Lord *Lechery,* Sir *Having Greedy,* with all the rest of our Nobility; and he hath said moreover, that if all men were of his mind, if possible, there is not one of these Noble-men should have any longer a being in this Town. Besides, he hath not been afraid to rail on you, my Lord, who are now appointed to be his Judge, calling you an ungodly villain, with many other such like vilifying terms, with which he hath bespattered most of the Gentry of our Town. When this *Pickthank* had told his tale, the Judge directed his speech to the Prisoner at the Bar, saying, Thou Runagate,[4] Heretick, and Traitor, hast thou heard what these honest Gentlemen have witnessed against thee.

4 Runagate: renegade

Faith. May I speak a few words in my own defence?

Judg. Sirrah, Sirrah, thou deserveth to live no longer, but to be slain immediately upon the place; yet that all men may see our gentleness towards thee, let us hear what thou hast to say.

Faith. 1. I say then in answer to what Mr. *Envy* hath spoken, I never said ought but this, *That what Rule, or Laws, or Custom, or People, were flat against the Word of God, are diametrically opposite to Christianity.* If I have said a miss in this, convince me of my errour, and I am ready here before you to make my recantation.

2. As to the second, to wit, Mr. *Superstition,* and his charge against me, I said only this, *That in the worship of God there is required a divine Faith; but there can be no divine Faith, without a divine Revelation of the will of God: therefore whatever is thrust into the worship of God, that is not agreeable to divine Revelation, cannot be done but by an humane Faith, which Faith will not profit to Eternal Life.*

3. As to what Mr. *Pickthank* hath said, I say, (avoiding terms, as that I am said to rail, and the like) That the Prince of this Town, with all the Rablement his Attendants, by this Gentleman named, are more fit for a being in Hell, then in this Town and Countrey; *and so the Lord have mercy upon me.*

Then the Judge called to the Jury (who all this while stood by, to hear and observe;) Gentlemen of the Jury, you see this man about whom so great an uproar hath been made in this Town: you have also heard what these worthy Gentlemen have witnessed against him; also you have heard his reply and confession: It lieth now in your brests to hang him, or save his life. But yet I think meet to instruct you into our Law.

There was an Act made in the days of *Pharaoh* the Great, Servant to our Prince, That lest those of a contrary Religion should multiply and grow too strong for him, their Miles should be thrown into the River. There was also an Act made in the days of *Nebuchadnezzar* the Great, another of his Servants, That whoever would not fall down and worship his golden Image, should be thrown into a fiery Furnace. There was also an Act made in the days of *Darius,* That who so, for some time, called upon any God but his, should be cast into the Lions Den. Now the substance of these Laws this Rebel has broken, not only in thought, (which is not to be born) but also in word and deed; which must therefore needs be intolerable.

For that of *Pharaoh,* his Law was made upon a supposition, to prevent mischief, no Crime being yet apparent; but here is a Crime apparent. For the second and third, you see he disputeth against our Religion; and for the Treason he hath confessed, he deserveth to die the death.

Then went the Jury out, whose names were Mr. *Blind-man,* Mr. *No-good,* Mr. *Malice,* Mr. *Love-lust,* Mr. *Live-loose,* Mr. *Heady,* Mr. *High-mind,* Mr. *Enmity,* Mr. *Lyar,* Mr. *Cruelty,* Mr. *Hate-light,* and Mr. *Implacable,* who every one gave in his private Verdict against him among themselves, and afterwards unanimously concluded to bring him in guilty before the Judge. And first Mr. *Blind-man,* the foreman, said, *I see clearly that this man is an Heretick.* Then said Mr. *No-good, Away with such a fellow from the Earth. Ay,* said Mr. *Malice, for I hate the very looks of him.* Then said Mr. *Love-lust, I could never indure him. Nor I,* said Mr. *Live-loose, for he would alwayes be condemning my way. Hang him, hang him,* said Mr. *Heady. A sorry Scrub,* said Mr. *High-mind. My heart riseth against him,* said Mr. *Enmity. He is a Rogue,* said Mr. *Lyar. Hanging is too good for him,* said Mr. *Cruelty. Lets dispatch him out of the way,* said Mr. *Hate-light.* Then said Mr. *Implacable, Might I have all the World given me, I could not be reconciled to him, therefore let us forthwith bring him in guilty of death:* And so they did, therefore he was presently Condemned, To be had from the place where he was, to the place from whence he came, and there to be put to the most cruel death that could be invented.

They therefore brought him out, to do with him according to their Law; and first they Scourged him, then they Buffetted him, then they Lanced his flesh with Knives; after that they Stoned him with Stones, then prickt him with their Swords, and last of all they burned him to Ashes at the Stake. Thus came *Faithful* to his end. Now, I saw that there stood behind the multitude, a Chariot and a couple of Horses, waiting for *Faithful,* who (so soon as his adversaries had dispatched him) was taken up into it, and straightway was carried up through the Clouds, with sound of Trumpet, the nearest way to the Cœlestial Gate. But as for *Christian,* he had some respit, and was remanded back to prison; so he there remained for a space: But he that over-rules all things, having the power of their rage in his own hand, so wrought it about, that *Christian* for that time escaped them, and went his way. . . .

. . .

Now I saw in my Dream, that by this time the Pilgrims were got over the Inchanted Ground, and entering into the Country of *Beulah*, whose Air was very sweet and pleasant, the way lying directly through it, they solaced themselves there for a season. Yea, here they heard continually the singing of Birds, and saw every day the flowers appear in the earth: and heard the voice of the Turtle in the Land. In this Countrey the Sun shineth night and day; wherefore this was beyond the Valley of the *shadow of death*, and also out of the reach of Giant *Despair;* neither could they from this place so much as see *Doubting-Castle.* Here they were within sight of the City they were going to: also here met them some of the Inhabitants thereof. For in this Land the shining Ones commonly walked, because it was upon the Borders of Heaven. In this Land also the contract between the Bride and the Bridgroom was renewed: Yea here, *as the Bridegroom rejoyceth over the Bride, so did their God rejoyce over them.* Here they had no want of Corn and Wine; for in this place they met with abundance of what they had sought for in all their Pilgrimage. Here they heard voices from out of the City, loud voices, saying, *Say ye to the daughter of* Zion, *Behold thy Salvation cometh, behold his reward is with him.* Here all the Inhabitants of the Countrey called them, *The holy People, the redeemed of the Lord, Sought out,* &c.

Now as they walked in this Land they had more rejoycing then in parts more remote from the Kingdom, to which they were bound; and drawing near to the City, they had yet a more perfect view thereof. It was builded of Pearls and Precious Stones, also the Street thereof was paved with Gold, so that by reason of the natural glory of the City, and the reflection of the Sunbeams upon it, *Christian*, with desire fell sick, *Hopeful* also had a fit or two of the same Disease: Wherefore here they lay by it a while, crying out because of their pangs, *If you see my Beloved, tell him that I am sick of love.*

But being a little strengthned, and better able to bear their sickness, they walked on their way, and came yet nearer and nearer, where were Orchards, Vineyards, and Gardens, and their Gates opened into the Highway. Now as they came up to these places, behold the Gardener stood in the way; to whom the Pilgrims said, Whose goodly Vineyards and Gardens are these? He answered, They are the Kings, and are planted here for his own delights, and also for the solace of Pilgrims, So the Gardiner had them into the Vineyards, and bid them refresh themselves with the Dainties; he also shewed them *there* the Kings Walks and the *Arbors* where he delighted to be: And here they tarried and slept.

Now I beheld in my Dream, that they talked more in their sleep at this time, then ever they did in all their Journey; and being in a muse there-about, the Gardiner said even to me, Wherefore musest thou at the matter? It is the nature of the fruit of the Grapes of these Vineyards to go down so sweetly, as to cause the lips of them that are asleep to speak.

So I saw that when they awoke, they addressed themselves to go up to the City. But, as I said, the reflections of the Sun upon the City, (for the City was pure Gold) was so extreamly glorious, that they could not, as yet, with open face behold it, but through an *Instrument* made for that purpose. So I saw, that as they went on, there met them two men, in Raiment that shone like Gold, also their faces shone as the light.

These men asked the Pilgrims whence they came? and they told them; they also asked them, Where they had lodg'd, what difficulties, and dangers, what comforts and pleasures they had met in the way? and they told them. Then said the men that met them, You have but two difficulties more to meet with, and then you are in the City.

Christian then and his Companion asked the men to go along with them, so they told them they would; but, said they, you must obtain it by your own faith. So I saw in my Dream that they went on together till they came within sight of the Gate.

Now I further saw, that betwixt them and the Gate was a River, but there was no Bridge to go over; the River was very deep; at the sight therefore of this River, the Pilgrims were much stounded, but the men that went with them, said, You must go through, or you cannot come at the Gate.

The Pilgrims then began to enquire if there was no other way to the Gate; to which they answered, Yes; but there hath not any, save two, to wit, *Enoch* and *Elijah,* been permitted to tread that path, since the foundation of the World, nor shall, untill the last Trumpet shall sound. The Pilgrims then, especially *Christian,* began to dispond in his mind, and looked this way and that, but no way could be found by them, by which they might escape the River. Then they asked the men if the Waters were all of a depth. They said no; yet they could not help them in that Case; for said they, *You shall find it deeper or shallower, as you believe in the King of the place.*

They then addressed themselves to the Water; and entring, *Christian* began to sink, and crying out to his good friend *Hopeful;* he said, I sink in deep Waters, the Billows go over my head, all his Waves go over me, *Selah.*[5]

Then said the other, Be of good chear, my Brother, I feel the bottom, and it is good. Then said *Christian,* Ah my friend, the sorrows of death have compassed me about, I shall not see the Land that flows with Milk and Honey. And with that, a great darkness and horror fell upon *Christian,* so that he could not see before him; also here he in great measure lost his senses, so that he could neither remember nor orderly talk of any of those sweet refreshments that he had met with in the way of his Pilgrimage. But all the words that he spake, still tended to discover that he had horror of mind, and hearty fears that he should die in that River, and never obtain entrance in at the Gate: Here also, as they that stood by, perceived, he was much in the troublesome thoughts of the sins that he had committed, both since and before he began to be a Pilgrim. 'Twas also observed, that he was troubled with apparitions of Hobgoblins and Evil Spirits. For ever and anon he would intimate so much by words. *Hopeful* therefore here had much adoe to keep his Brothers head above water, yea sometimes he would be quite gone down, and then ere a while he would rise up again half dead. *Hopeful* also would endeavour to comfort him, saying, Brother, I see the Gate, and men standing by it to receive us. But *Christian* would answer, 'Tis you, 'tis you they wait for, you have been *Hopeful* ever since I knew you: and so have you, said he to *Christian.* Ah Brother, said he, surely if I was right, he

5 *Selah:* Hebrew musical or liturgical direction, frequently occurring at the end of a verse in the Psalter

would now arise to help me; but for my sins he hath brought me into the snare, and hath left me. Then said *Hopeful*, My Brother, you have quite forgot the Text, where its said of the wicked, *There is no band in their death, but their strength is firm, they are not troubled as other men, neither are they plagued like other men.* These troubles and distresses that you go through in these Waters, are no sign that God hath forsaken you, but are sent to try you, whether you will call to mind that which heretofore you have received of his goodness, and live upon him in your distresses.

Then I saw in my Dream that *Christian* was as in a muse a while; to whom also *Hopeful* added this word, *Be of good cheer, Jesus Christ maketh thee whole:* And with that, *Christian* brake out with a loud voice, Oh I see him again! and he tells me, *When thou passest through the waters, I will be with thee, and through the Rivers, they shall not overflow thee.* Then they both took courage, and the enemy was after that as still as a stone, until they were gone over. *Christian* therefore presently found ground to stand upon; and so it followed that the rest of the River was but shallow. Thus they got over. Now upon the bank of the River, on the other side, they saw the two shining men again, who there waited for them. Wherefore being come up out of the River, they saluted them, saying, *We are ministring Spirits, sent forth to minister for those that shall be Heirs of Salvation.* Thus they went along towards the Gate, now you must note that the City stood upon a mighty hill, but the Pilgrims went up that hill *with ease,* because they had these two men to lead them up by the Arms; also they had left their *Mortal* Garments behind them in the River: for though they went in with them, they came out without them. They therefore went up here with much agility and speed, though the foundation upon which the City was framed was higher then the Clouds. They therefore went up through the Regions of the Air, sweetly talking as they went, being comforted, because they safely got over the River, and had such glorious Companions to attend them.

The talk that they had with the shining Ones, was about the glory of the place, who told them, that the beauty, and glory of it was inexpressible. There, said they, is the Mount *Sion*, the heavenly *Jerusalem*, the inumerable company of Angels, and the Spirits of Just Men made perfect: You are going now, said

they, to the Paradice of God, wherein you shall see the Tree of
Life, and eat of the never-fading fruits thereof: And when you
come there, you shall have white Robes given you, and your
walk and talk shall be every day with the King, even all the days
of eternity. There you shall not see again, such things as you
saw when you were in the lower Region upon the earth, to wit,
sorrow, sickness, affliction, and death, *for the former things are
passed away*. You are going now to *Abraham,* to *Isaac,* and
Jacob, and to the Prophets; men that God hath taken away
from the evil to come, and that are now resting upon their Beds,
each one walking in his rightousness. The men then asked,
What must we do in the holy place? To whom it was answered,
You must there receive the comfort of all your toil, and have
joy for all your sorrow; you must reap what you have sown,
even the fruit of all your Prayers and Tears, and sufferings for
the King by the way. In that place you must wear Crowns of
Gold, and enjoy the perpetual sight and Visions of the *Holy One,
for there you shall see him as he is.* There also you shall serve
him continually with praise, with shouting and thanksgiving,
whom you desired to serve in the World, though with much
difficulty, because of the infirmity of your flesh. There your eyes
shall be delighted with seeing, and your ears with hearing, the
pleasant voice of the mighty One. There you shall enjoy your
friends again, that are got thither before you; and there you
shall with joy receive, even every one that follows into the Holy
place after you. There also you shall be cloathed with Glory and
Majesty, and put into an equipage fit to ride out with the King
of Glory. When he shall come with sound of Trumpet in the
Clouds, as upon the wings of the Wind, you shall come with
him; and when he shall sit upon the Throne of Judgement, you
shall sit by him; yea, and when he shall pass Sentence upon all
the workers of Iniquity, let them be Angels or Men, you also
shall have a voice in that Judgement, because they were his and
your Enemies. Also when he shall again return to the City, you
shall go too, with sound of Trumpet, and be ever with him.

Now while they were thus drawing towards the Gate, behold
a company of the Heavenly Host came out to meet them: To
whom it was said, by the other two shining Ones, These are the
men that have loved our Lord, when they were in the World,
and that have left all for his holy Name, and he hath sent us

to fetch them, and we have brought them thus far on their desired Journey; that they may go in and look their Redeemer in the face with joy. Then the Heavenly Host gave a great shout, saying, *Blessed are they that are called to the Marriage Supper of the Lamb.*

There came out also at this time to meet them, several of the Kings Trumpeters, cloathed in white and shining Rayment, who with melodious noises, and loud, made even the Heavens to eccho with their sound. These Trumpeters saluted *Christian* and his Fellow with ten thousand welcomes from the world: And this they did with shouting, and sound of Trumpet.

This done, they compassed them round on every side; some went before, some behind, and some on the right hand, some on the left (as 'twere to guard them through the upper Regions) continually sounding as they went, with melodious noise, in notes on high; so that the very sight was to them that could behold it, as if Heaven it self was come down to meet them. Thus therefore they walked on together, and as they walked, ever and anon, these Trumpeters, even, with joyful sound, would, by mixing their Musick, with looks and gestures, still signifie to *Christian* and his Brother, how welcome they were into their company, and with what gladness they came to meet them: And now were these two men, as 'twere, in Heaven, before they came at it; being swallowed up with the sight of Angels, and with hearing of their melodious notes. Here also they had the City it self in view, and they thought they heard all the Bells therein to ring, to welcome them thereto: but above all, the warm and joyful thoughts that they had about their own dwelling there, with such company, and that for ever and ever. Oh! by what tongue or pen can their glorious joy be expressed: and thus they came up to the Gate.

Now when they were come up to the Gate, there was written over it, in Letters of Gold, *Blessed are they that do his commandments, that they may have right to the Tree of Life; and may enter in through the Gates into the City.*

Then I saw in my Dream, that the shining men bid them call at the Gate, the which when they did, some from above looked over the Gate; to wit, *Enoch, Moses,* and *Elijah, &c.* to whom it was said, These Pilgrims are come from the City of *Destruction,* for the love that they bear to the King of this place: and then the Pilgrims gave in unto them each man his Certificate, which they had received in the beginning; those therefore were carried into the King, who when he had read them, said, Where are the men? to whom it was answered, They are standing without the Gate. The King then commanded to open the Gate; *That the righteous Nation*, said he, *that keepeth Truth may enter in.*

Now I saw in my Dream, that these two men went in at the Gate; and loe, as they entered, they were transfigured, and they had Raiment put on that shone like Gold. There was also that met them with Harps and Crowns, and gave them to them; The Harp to praise withal, and the Crowns in token of honor: Then I heard in my Dream, that all the Bells in the City Rang again for joy; and that it was said unto them, *Enter ye into the joy of your Lord.* I also heard the men themselves, that they sang with a loud voice, saying, *Blessing, Honour, Glory, and Power, be to him that sitteth upon the Throne, and to the Lamb for ever and ever.*

Now just as the Gates were opened to let in the men, I looked in after them; and behold, the City shone like the Sun, the Streets also were paved with Gold, and in them walked many men, with Crowns on their heads, Palms in their hands, and golden Harps to sing praises withall.

There were also of them that had wings, and they answered one another without intermission, saying, *Holy, Holy, Holy, is the Lord.* And after that, they shut up the Gates: which when I had seen, I wished my self among them.

Now while I was gazing upon all these things, I turned my head to look back, and saw *Ignorance* come up to the River side: but he soon got over, and that without half that difficulty which the other two men met with. For it happened, that there was then in that place one *Vain-hope* a Ferry-man, that with his Boat helped him over: so he, as the other I saw, did ascend the Hill to come up to the Gate, only he came alone; neither did any man meet him with the least incouragement. When he was come up to the Gate, he looked up to the writing that was above; and then began to knock, supposing that entrance should have been quickly administred to him: But he was asked by the men that lookt over the top of the Gate, Whence came you? and what would you have? He answered, I have eat and drank in the presence of the King, and he has taught in our Streets. Then they asked him for his Certificate, that they might go in and shew it to the King. So he fumbled in his bosom for one, and found none. Then said they, Have you none? But the man answered never a word. So they told the King but he would not come down to see him; but commanded the two shining Ones that conducted *Christian* and *Hopeful* to the City to go out and take *Ignorance* and bind him hand and foot, and have him away. Then they took him up, and carried him through the air to the door that I saw in the side of the Hill, and put him in there. Then I saw that there was a way to Hell, even from the Gates of Heaven, as well as from the City of *Destruction*. So I awoke, and behold it was a Dream.

Thomas Traherne

Thomas Traherne was born in Hereford sometime between 1637 and 1639. He entered Brasenose College, Oxford, in 1656, from which he received his B.A., M.A., and B.D. degrees. From 1667 to 1672 he acted as chaplain to Sir Orlando Bridgeman, the Lord Keeper, with whom he retired to Teddington, where he died in 1674. Christian Ethicks *was published in the following year, and* A Serious and Patheticall Contemplation of the Mercies of God *in 1699, but the poems and* Centuries of Meditations *were not known until 1896–7, when the manuscripts were discovered in London (published 1903 and 1908).*

FROM

Centuries of Meditations:

THE THIRD CENTURY

1

Will you see the Infancy of this sublime and celestial Greatness? Those Pure and Virgin Apprehensions I had from the Womb, and that Divine Light wherewith I was born, are the Best unto this Day, wherin I can see the Universe. By the Gift of GOD they attended me into the World, and by his Special favor I remember them till now. Verily they seem the Greatest Gifts His Wisdom could bestow. for without them all other Gifts had been Dead and Vain They are unattainable by Book, and therfore I will teach them by Experience. Pray for them earnestly: for they will make you Angelical, and wholy Celestial. Certainly Adam in Paradice had not more sweet and Curious Apprehensions of the World, then I when I was a child.

2

All appeared New, and Strange at the first, inexpressibly rare, and Delightfull, and Beautifull. I was a little Stranger which at my Enterance into the World was Saluted and Surrounded with innumerable Joys. My Knowledg was Divine. I knew by Intuition those things which since my Apostasie, I Collected again, by the Highest Reason. My very Ignorance was Advantageous. I seemed as one Brought into the Estate of Innocence. All Things were Spotles and Pure and Glorious: yea, and infinitly mine, and Joyfull and Precious. I Knew not that there were any Sins,

or Complaints, or Laws. I Dreamed not of Poverties Contentions
or Vices. All Tears and Quarrels, were hidden from mine Eys.
Evry Thing was at Rest, Free, and Immortal. I Knew Nothing
of Sickness or Death, or Exaction, in the Absence of these I was
Entertained like an Angel with the Works of GOD in their Splendor and Glory; I saw all in the Peace of Eden; Heaven and Earth
did sing my Creators Praises and could not make more Melody
to Adam, then to me. All Time was Eternity, and a Perpetual
Sabbath. Is it not Strange, that an Infant should be Heir of the
World, and see those Mysteries which the Books of the Learned
never unfold?

<h1 style="text-align:center">3</h1>

The Corn was Orient[1] and Immortal Wheat, which never should
be reaped, nor was ever sown. I thought it had stood from ever-
lasting to everlasting. The Dust and Stones of the Street were as
Precious as GOLD. The Gates were at first the End of the World,
The Green Trees when I saw them first through one of the Gates
Transported and Ravished me; their Sweetnes and unusual
Beauty made my Heart to leap, and almost mad with Extasie,
they were such strange and Wonderfull Thing: The Men! O
what Venerable and Reverend Creatures did the Aged seem!
Immortal Cherubims! And yong Men Glittering and Sparkling
Angels and Maids strange Seraphick Pieces of Life and Beauty!
Boys and Girles Tumbling in the Street, and Playing, were mov-
ing Jewels. I knew not that they were Born or should Die. But
all things abided Eternaly as they were in their Proper Places.
Eternity was Manifest in the Light of Day, and som thing
infinit Behind evry thing appeared: which talked with my Ex-
pectation and moved my Desire. The Citie seemed to stand in
Eden, or to be Built in Heaven. The Streets were mine, the Tem-
ple was mine, the People were mine, their Clothes and Gold
Silver was mine, as much as their Sparkling Eys Fair Skins and
ruddy faces. The Skies were mine, and so were the Sun and
Moon and Stars, and all the World was mine, and I the only
Spectator and Enjoyer of it. I knew no Churlish Proprieties[2] nor
Bounds nor Divisions: but all Proprieties and Divisions were
mine: all Treasures and the Possessors of them. So that with

---

1 Orient: shining, brilliant
2 Proprieties: properties

much adoe I was corrupted; and made to learn the Dirty Devices of this World. Which now I unlearn, and becom as it were
a little Child again, that I may enter into the Kingdom of GOD.

. . .

5

Our Saviors Meaning, when He said, He must be Born again and
becom a little Child that will enter into the Kingdom of Heaven:
is Deeper far then is generally believed. It is not only in a Careless Reliance upon Divine Providence, that we are to becom Little Children, or in the feebleness and shortness of our Anger and
Simplicity of our Passions: but in the Peace and Purity of all
our Soul. Which Purity also is a Deeper Thing then is commonly
apprehended. for we must disrobe our selvs of all fals Colors,
and unclothe our Souls of evil Habits; all our Thoughts must be
Infant-like and Clear: the Powers of our Soul free from the
Leven of this World, and disentangled from mens conceits and
customs. Grit in the Ey or the yellow Jandice will not let a Man
see those Objects truly that are before it. And therfore it is req-
uisit that we should be as very Strangers to the Thoughts Customs and Opinions of men in this World as if we were but little
Children. So those Things would appear to us only which do to
Children when they are first Born. Ambitions, Trades, Luxuries,
inordinat Affections, Casual and Accidental Riches invented
since the fall would be gone, and only those Things appear,
which did to Adam in Paradice, in the same Light, and in the
same Colors. GOD in His Works, Glory in the Light, Lov in our
Parents, Men, our selvs, and the Face of Heaven. Evry Man
naturaly seeing those Things, to the Enjoyment of which He
is Naturaly Born.

6

Evry one provideth Objects, but few prepare Senses wherby, and
Light wherin to see them. Since therfore we are Born to be a
Burning and Shining Light, and whatever men learn of others,
they see in the Light of others Souls: I will in the Light of my
Soul shew you the Univers. Perhaps it is Celestial, and will teach
you how Beneficial we may be to each other. I am sure it is a
Sweet and Curious Light to me: which had I wanted: I would

hav given all the Gold and Silver in all Worlds to hav Purchased.
But it was the Gift of GOD and could not be bought with Mony.
And by what Steps and Degrees I proceeded to that Enjoyment
of all Eternity which now I possess I will likewise shew you. A
Clear, and familiar Light it may prove unto you.

7

The first Light which shined in my Infancy in its Primitive and
Innocent Clarity was totaly ecclypsed: insomuch that I was fain
to learn all again. If you ask me how it was ecclypsed? Truly by
the Customs and maners of Men, which like Contrary Winds
blew it out: by an innumerable company of other Objects, rude
vulgar and Worthless Things that like so many loads of Earth
and Dung did over whelm and Bury it: by the Impetuous Torrent of Wrong Desires in all others whom I saw or knew that
carried me away and alienated me from it: by a Whole Sea of
other Matters and Concernments that Covered and Drowned it:
finaly by the Evil Influence of a Bad Education that did not
foster and cherish it. All Mens thoughts and Words were about
other Matters; They all prized New Things which I did not
dream of. I was a stranger and unacquainted with them; I was
little and reverenced their Authority; I was weak, and easily
guided by their Example: Ambitious also, and Desirous to approve my self unto them. And finding no one Syllable in any
mans Mouth of those Things, by Degrees they vanishd, My
Thoughts, (as indeed what is more fleeting then a Thought)
were blotted out. And at last all the Celestial Great and Stable
Treasures to which I was born, as wholy forgotten, as if they
had never been.

8

Had any man spoken of it, it had been the most easy Thing in
the World, to hav taught me, and to hav made me believ, that
Heaven and Earth was GODs Hous, and that He gav it me. That
the Sun was mine and that Men were mine, and that Cities and
Kingdoms were mine also: that Earth was better then Gold, and
that Water was, every Drop of it, a Precious Jewel. And that
these were Great and Living Treasures: and that all Riches
whatsoever els was Dross in Comparison. From whence I clearly
find how Docible our Nature is in natural Things, were it rightly

entreated. And that our Misery proceedeth ten thousand times more from the outward Bondage of Opinion and Custom, then from any inward corruption or Depravation of Nature: And that it is not our Parents Loyns, so much as our Parents lives, that Enthrals and Blinds us. Yet is all our Corruption Derived from Adam: inasmuch as all the Evil Examples and inclinations of the World arise from His Sin. But I speak it in the presence of GOD and of our Lord Jesus Christ, in my Pure Primitive Virgin Light, while my Apprehensions were natural, and unmixed, I can not remember, but that I was ten thousand times more prone to Good and Excellent Things, then evil. But I was quickly tainted and fell by others.

9

It was a Difficult matter to persuade me that the Tinsild Ware upon a Hobby hors was a fine thing. They did impose upon me and Obtrude their Gifts that made me believ a Ribban or a Feather Curious. I could not see where the Curiousness or fineness: And to Teach me that A Purs of Gold was of any valu seemed impossible, the Art by which it becomes so, and the reasons for which it is accounted so were so Deep and Hidden to my Inexperience. So that Nature is still nearest to Natural Things. and farthest off from preternatural, and to esteem that the Reproach of Nature, is an Error in them only who are unacquainted with it. Natural Things are Glorious, and to know them Glorious: But to call things preternatural Natural, Monstrous. Yet all they do it, who esteem Gold Silver Houses Lands Clothes &c. the Riches of Nature, which are indeed the Riches of Invention. Nature Knows no such Riches. but Art and Error makes them. Not the God of Nature, but Sin only was the Parent of them. The Riches of Nature are our Souls and Bodies, with all their Faculties Sences and Endowments. And it had been the Easiest thing in the whole World, that all felicity consisted in the Enjoyment of all the World, that it was prepared for me before I was born, and that Nothing was more Divine and Beautifull.

10

Thoughts are the most Present things to Thoughts, and of the most Powerfull Influence. My Soul was only Apt and Disposed to Great Things; But Souls to Souls are like Apples to Apples, one being rotten rots another. When I began to speak and goe. Nothing began to be present to me, but what was present in their Thoughts. Nor was any thing present to me any other way, then it was so to them. The Glass of Imagination was the only Mirror, wherein any thing was represented or appeared to me. All Things were Absent which they talkt not of. So I began among my Play fellows to prize a Drum, a fine Coat, a Peny, a Gilded Book &c. who before never Dreamd of any such Wealth. Goodly Objects to drown all the Knowledg of Heaven and Earth: As for the Heavens and the Sun and Stars they disappeared, and were no more unto me than the bare Walls. So that the Strange Riches of Mans Invention quite overcame the Riches of Nature. Being learned more laboriously and in the second Place.

11

By this let Nurses, and those Parents that desire Holy Children learn to make them Possessors of Heaven and Earth betimes. to remove silly Objects from before them, to Magnify nothing but what is Great indeed, and to talk of God to them and of His Works and Ways before they can either Speak or go. For Nothing is so Easy as to teach the Truth becaus the Nature of the Thing confirms the Doctrine. As when we say The Sun is Glorious, A Man is a Beautifull Creature, Soveraign over Beasts and Fowls and Fishes, The Stars Minister unto us, The World was made for you, &c. But to say This Hous is yours, and these Lands are another Mans and this Bauble is a Jewel and this Gugaw a fine Thing, this Rattle makes Musick &c. is deadly Barbarous and uncouth to a little Child; and makes him suspect all you say, becaus the Nature of the Thing contradicts your Words. Yet doth that Blot out all Noble and Divine Ideas, Dissettle his foundation, render him uncertain in all Things, and Divide him from GOD. To teach him those Objects are little vanities, and that tho GOD made them, by the Ministery of Man, yet Better and more Glorious Things are more to be Esteemed, is Natural and Easy.

12

By this you may see who are the Rude and Barbarous Indians For verily there is no Salvage Nation under the Cope of Heaven,

that is more absurdly Barbarous than the Christian World. They
that go Naked and Drink Water and liv upon Roots are like
Adam, or Angels in Comparison of us. But they indeed that call
Beads and Glass Buttons Jewels, and Dress them selvs with
feather, and buy pieces of Brass and broken hafts of Knives of
our Merchants are som what like us. But We Pass them in
Barbarous Opinions, and Monstrous Apprehensions: which we
Nick Name Civility, and the Mode, amongst us. I am sure those
Barbarous People that go naked, com nearer to Adam God, and
Angels in the Simplicity of their Wealth, tho not in Knowledg.

13

You would not think how these Barbarous Inventions spoyle
your Knowledg. They put Grubs and Worms in Mens Heads:
that are Enemies to all Pure and True Apprehensions, and eat
out all their Happines. They make it impossible for them, in
whom they reign, to believ there is any Excellency in the Works
of GOD, or to taste any Sweetness in the Nobility of Nature,
or to Prize any Common, tho never so Great a Blessing. They
alienat men from the Life of GOD, and at last make them to
live without GOD in the World. To liv the Life of GOD is to live
to all the Works of GOD, and to enjoy them in His Image, from
which they are wholy Diverted that follow fashions. Their fancies are corrupted with other Gingles.

14

Being Swallowed up therfore in the Miserable Gulph of idle talk
and worthless vanities, thenceforth I lived among Shadows,
like a Prodigal Son feeding upon Husks with Swine. A Com-
fortless Wilderness full of Thorns and Troubles the World was,
or wors: a Waste Place covered with Idleness and Play, and
Shops and Markets and Taverns. As for Churches they were
things I did not understand. And Scholes were a Burden: so
that there was nothing in the World worth the having, or Enjoying, but my Game and Sport, which also was a Dream and
being passed wholy forgotten. So that I had utterly forgotten
all Goodness Bounty Comfort and Glory: which things are the
very Brightness of the Glory of GOD: for lack of which therfore
He was unknown.

15

Yet somtimes in the midst of these Dreams, I should com a litle
to my self. so far as to feel I wanted som thing, secretly to Ex-
postulate with GOD for not giving me Riches, to long after an
unknown Happiness, to griev that the World was so empty, and
to be dissatisfied with my present State becaus it was vain and
forlorn. I had heard of Angels, and much admired that here
upon earth nothing should be but Dirt and Streets and Gutters.
for as for the Pleasures that were in Great Mens Houses I had
not seen them: and it was my real Happiness they were unknown. for becaus Nothing Deluded me, I was the more Inquisitive.

16

Once I remember (I think I was about 4 yeer old, when) I thus
reasoned with my self. sitting in a little Obscure Room in my
Fathers poor House. If there be a God, certainly He must be
infinit in Goodness. And that I was prompted to, by a real
Whispering Instinct of Nature. And if He be infinit in Goodness,
and a Perfect Being in Wisdom and Love, certainly He must do
most Glorious Things: and giv us infinit Riches; how comes it
to pass therfore that I am so poor? of so Scanty and Narrow a
fortune, enjoying few and Obscure Comforts? I thought I could
not believ Him a GOD to me, unless all His Power were Em-
ployd to Glorify me. I knew not then my Soul, or Body: nor did
I think of the Heavens and the Earth, the Rivers and the Stars,
the Sun or the Seas: all those were lost, and Absent from me.
But when I found them made out of Nothing for me, then I had
a GOD indeed, whom I could Prais, and rejoyce in.

17

Som times I should be alone, and without Employment, when
suddainly my Soul would return to it self, and forgetting all
Things in the whole World which mine Eys had seen, would be
carried away to the Ends of the Earth: and my Thoughts would
be deeply Engaged with Enquiries, How the Earth did End?
Whether Walls did Bound it, or Suddain Precipices, or Whether
the Heavens by Degrees did com to touch it; so that the face
of the Earth and Heaven were so neer, that a Man with Diffi-

culty could Creep under? Whatever I could imagin was incon-
venient, and my Reason being Posed was Quickly Wearied. What
also upheld the Earth (becaus it was Heavy) and kept it from
falling; Whether Pillars, or Dark Waters? And if any of these,
What then upheld those, and what again those, of which I saw
there would be no End? Little did I think that the Earth was
Round, and the World so full of Beauty, Light, and Wisdom.
When I saw that, I knew by the Perfection of the Work there
was a GOD, and was satisfied, and Rejoyced. People underneath
and feilds and flowers with another Sun and another Day
Pleased me mightily: but more when I knew it was the same
Sun that served them by night, that served us by Day.

18

Som times I should Soar abov the Stars and Enquire how the
Heavens Ended, and what was beyond them? concerning which
by no means could I receiv satisfaction. som times my Thoughts
would carry me to the Creation, for I had heard now, that the
World which at first I thought was Eternal, had a Beginning:
how therfore that Beginning was, and Why it was; Why it was
no sooner, and what was before; I mightily desired to Know. By
all which I easily perceiv that my Soul was made to live in Communion with GOD, in all Places of his Dominion, and to be
satisfied with the Highest Reason in all Things. After which it
so Eagerly aspired, that I thought all the Gold and Silver in the
World but Dirt, in comparison of satisfaction in any of these.
Som times I Wondered Why Men were made no Bigger? I would
have had a Man as Big as a Giant, a Giant as big as a Castle,
and a Castle as big as the Heavens. Which yet would not serv:
for there was infinit Space beyond the Heavens, and all was
Defectiv and but little in Comparison: And for him to be made
infinit, I thought it would be to no Purpose, and it would be in-
convenient. Why also there was not a Better Sun, and better
Stars, a Better Sea and Better Creatures I much admired. Which
thoughts produced that Poem upon Moderation, which afterwards was written. Som part of the verses are these. . . .

.   .   .

20

The Excellencies of the Sun I found to be of another kind then
that Splendor after which I sought, even in unknown and invisible Services; And that GOD by Moderation Wisely Bounding His
Almighty power, had to my Eternal Amazement and Wonder,
made all Bodies far Greater then if they were infinit: there not
being a Sand nor Mote in the Air that is not more Excellent then
if it were infinit. How Rich and Admirable then is the Kingdom
of GOD; where the Smallest is Greater then an infinit Treasure!
Is not this Incredible? Certainly to the Placits[3] and Doctrines of
the Scholes: Till we all Consider, That infinit Worth shut up in
the Limits of a Material Being, is the only way to a Real Infinity.
GOD made Nothing infinit in Bulk, but evry thing there where
it ought to be. Which, becaus Moderation is a Vertu observing
the Golden Mean, in som other parts of the former Poem, is
thus Expressed. . . .

.   .   .

22

These Liquid Clear Satisfactions, were the Emanations of the
Highest Reason, but not atchieved till a long time afterwards In
the mean time I was som times tho seldom visited and inspired
with New and more vigorous Desires after that Bliss which Nature Whispered and Suggested to me. Evry New Thing Quick-
ened my Curiosity and raised my Expectation. I remember once,
the first time I came into a Magnificent or Noble Dining Room,
and was left there alone, I rejoyced to see the Gold and State and
Carved Imagery. but when all was Dead, and there was no Motion, I was weary of it, and departed Dissatisfied. But afterwards,
when I saw it full of Lords and Ladies and Musick and Dancing,
the Place which once seemed not to differ from a Solitary Den,
had now Entertainment and nothing of Tediousness but pleasure
in it. By which I perceived (upon a Reflexion made long after)
That Men and Women are when well understood a Principal
Part of our True felicity. By this I found also that nothing that
stood still, could by doing so be a Part of Happiness: and that
Affection, tho it were invisible, was the best of Motions. But the

3 Placits: judgments, decrees, opinions

August and Glorious Exercise of Virtue, was more Solemn and Divine which yet I saw not. And that all Men and Angels should appear in Heaven.

23

Another time, in a Lowering and sad Evening, being alone in the field, when all things were dead and quiet, a certain Want and Horror fell upon me, beyond imagination. The unprofitableness and Silence of the Place dissatisfied me, its Wideness terrified me, from the utmost Ends of the Earth fears surrounded me. How did I know but Dangers might suddainly arise from the East, and invade me from the unknown Regions beyond the Seas? I was a Weak and little child, and had forgotten there was a man alive in the Earth. Yet som thing also of Hope and Expectation comforted me from every Border. This taught me that I was concerned in all the World: and that in the remotest Borders the Causes of Peace delight me, and the Beauties of the Earth when seen were made to entertain me: that I was made to hold a Communion with the Secrets of Divine Providence in all the World: that a Remembrance of all the Joys I had from my Birth ought always to be with me: that the Presence of Cities Temples and Kingdoms ought to Sustain me, and that to be alone in the World was to be Desolate and Miserable. The Comfort of Houses and friends, and the clear Assurance of Treasures evry where, Gods Care and Lov, His Goodnes Wisdom, and Power, His presence and Watchfulness in all the Ends of the Earth, were my Strength and Assurance for ever: and that these things being Absent to my Ey, were my Joys and consolations: as present to my Understanding as the Wideness and Emptiness of the Universe which I saw before me.

24

When I heard of any New Kingdom beyond the seas, the Light and Glory of it pleased me immediatly, enterd into me, it rose up within me and I was Enlarged Wonderfully. I entered into it, I saw its Commodities, Rarities, Springs, Meadows, Riches, Inhabitan[t]s, and became Possessor of that New Room, as if it had been prepared for me, so much was I Magnified and Delighted in it. When the Bible was read my Spirit was present in other Ages. I saw the Light and Splendor of them: the Land of Canaan, the

Israelites entering into it, the ancient Glory of the Amorites, their Peace and Riches, their Cities Houses Vines and Fig trees, the long Prosperity of their Kings, their Milk and Honie, their slaughter and Destruction, with the Joys and Triumphs of GODs People all which Entered into me, and GOD among them. I saw all and felt all in such a lively maner, as if there had been no other Way to those Places, but in Spirit only. This shewd me the Liveliness of interior presence, and that all Ages were for most Glorious Ends, Accessible to my Understanding, yea with it, yea within it, for without changing Place in my self I could behold and Enjoy all those. Any thing when it was proposed, tho it was 10,000 Ages agoe, being always before me.

25

When I heard any News I received it with Greediness and Delight, becaus my Expectation was awakend with som Hope that My Happiness and the Thing I wanted was concealed in it. Glad Tidings you know from a far Country brings us our Salvation: And I was not deceived. In Jury was Jesus Killed, and from Jerusalem the Gospel came. Which when I once knew I was very Confident that evry Kingdom contained like Wonders and Causes of Joy, tho that was the fountain of them. As it was the First fruits so was it the Pledg of what I shall receiv in other Countries. Thus also when any curious Cabinet, or secret in Chymistrie, Geometry or Physick was offered to me, I diligently looked in it, but when I saw it to the Bottom and not my Happiness I despised it.

. . .

27

Among other things, there befel me a most infinit Desire of a Book from Heaven. for observing all things to be rude and superfluous here upon Earth I thought the Ways of felicity to be known only among the Holy Angels: and that unless I could receiv information from them, I could never be Happy. This Thirst hung upon me a long time; Till at last I perceived that the God of Angels had taken Care of me, and prevented my Desires. For He had sent the Book I wanted before I was Born: and prepared it for me, and also commended, and sent it unto me, in a far better maner then I was able to imagine. Had som Angel brought it to me, which was the best way wherin I could then desire it, it would hav been a peculiar favor, and I should hav thought myself therin Honored abov all Mankind. It would hav been the Soul of this world, the Light of my Soul, the Spring of Life, and a fountain of Happiness. You cannot think what Riches and Delights I promised myself therin. It would hav been a Mine of Rarities, Curiosities and Wonders, to hav entertained the Powers of my Soul, to hav directed me in the Way of Life, and to hav fed me with Pleasures unknown to the whole World.

28

Had som Angel brought it miraculously from Heaven, and left it at my foot, it had been a Present meet for Seraphims. Yet had it been a Dream in comparison of the Glorious Way wherin GOD prepared it. I must hav spent time in studying it, and with great Diligence, hav read it daily to drink in the Precepts and Instructions it contained. It had in a narrow Obscure maner com unto me, and all the World had been Ignorant of felicity but I. Wheras now there are thousands in the World, of whom I being a Poor Child was Ignorant, that in Temples, Universities and Secret Closets enjoy felicity. whom I saw not in Shops, or Scholes or Trades; whom I found not in Streets, or at feasts, or Taverns: and therfore thought not to be in the World: Who Enjoy Communion with God, and hav fellowship with the Angels evry Day. And these I discerned to be a Great Help unto me.

29

This put me upon two things: upon Enquiring into the Matter contained in the Bible, and into the Maner wherin it came unto me. In the matter I found all the Glad Tidings my Soul longed after, in its Desire of News. in the maner, that the Wisdom of GOD was infinitly Greater then mine and that He had appeared in His Wisdom exceeding my Desires. Abov all things I desired som Great Lord or Mighty King, that having Power in his hand, to give me all Kingdoms Riches and Honors, was willing to do it. And by that Book I found that there was an eternal GOD, who loved me infinitly, that I was his Son, that I was to overcom Death, and to liv for ever, that He Created the World for me, that I was to Reign in His Throne and to inherit all Things. Who

would hav believed this had not that Book told me? It told me
also that I was to liv in Communion with Him, in the Image of
His Life and Glory, that I was to Enjoy all His Treasures and
Pleasures, in a more perfect maner then I could Devise, and
that all the truly Amiable and Glorious Persons in the World
were to be my friends and Companions.

30

Upon this I had enough. I desired no more the Honors and Pleasures of this World, but gav my self to the Illimited and Clear
fruition of that: and to this Day see nothing wanting to my
Felicity but mine own Perfection. All other Things are well; I
only, and the Sons of Men about me are Disorderd. Nevertheless
could I be what I ought, their very Disorders would be my Enjoyments, for all things shall work together for Good to them that
lov GOD. And if the Disorders then certainly the Troubles, and if
the Troubles, much more the Vanities of Men would be mine.
Not only their Enjoyments, but their very Errors and Distractions
increasing my Felicity. So that being Heir of the Whole World
alone, I was to walk in it, as in a Strange Marvellous and Amiable
Possession, and alone to render Praises unto God for its Enjoyment.

31

This taught me that those Fashions and Tinsild vanities, which
you and I despised ere while, fetching a litle Cours about, became ours. And that the Wisdom of God in them also was very
Conspicuous. For it becometh His Goodness to make all Things
Treasures: and His Power is able to bring Light out of Darkness,
and Good out of Evil. Nor would His Lov endure, but that I also
should hav a Wisdom, wherby I could draw Order out of Confusion. So that it is my Admiration and Joy, that while so many
thousand wander in Darkness, I am in the Light, and that while
so many Dote upon fals Treasures and Pierce themselvs thorow
with many Sorrows, I liv in Peace, and Enjoy the Delights of
God and Heaven.

32

In respect of the Matter, I was very sure that Angels and Cherubims could not bring unto me better Tidings then were in the

Scriptures contained: could I but believ them to be true. but I was
Dissatisfied about the Maner, and that was the Ground of my
Unbelief. For I could not think that GOD being LOV would neglect His Son, and therfore surely I was not His Son, nor He Lov:
becaus He had not Ascertaind me more carefully, that the Bible
was His Book from Heaven. Yet I was encouraged to hope well,
becaus the Matter was so Excellent, abov my Expectation. And
when I searched into it, I found the Way infinitly better then if
all the Angels in Heaven had brought it to me.

33

Had the Angels brought it to me alone, these Several Inconveni-
ences had attended the Vision. 1. It had been but one Suddain
Act wherin it was sent me: wheras Now GOD hath been all
Ages in preparing it. 2. It hath been don by inferior Ministers,
wheras now it is don by GOD Himself. 3. Being Satan is able to
Transform Him self into an Angel of Light, I had been still
Dubious, till having recours to the Excellency of the Matter, by
it I was informed and Satisfied. 4. Being Corrupted, that one
Miracle would hav been but like a Single Spark upon green
Wood, it would hav gon out immediatly: wheras I needed 10,000
Miracles to Seal it, yea and to awaken me to the Meditation of
the Matter that was revealed to me. 5. Had it been revealed no
other Way, all the World had been Dark and Empty round about
me: Wheras now it is my Joy and my Delight and Treasure,
being full of Knowledg, Light, and Glory. 6. Had it been revealed
at no other Time, God had now only been Good unto me, wheras
He hath Manifested His Lov in all Ages, and been Carefully and
most Wisely Revealing it from the Beginning of the World. 7.
Had He revealed it to no other Person, I had been Weak in faith
being Solitary, and sitting alone like a Sparrow upon the Hous
top, who now hav the Concurrent and joynt affections of Kingdoms and Ages. Yea notwithstanding the Disadvantage of this
Weakness, I must hav gon abroad, and Published this faith to
others, both in lov to God, and Lov to Men. for I must hav don
my Duty, or the Book would hav don me no Good, and Lov to
God and Men must hav been my Duty. for without that I could
never be Happy. Yea finaly had not the Book been revealed before
neither had GOD been Glorious, nor I Blessed, for He had been
Negligent of other Persons, His Goodness had been Defectiv to

all Ages, Whom now I Know to be GOD by the Universality of
His Lov unto Mankind: and the Perfection of His wisdom to evry
Person.

34

To talk now of the Necessity of bearing all Calamities and Persecutions in preaching, is little: to consider the Reproaches,
Mockings and Derisions I must have endured of all the World,
while they scoffed at me, for pretending to be the only man, that
had a Book from Heaven; is Nothing; nor is it much to Mention
the Impossibility of Convincing others, all the World having been
full of Darkness, and God always Silent before. All Ages had
been void of Treasure had not the Bible been revealed till the
other Day, wherin now I can Expatiat with Perfect Liberty, and
evry where See the Lov of GOD to all Mankind Lov to me alone.
All the World being adorned with Miracles Prophets Patriarchs
Apostles, Martyrs, Revelations from Heaven, Lively Examples
Holy Souls, Divine Affairs, for my Enjoyment. The Glory of God
and the Light of Heaven appearing evrywhere, as much as it
would hav don in that seeming Instant, had the Book I desired
com unto me any other Way.

35

You will not believ what a World of Joy this one Satisfaction and
Pleasure brought me. Thenceforth I thought the Light of Heaven
was in this World: I saw it Possible, and very Probable, that I
was infinitly Beloved of Almighty God, the Delights of Paradice
were round about me, Heaven and Earth were open to me, all
Riches were little Things, this one Pleasure being so Great that
it exceeded all the Joys of Eden. So Great a Thing it was to me,
to be satisfied in the Maner of Gods Revealing Himself unto Mankind. Many other Enquiries I had concerning the Maner of His
Revealing Himself, in all which I am infinitly satisfied.

36

Having been at the University, and received there the Taste and
Tincture of another Education, I saw that there were Things in
this World of which I never Dreamed, Glorious Secrets, and
Glorious Persons past Imagination. There I saw that Logick,
Ethicks, Physicks, Metaphysicks, Geometry, Astronomy, Poesie,

Medicine, Grammer, Musick, Rhetorick, all kind of Arts Trades
and Mechanicismes that Adorned the World pertained to felicity.
At least there I saw those Things, which afterwards I knew to
pertain unto it: And was Delighted in it. There I saw into the
Nature of the Sea, the Heavens, the Sun, the Moon and Stars,
the Elements, Minerals and Vegetables All which appeared
like the Kings Daughter, All Glorious within, and those Things
which my Nurses and Parents should hav talkt of, there were
taught unto Me.

37

Nevertheless som things were Defectiv too. There was never a
Tutor that did professely Teach Felicity: tho that be the Mistress
of all other Sciences. Nor did any of us Study these things but as
Aliena, which we ought to hav Studied as our own Enjoyments.
We Studied to inform our Knowledg, but Knew not for what End
we so Studied. And for lack of aiming at a Certain End, we
Erred in the Maner. How beit there we received all those Seeds of
Knowledg that were afterwards improved; and our Souls were
Awakened to a Discerning of their faculties, and Exercise of their
Powers.

38

The Maner is in evry thing of greatest Concernment. Whatever
Good thing we do, neither can we pleas God, unless we do it
Well: nor can He pleas us, whatever Good He does, unless He do
it *well.* Should He giv us the most Perfect Things in Heaven and
Earth to make us Happy, and not giv them to us in the Best of all
Possible Maners, He would but Displeas us, and it were Impossible for Him to make us Happy. It is not Sufficient therfore for
us to Study, the most excellent Things unless we do it in the most
Excellent of Maners. And what that is it is impossible to find till
we are Guided therunto by the Most Excellent End, with a Desire
of which I flagrantly Burned.

39

The Best of all Possible Ends is the Glory of GOD, but Happiness
was that I thirsted after. And yet I did not erre. for the Glory of
God is to make us Happy. Which can never be don but by giving
us most Excellent Natures and Satisfying those Natures: by

Creating all Treasures of infinit Valu, and giving them to us in
an infinit maner, to wit both in the Best that to Omnipotence was
possible. This led me to Enquire, Whither all things were Excellent and of Perfect Valu, and whither they were mine in Pro-
priety?

40

It is the Glory of God to giv all Things to us in the Best of all
possible maners. To Study Things therfore under the Double
Notion of Interest and Treasure, is to study all Things in the Best
of all possible Maners. Becaus in Studying so we Enquire after
GODs Glory and our own Happiness. And indeed enter into the
Way that leadeth to all Contentments Joys and Satisfactions, to
all Praises Triumphs and Thanksgivings, to All Virtues Beauties
Adorations and Graces, to all Dominion Exaltation Wisdom and
Glory, to all Holiness, Union and Communion with GOD, to all
Patience and Courage and Blessedness, which it is impossible to
meet any other Way. So that to Study Object for Ostentation,
vain Knowledg or Curiosity is fruitless Impertinence. tho GOD
Himself, and Angels, be the Object. But to Study that which will
Oblige us to lov Him, and Feed us with Nobility and Goodness
toward Men, that is Blessed. And so is it to Study that, which will
lead us to the Temple of Wisdom, and Seat us in the Throne of
Glory.

A Miscellany

Augustine Baker
1575–1641

Benedictine monk, ecclesiastical historian,
author of devotional works

FROM

Treatise of the Venerable Father Augustin Baker
concerning his own Life

. . . But the said Queen Mary in the fift year of her reign dying, and Queen Elizabeth succeeding, she being affected to heresy soon brought it to be the publick and universall profession of the land; the Catholick religion being, as to all publick use of it, clean suppressed. And those parents accommodated themselves at least exteriorly to the common though schismaticall service of the land. And indeed at the first, and for some years after the said change made by Queen Elizabeth, the greatest part even of those who in their judgments and affections had before bin Catholickes, did not well discern any great fault, novelty, or difference from the former religion, that was Catholick, in this new sett up by Queen Elizabeth; save only change of language, as bringing in service in the English tongue, in lieu of that which had bin in the Latin; in the which difference they conceived nothing of substance or essence to be. And so easily digested the new religion and accommodated themselves thereto; especially in Wales and other such like places, remotest from London, in the which remotest places there was not as yet so much formall heresy, as meer ignorance of what was to be beleived and exercised by a true Christian. But after a dozen years past or somewhat more, matters came to be more discerned and distinguished concerning religion: as the publick profession of England to be by Catholicks and those that were Catholickly affected to be but hereticall or schismaticall; and that, which in verity was the true Catholick religion, to be abhorred and persecuted in the professors thereof, so far as such were and could be discerned, by the schismaticall State of England and the members thereof Protestants and Puritans.

By these means and occasions those parents, with thousands of others that likewise in their younger years had bin professors of the Catholick religion (besides those that proved enemies thereto, as being Protestants) in tract of time and *sensim*,[1] and indeed as it were unawares to themselves, became neutrals in religion, viz. neither indeed true Catholicks, for perfect knowledg, beleif and practice, nor yet meer Protestants or otherwise hereticks in their beleif, though schismaticall, by their externall accommodation of themselves to the schismaticall service of the English Church. Those neutrals, as far as they had any religion in them, serving God but in a certain naturall manner, which God knows, even as naturall, could not [but] be very defective, wanting the light and grace of faith, without which nature is very blind in man corrupted by sin, even as to the true and perfect naturall worship and service of God. Of the number or quality of those kind of neutrals, do I imagine, by what I have heard and of myself do conceive, the said parents, in the said later condition of theirs, to have bin and remained. The which kind of religion, as not having verity in it, could not have any true zeal at all in it, nor indeed any zeal even of its own quality of religion, as being but a state of mere coldnesse and lulling in a state of sleep and resting in mere nature; whereas yet formal heresy hath

1 *sensim:* gradually, by degrees

much zeal in it, but a naughty and malicious one. By zeal, I here mean a desire of propagating and maintaining such religion, though vain and false, in and towards others, as well as in their ownselves. The which zeal, so far as it may be termed zeal, was not yet in the said parents, or others suchlike; by reason whereof they gave no education at all (which is the sole point that makes for my present purpose) as to any religion to their children; but regarded only in them a good moral extern carriage, to which through nature they were even of their own selves well disposed. But what their childrens beleife or practice should be, in matter of religion, they heeded not. And thereupon, sending those their children (for some or the most part of them) to London or thereabouts, as for better education, they regarded not nor thought of what would become of them as to religion. By means of which sending of them to those places and keeping them there for some years, where was more exercise of formall heresy, the children could not but be more corrupted in beleif, then before they were even by their natures; though for some of them, it pleased God afterwards to enlighten them with the true faith, and to bring them into the fold of His Holy Church. . . .

Lancelot Andrewes
1555–1626

*Bishop of Winchester, contributor to translation
of King James' version of the Bible, eminent for
his learning and piety*

FROM

A Sermon Preached before the King's Majestie,
AT WHITE-HALL, ON *Wednesday,*
THE XXV OF *December,* A.D. MDCXXII,
BEING CHRISTMASSE DAY

. . . Now, to *Venimus,* their *Comming* it selfe. And it followes
well. For it is not a *starr* only, but a *Lode-starr:* And, whither
should *stella Eius ducere,* but *ad Eum?* whither lead us, but to
Him, whose the *starr* is? The *starr,* to the *Starr's Master.*

All this while we have been at *dicentes,* saying and seeing:
Now we shall come to *Facientes,* see them do some-what upon it.
It is not *saying,* nor *seeing* will serve *Saint James:* He will call,
and be still calling for *Ostende mihi, shew me* thy Faith by some
Worke. And, well may he be allowed to call for it, this *Day:* It is
the day of *Vidimus,* Appearing, Beeing seen. You have seen His
starr; Let Him now see your starr, another while. And, so they
do. Make your Faith to be seen: So it is: Their *Faith,* in the
stepps of their *Faith.* And, so was *Abraham's* first, by *comming*
forth of his Countrey; As, these heer do, and so *walke in the
stepps of the faith of Abraham;* do his first worke.

It is not commended, to stand *gazing up into Heaven* too long,
Not *on* CHRIST *Himselfe ascending:* Much lesse on His *starr.*
For, they sat not still gazing on the *starr.* Their *Vidimus* begatt
Venimus; their *seeing* made them *come;* come, a great journey.
Venimus is soone sayd; but a *short word:* But, many a wide and

weary stepp they made, before they could come to say *Venimus,*
Lo, *heer we are come; Come,* and at our journeys end. To looke a
little on it. In this their *Comming,* we consider, 1. First, the *distance* of the Place, they came from. It was not hard by, as the
shepheard's (but a step to *Bethlehem,* over the fields:) This was
riding many a hundred miles, and cost them many a dayes journey. 2. Secondly, we consider the *Way,* that they came: If it be
pleasant, or plaine and *easy:* For, if it be, it is so much the better.
1. This was nothing *pleasant;* for, through *deserts:* all the way
wast and desolate. 2. Nor (secondly) *easy* neither: For, over the
Rocks and craggs of both *Arabies* (specially *Petræa*[1]) their journey lay. 3. Yet, if safe: But, it was not; but exceeding dangerous,
as lying through the middest of the *Black Tents of Kedar,* a Nation of *Theeves* and Cut-throtes; To pass over the *hills* of *Rob-
bers;* Infamous then, and infamous to this day. No passing
without great troop, or Convoy. 4. Last, we consider the *time* of
their comming, the season of the yeare. It was no *summer Prog-
resse.* A cold comming they had of it, at this time of the yeare;
just, the worst time of the yeare, to take a journey, and specially
a long journey, in. The waies deep, the weather sharp, the daies
short, the sunn farthest of *in solstitio brumali,* the very dead of
Winter: Venimus, We are come, if that be one; Venimus, We are
(now) come, come at this time, that (sure) is another.

All these difficulties they overcame, of a *wearisome, irksome,
troublesome, dangerous, unseasonable* journey: And for all this,
they *came.* And, came it cheerefully, and quickly; As appeareth,
by the speed they made. It was but *Vidimus, Venimus,* with
them; They *saw,* and they *came:* No sooner *saw,* but they set out
presently. So, as upon the first appearing of the *Starre* (as it
might be, last night) they knew, it was *Balaam's starre;* it called
them away, they made ready streight to begin their journey this
morning. A signe, they were highly conceited of [2] His *Birth,* believed some great matter of it, that they tooke all these paines,
made all this haste, that they might be there to *worship Him,*
with all the possible speede they could. Sorie for nothing so
much, as that they could not be there soone enough, with the
verie first, to do it even this *day,* the *day* of His *Birth.* All considered, there is more in Venimus then shewes at the first sight.

1 *Petræa:* rocks, crags
2 highly conceited of: held a high estimation of

It was not for nothing, it was said (in the first Verse) *Ecce Vene-runt;* their *comming* hath an *Ecce*[3] on it: it well deserves it.

And we, what should we have done? Sure, these men of the *East* shall *rise in Judgement against the men of the West,* that is, us: and their *faith,* against ours, in this point. With them, it was but *Vidimus, Venimus:* With us, it would have been but *Venie-mus*[4] at most. Our fashion is, to see and see againe, before we stirre a foot: Specially, if it be to the worship of CHRIST. Come such a Journey, at such a time? No: but fairely have put it off to the Spring of the yeare, till the dayes longer, and the waies fairer, and the weather warmer; till better travailing to CHRIST. Our *Epiphanie* would (sure) have fallen in *Easter-weeke* at the soonest.

But then, for the *distance, desolatenesse, tediousnesse,* and the rest, any of them were enough to marre our *Venimus* quite. It must be no great way (first) we must come: we love not that. Well fare the *Shepheards* yet, they came but hard by: Rather like them then the *Magi.* Nay, not like them neither. For, with us, *the neerer* (lightly) *the further off:* Our Proverbe is (you know) *The neerer the Church the further from* GOD.

Nor, it must not be through no *Desert,* over no *Petræa.* If rugged, or uneven the way; if the weather ill disposed; if any never so little danger, it is enough to stay us. To CHRIST we cannot travaile, but weather and way and all must be faire. If not, no journey, but sit still and see further. As indeed, all our Religion is rather *Vidimus,* a *Contemplation,* then *Venimus,* a *Motion,* or stirring to doe ought.

But, when we do it, we must be allowed leisure. Ever, *Venie-mus;* never *Venimus:* Ever, *comming;* never, come. We love to make no very great haste. To other things, perhapps: Not, to *Adorare,* the Place of the worship of GOD. Why should we? CHRIST, is no wild catt. What talke you of *twelve* dayes? And it be *fortie* dayes hence, ye shall be sure to finde His *Mother* and *Him;* She cannot be *churched* till then: What needes such haste? The truth is, we conceipt Him and His *Birth* but slenderly, and our haste is even thereafter. But, if we be at that point, we must be out of this *Venimus:* they like enough to leave us behind. Best,

---

3 *Ecce:* behold
4 *Veniemus:* we are going to come

get us a new *Christ-masse* in *September:* we are not like to come to CHRIST at this Feast. Enough, for *venimus* . . .

Edward Lord Herbert
1583–1648

Eldest brother of the poet, courtier, ambassador, author of DE VERITATE *in which he formulated the principles of natural religion*

FROM

The Life of EDWARD Lord HERBERT of CHERBURY.
WRITTEN BY HIMSELF

. . . My book De Veritate . . . having been begun by me in England, and formed there in all its principal Parts, was about this time finished; all the spare hours which I could get from my Visits and Negotiations, being imployed to perfect this Work, which was no sooner done, but that I communicated it to Hugo Grotius that great Scholar, who having escaped his Prison in the Low Countreys, came into France, and was much welcomed by me and Monsieur Tieleners also, one of the greatest Scholars of his time, who after they had perused it, and given it more Commendations than is fit for me to repeat, exhorted me earnestly to print and publish it; howbeit as the frame of my whole Book was so different from any thing which had been written heretofore, I found I must either renounce the Authority of all that had written formerly, concerning the Method of finding out Truth, and consequently insist upon my own way, or hazard myself to a general Censure, concerning the whole Argument of my Book; I must confess it did not a little animate me, that the two great Persons abovementioned did so highly value it, yet as I knew it

wou'd meet with much opposition, I did consider whether it was
not better for me a while to suppress it: Being thus doubtfull in
my Chamber, one fair day in the Summer, my Casement being
opened towards the South, the Sun shining clear and no Wind
stirring, I took my book De Veritate in my Hand, and kneeling
on my Knees devoutly said these words,

O Thou Eternal God, Authour of the Light which now shines
upon me, and Giver of all inward Illuminations, I do beseech
Thee of thy infinite Goodness to pardon a greater Request than a
Sinner ought to make; I am not satisfied enough whether I shall
publish This Book De Veritate; if it be for thy Glory, I beseech
thee give me some Sign from Heaven; if not I shall suppress it.

I had no sooner spoken these words, but a loud tho yet gentle
Noise came from the Heavens (for it was like nothing on Earth)
which did so comfort and cheer me, that I took my Petition as
granted, and that I had the Sign I demanded, whereupon also I
resolved to print my Book: This (how strange soever it may
seem) I protest before the Eternal God is true, neither am I any
way superstitiously deceived herein, since I did not only clearly
hear the Noise, but in the serenest Skye that ever I saw, being
without all Cloud, did to my thinking see the place from whence
it came. . . .

George Herbert
1593–1633

*Rector of Bemerton, widely read author of religious
lyric poetry collected in* THE TEMPLE

FROM

A PRIEST to the TEMPLE,
OR, THE COUNTREY PARSON HIS CHARACTER,
AND RULE OF HOLY LIFE

CHAPTER VII:
THE PARSON PREACHING

The Countrey Parson preacheth constantly, the pulpit is his joy
and his throne: if he at any time intermit, it is either for want of
health, or against some great Festivall, that he may the better
celebrate it, or for the variety of the hearers, that he may be
heard at his returne more attentively. When he intermits, he is
ever very well supplyed by some able man who treads in his
steps, and will not throw down what he hath built; whom also
he intreats to press some point, that he himself hath often urged
with no great success, that so in the mouth of two or three witnesses the truth may be more established. When he preacheth,
he procures attention by all possible art, both by earnestnesse of
speech, it being naturall to men to think, that where is much
earnestness, there is somewhat worth hearing; and by a diligent,
and busy cast of his eye on his auditors, with letting them know,
that he observes who marks, and who not; and with particulariz-
ing of his speech now to the younger sort, then to the elder, now
to the poor, and now to the rich. This is for you, and This is for
you; for particulars ever touch, and awake more then generalls.
Herein also he serves himselfe of the judgements of God, as of

those of antient times, so especially of the late ones; and those most, which are nearest to his Parish; for people are very attentive at such discourses, and think it behoves them to be so, when God is so neer them, and even over their heads. Sometimes he tells them stories, and sayings of others, according as his text invites him; for them also men heed, and remember better then exhortations; which though earnest, yet often dy with the Sermon, especially with Countrey people; which are thick, and heavy, and hard to raise to a poynt of Zeal, and fervency, and need a mountaine of fire to kindle them; but stories and sayings they will well remember. He often tels them, that Sermons are dangerous things, that none goes out of Church as he came in, but either better, or worse; that none is careless before his Judg, and that the word of God shal judge us. By these and other means the Parson procures attention; but the character of his Sermon is Holiness; he is not witty, or learned, or eloquent, but Holy. A Character, that *Hermogenes* never dream'd of, and therefore he could give no precepts thereof. But it is gained, first, by choosing texts of Devotion, not Controversie, moving and ravishing texts, whereof the Scriptures are full. Secondly, by dipping, and seasoning all our words and sentences in our hearts, before they come into our mouths, truly affecting, and cordially expressing all that we say; so that the auditors may plainly perceive that every word is hart-deep. Thirdly, by turning often, and making many Apostrophes to God, as, Oh Lord blesse my people, and teach them this point; or, Oh my Master, on whose errand I come, let me hold my peace, and doe thou speak thy selfe; for thou art Love, and when thou teachest, all are Scholers. Some such irradiations scatteringly in the Sermon, carry great holiness in them. The Prophets are admirable in this. So *Isa.* 64. *Oh that thou would'st rent the Heavens, that thou wouldst come down,* &c. And *Jeremy,* Chapt. 10. after he had complained of the desolation of *Israel,* turnes to God suddenly, *Oh Lord, I know that the way of man is not in himself,* &c. Fourthly, by frequent wishes of the peoples good, and joying therein, though he himself were with Saint *Paul* even sacrificed upon the service of their faith. For there is no greater sign of holinesse, then the procuring, and rejoycing in anothers good. And herein St *Paul* excelled in all his Epistles. How did he put the *Romans* in all his prayers? *Rom.* 1.9. And ceased not to give thanks for the *Ephesians, Eph.*

1.16. And for the *Corinthians, chap.* 1.4. And for the *Philippians* made request with joy, *ch.* 1.4. And is in contention for them whither to live, or dy; be with them, or Christ, *verse* 23. which, setting aside his care of his Flock, were a madnesse to doubt of. What an admirable Epistle is the second to the *Corinthians?* how full of affections? he joyes, and he is sorry, he grieves, and he gloryes, never was there such care of a flock expressed, save in the great shepherd of the fold, who first shed teares over *Jerusalem*, and afterwards blood. Therefore this care may be learn'd there, and then woven into Sermons, which will make them appear exceeding reverend, and holy. Lastly, by an often urging of the presence, and majesty of God, by these, or such like speeches. Oh let us all take heed what we do, God sees us, he sees whether I speak as I ought, or you hear as you ought, he sees hearts, as we see faces: he is among us; for if we be here, hee must be here, since we are here by him, and without him could not be here. Then turning the discourse to his Majesty, And he is a great God, and terrible, as great in mercy, so great in judgement: There are but two devouring elements, fire, and water, he hath both in him; *His voyce is as the sound of many waters, Revelations* 1. And he himselfe *is a consuming fire, Hebrews* 12. Such discourses shew very Holy. The Parsons Method in handling of a text consists of two parts; first, a plain and evident declaration of the meaning of the text; and secondly, some choyce Observations drawn out of the whole text, as it lyes entire, and unbroken in the Scripture it self. This he thinks naturall, and sweet, and grave. Whereas the other way of crumbling a text into small parts, as, the Person speaking, or spoken to, the subject, and object, and the like, hath neither in it sweetnesse, nor gravity, nor variety, since the words apart are not Scripture, but a dictionary, and may be considered alike in all the Scripture. The Parson exceeds not an hour in preaching, because all ages have thought that a competency, and he that profits not in that time, will lesse afterwards, the same affection which made him not profit before, making him then weary, and so he grows from not relishing, to loathing.

Isaac Barrow
1630–1677

Master of Trinity College, Cambridge,
Anglican priest and author of theological works, eminent classicist,
mathematician second in reputation only
to his student Isaac Newton

FROM

A Sermon:
OF THE GOODNESS OF GOD

. . . There is no argument from natural effects discernible by
us, which proveth God's existence (and innumerable such there
are, every sort of things well studied may afford some), the
which doth not together persuade God to be very kind and benign; careful to impart to us all befitting good, suitable to our
natural capacity and condition; and unwilling that any considerable harm, any extreme want or pain should befall us. (I in-
terpose such limitations, for that an absolute, or universal and
perpetual exemption from all kinds, or degrees of inconvenience,
and accumulation of all sorts of appearing good upon us, doth
not become, or suit our natural state of being, or our rank in perfection among creatures; neither, all things being duly stated
and computed, will it turn to best account for us.) The best (no
less convincing than obvious) arguments, asserting the existence
of a Deity, are deduced from the manifold and manifest footsteps
of admirable wisdom, skill, and design apparent in the general
order, and in the particular frame of creatures; the beautiful
harmony of the whole, and the artificial contrivance of each part
of the world; the which it is hardly possible that any unprejudiced and undistempered mind should conceive to proceed from
blind chance, or as blind necessity. But with this wisdom are always complicated no less evident marks of goodness. We cannot

in all that vast bulk of the creation, and numberless variety of things, discover any piece of mere pomp, or dry curiosity; every thing seems to have some beneficial tendency; according to which it confers somewhat to the need, convenience, or comfort of those principal creatures, which are endued with sense and capacity to enjoy them. Most of them have a palpable relation to the benefit (to the subsistence or delight) of living creatures; and especially in an ultimate relation to the benefit of man; and the rest, although their immediate use be not to our dim sight so discernible, may therefore be reasonably presumed in their natural designation to regard the same end. Wherefore as upon consideration of that ample provision, which is made in nature for the necessary sustenance, defence, and relief, for the convenience, delight, and satisfaction of every creature, any man, who is not careless or stupid, may be induced to cry out with the Psalmist: *O Lord, how manifold are thy works? In wisdom hast thou made them all. . . .*

Thomas Sprat
1635–1713

Bishop of Rochester and Dean of Westminster,
author of THE HISTORY OF THE ROYAL SOCIETY (1667),
editor and biographer of the poet Abraham Cowley

FROM

A SERMON Preached before the KING at White-Hall,
Decemb. THE 24TH, 1676

First, towards our right instruction in the Doctrines of the Gospel, we should all labour to bring our minds clear, unprejudiced, clean, uncorrupt. For the being void of errors, is the first great step to the greatest knowledge, and that understanding, in which tho little is written, yet nothing is blotted, that which is not disfigured by ill impressions, is a subject most capable of the best. There nothing is required but plain Teaching; whereas the mind that is either perverted by false knowledge, or made crooked by deceitful prejudices, must not only be taught, but first untaught that ill it had Learn'd: And to unteach is a much more difficult work than to teach.

Such a pure, simple, undefil'd disposition of mind, by nature we cannot pretend to; because of the Original Corruption of our nature; but by the Grace of God in the Gospel we may attain it: And it is the chief design of the Gospel to direct us in the way of it.

That teaches us to cleanse, and repair by repentance, and amendment, our natural decays, and pollutions, to be constantly watchful in keeping our Souls free from carnal, moral, nay, spiritual prejudices against Religion; to endeavour sincerely, that our minds be not often overthrown by violent passions, nor too much disordered by Worldly Affections; not seduced by secular ends, that secretly undermine the Soul; not corrupted by bodily lusts, that openly war against the Soul; especially that they be not infected by false Enthusiastical conceptions, concerning God, and Religion; which are wont most dangerously to insinuate themselves into the Soul, as seeming to come from Heaven, and coming under the shadow of Religion it self.

John Tillotson
1630–1694

Archbishop of Canterbury, eminent as a preacher

FROM

A Sermon:
THE PRECEPTS OF CHRISTIANITY NOT GRIEVOUS

. . . God will not so much disparage eternal life and happiness, as to bestow it upon those who have conceived so low an opinion of it, as not to think it worth the labouring for. And, surely, this is sufficient to recommend religion to any considerate man, if the advantages of it be much greater than of any worldly design that we can propound to ourselves, and the difficulties of it not greater. If the same seriousness, and industry of endeavour, which men commonly use, to raise a fortune, and advance themselves in the world, will serve to make a man a good man, and to bring him to heaven, what reason hath any man to complain of the hard terms of religion? And I think I may truly say, that usually less than this does it: for God considers our condition in this world, and the pressing necessities of this life; that we are flesh, as well as spirit; and that we have great need of these things; and therefore he allows us to be very sedulous and industrious about them. However, this I am sure of, that if men would be as serious to save their immortal souls, as they are to support these dying bodies; if they would but provide for eternity with the same solicitude and real care as they do for this life; if they would but seek heaven with the same ardour of affection, and vigour of prosecution, as they seek earthly things; if they would but love God as much as many men do the world, and mind godliness as much as men usually do gain; if they would but go to church with as good will as men ordinarily do to their markets and fairs, and be in as good earnest at their devotions as men commonly are in driving a bargain; if they would but endure some troubles and inconveniencies in the ways of religion, with the same patience and constancy as they can do storms, and foul ways and mischances, when they are travelling about their worldly occasions; if they would but avoid bad company, as men use to do cheaters, and reject the temptations of the devil and the world, as they would do the kind words and insinuations of a man whom they verily believe to have a design to over-reach them: I am confident that such a one could not fail of heaven; and would be much surer of it upon these terms, than any man that doth all the other things could be of getting an estate, or of attaining any thing in this world. . . .

Benjamin Whichcote
1609–1683

Provost of King's College, Cambridge, until ejected at the Restoration, earliest of a group of philosophical divines known as the Cambridge Platonists

FROM

Moral and Religious Aphorisms

The *Rule* of Right is the Reason of Things; the *Judgment* of Right is the Reason of our Minds, *perceiving* the Reason of things.

Men have an itch rather to *make* Religion, than to *use* it: but we are to use our Religion; not to make it.

To use *Power*, to controul the Principles of Human Nature; (the Use of *Reason*, the Exercise of *Liberty*) is as strange a *Phænomenon*, as to cross or pervert the common Course of Natural Agents; to bring the Sun back again, or to make it fill the world with darkness. God does not this: if he did, he would contest with himself; his *Power* would rise-up against his *Wisdom;* and he would disparage and frustrate his own workmanship. Why should We think to do that, which God will not do—to over-bear *Reason* with *Violence!*

There is no solid Satisfaction; but in a mental Reconciliation with the Nature of God, and the Law of righteousness.

He that never *changed* any of his opinions, never *corrected* any of his Mistakes: and He, who was never *wise* enough, to find out any mistakes in Himself; will not be *charitable* enough, to excuse what he reckons mistakes in Others.

A man must *cultivate* his Mind, by enquiries after the Measures and Reasons of his duty; by Reconciliation of his Temper to those Measures, upon those Reasons: and he must cultivate his Life, by acting according to the Improvement of his Mind.

We are only so *Free;* that Others may be free, as well as We.

Those that *differ* upon Reason, may come together by Reason.

Conscience, without Judgment, is *Superstition;* Judgment without Conscience, is *Self-condemnation.*

Every man is Born with the *Faculty* of Reason, and the Faculty of Speech: but why should he be able to Speak, before he has any thing to say?

It is not to be expected, that *another* man should Think as I would, to please *me;* since I cannot think as I would, to please *myself;* it is neither in His nor My power, to think as we will; but as we see reason, and find cause.

To go against *Reason,* is to go against *God:* it is the self same thing, to do that which the Reason of the Case doth require; and that which God Himself doth appoint: Reason is the *Divine* Governor of Man's Life; it is the very Voice of God.

When the *Doctrine of the Gospel* becomes the Reason of our Mind, it will be the Principle of our Life.

If Reason may not *command,* it will *condemn.*

Reason *discovers* what is Natural; and Reason *receives* what is Supernatural.

Nothing is *worse* done than what is *ill* done *for* Religion. That must not be done, in the *Defence* of Religion, which is *contrary* to Religion.

I will not make a Religion for *God:* nor suffer any to make a Religion for *me.*

Nothing spoils human Nature more than false Zeal. The *Good-nature* of a Heathen is more God-like than the furious *Zeal* of a Christian.

Our Fallibility and the Shortness of our Knowledge should make us peaceable and gentle: because I *may* be Mistaken, I *must* not be dogmatical and confident, peremptory and imperious. I *will* not break the certain Laws of Charity, for a doubtful Doctrine or of uncertain Truth.

Certainly our *Saviour* accepts of no other Separation of *His Church* from the other part of the world than what is made by Truth, Virtue, Innocency, and Holiness of Life.

Richard Baxter
1615–1691

*Presbyterian divine,
author of a remarkably large body of political, historical,
and philosophical as well as religious writings*

FROM

The Saints Everlasting Rest;
OR, A TREATISE OF THE BLESSED STATE
OF THE SAINTS IN THEIR ENJOYMENT
OF GOD IN GLORY

And now, *Reader,* having laid thee down these undeniable Arguments, I do here in the name of God demand thy Resolution; What sayst thou? Wilt thou yeeld obedience, or not? I am confident thy Conscience is convinced of thy Duty: Darest thou now go on in thy common careless course, against the plain Evidence of Reason, and Commands of God, and against the light of thy own Conscience? Darest thou live as loosely? and sin as boldly? and pray as seldom and as coldly as before? Darest thou now as carnally spend the Sabbath? and slubber over the Service of God as sleightily? and think of thine Everlasting state as carelessly as before? Or dost thou not rather resolve to gird up the loins of thy minde? and to set thy self wholy about the work of thy Salvation? and to do it with all thy strength and might? and to break over all the oppositions of the world? and to sleight all their scorns and persecutions? to cast off the weight that hangeth on thee, and the sin that doth so easily beset thee, and to run with patience and speed the race that is before thee? I hope these are thy full Resolutions: if thou be well in thy wits, I am sure they are.

Yet because I know the strange obstinacy and Rockiness of the heart of man, and because I would fain drive this nail to the head, and leave these perswasions fastened in thy heart, that so, if it be possible, thou mightest be awakened to thy Duty, and thy Soul might live; I shall therefore proceed with thee yet a little further: And I once more intreat thee to stir up thy attention, and go along with me in the free and sober use of thy Reason, while I propound to thee these following Questions: And I command thee from God, that thou stifle not thy Conscience, and resist not conviction; but Answer them faithfully, and obey accordingly.

1 Question: If you could grow Rich by Religion, or get Lands and Lordships by being diligent in godliness; or if you could get honor or preferment by it in the world; or could be recovered from sickness by it, or could live for ever in prosperity on Earth; What kind of lives would you then lead? and what pains would you take in the Service of God? And is not the Rest of the Saints a more excellent Happiness then all this?

2 Question: If the Law of the Land did punish every breach of the Sabbath, or every omission of family duties, or secret duties, or every cold and heartless prayer with Death; If it were Felony or Treason to be ungodly and negligent in Worship, and loose in your lives; What manner of persons would you then be? and what lives would you lead? And is not Eternal death more terrible then all this? Give but Reason leave to speak.

.　　.　　.

4 Question: If one of your old acquaintance and companions in sin, should come from the dead, and tell you, that he suffereth the Torments of Hell for those sins that you are guilty of, and for neglecting those duties which you neglect, and for living such a careless, worldly, ungodly life as you now live, and should therfore advise you to take another course; If you should meet such a one in your Chamber when you are going to bed, and he should say to you, Oh take heed of this carnal unholy life! Set your self to seek the Lord with all your might; neglect not your Soul, Prepare for Eternity, that you come not to the place of Torment that I am in: How would this take with you: and what manner of persons would you afterwards be? It is written in the life of Bruno, that a Doctor of great note for learning and godliness being dead, and being brought to the Church to be buried, while they were in their Popish Devotions, and came to the words *Responde mihi,* the Corps arose in the Beir, and with a terrible voyce cryed out, *Justo Dei Judicio accusatus sum,* I am accused in the Just Judgment of God: At which voyce the people run all out of the Church affrighted. On the morrow when they came again to perform the Obsequies, at the same words as before, the Corps arose again, and cryed with a hideous voyce, *Justo Dei Judicio Judicatus sum,* I am Judged at the righteous Judgment of God: Whereupon the people run away again amazed. The third day almost all the City came together, and when they came to the same words as before, the Corps rose again, and cryed with a more doleful voyce then before, *Justo Dei Judicio Condemnatus Sum,* I am condemned at the Just Judgment of God. The consideration whereof, that a man reputed so upright should yet by his own confession be damned, caused Bruno, and the rest of his companions, to enter into that strict order of the Carthusians. If the voyce of the dead man could affright them into Superstition, should not the warnings of God affright thee into true Devotion?

5 *Question:* If you knew that this were the last day you had to live in the world, how would you spend this day? If you were sure when you go to bed that you should never rise again, would not your thoughts of another life be more serious that night? If you knew when you are praying that you should never pray more, would you not be more earnest and importunate in that prayer? Or if you knew when you are preaching, or hearing, or exhorting, your sinful acquaintance, that this were the last opportunity you should have, would you not ply it more closely then usually you

do? Why you do not know but it may be the last; and you are sure your last is near at hand.

George Fox
1624–1691

*Founder of the Society of Friends,
missionary, preacher, and prolific pamphleteer*

FROM

The Journal of George Fox

And then (it may be) another Company would come, that wold bee talkeing of the Scriptures and pleading for sinne, and I would aske them have you any faithe? and they wold say, yes, and that they were Christians.—And I said what Faith is it; will it give Victorie over sin? and over the Divell? and Purifie your heartes? and bring you to have accesse to God againe? and to please God, which faith is held in a pure Conscience, and they could not Endure to hear talke of puritye nor victory over sin and the Divell heere upon the earth, and then I bid them also Give over talkeing and babling of the Scriptures that were Given forth by holy Men, as they were moved by the holye Ghost, and the keeper beinge a great Professor was in a mighty rage against mee, yet it pleased the Lord to strike him soe one day that as I was walkeing in my Chamber I heard A dolefull Noise and I made a stand, and hee was speaking to his wife How that hee saw the Day or Judgment and hee saw Georg there and Hee was afraid of him because that Hee had done him soe much wronge and spoke soe much against him to Professors and Justices and the Preists and in Tavernes and Alehouses, etc., and soe toward Evening hee came up into my Chamber and said to mee, I have bin as a Lyon against you, but Now I come like a Lamb, and come like the Goaler that came to Paul and Silas trembling and desired that hee might Lye with mee, and I tould him that I was in his power, hee might doe what hee would, and hee said nay, hee wold have my Leave, and hee could desire to be allways with mee, but not to have mee as a Prisoner, and said that hee had bin plagued, and his house was plagued for my sake like Pharohs and Abimelecks concerning Abraham and Isaack, and soe I suffred Him to lye with mee, and then he tould mee all his heart and believed what I said to be true of the true faith, and hope, etc., and wondred that the other man did not stand to itt that was putt into prison with mee and said Hee was a knave and I was an honnest man etc., and soe hee went to the Justices and tould them hee and his house had been plagued for my sake and the Justices said that the plagues was on them too for keepinge mee in prison, this was Justice Bennett of Darby that first called Us Quakers because wee bid them tremble att the Word of God and this was in the year 1650.

Bibliography

GENERAL BACKGROUND

BUSH, DOUGLAS. *English Literature in the Earlier Seventeenth Century.* Oxford: Clarendon Press, 1962.

CRAGG, G. R. *From Puritanism to the Age of Reason.* Cambridge: Cambridge University Press, 1950.

MITCHELL, W. FRASER. *English Pulpit Oratory from Andrewes to Tillotson.* London: Society for Promoting Christian Knowledge, 1932.

WILLEY, BASIL. *The Seventeenth-Century Background.* London: Chatto & Windus, 1934.

CATHOLICISM

MAGEE, BRIAN. *The English Recusants.* London: Burns, Oates and Washbourne, 1938.

MATHEW, D. *Catholicism in England.* London: Eyre and Spottiswoode, 1955.

ANGLICANISM

BOSHER, R. S. *The Making of the Restoration Settlement.* London: Dacre Press, 1951.

FULLER, THOMAS. *The Church-History of Britain.* London: W. Legg, 1868.

MCADOO, H. R. *The Structure of Caroline Moral Theology.* London: Longmans, 1949.

MORE, P. E. and CROSS, F. L. *Anglicanism.* New York: Macmillan, 1957.

USHER, R. G. *The Reconstruction of the English Church.* New York: D. Appleton, 1910.

PURITANISM

DAVIES, HORTON. *The Worship of the English Puritans.* London: Dacre Press, 1948.

GEORGE, C. and K. *The Protestant Mind of the English Reformation.* Princeton: Princeton University Press, 1961.

HALLER, WILLIAM. *The Rise of Puritanism.* New York: Columbia University Press, 1947.

KNAPPEN, M. M. *Tudor Puritanism.* Gloucester, Mass.: P. Smith, 1963.

NUTTALL, G. F. *The Holy Spirit in Puritan Faith and Experience.* Oxford: Blackwell, 1947.

SASEK, LAWRENCE. *The Literary Temper of the English Puritans.* Baton Rouge: Louisiana State University Press, 1961.

WOODHOUSE, A. S. P., ed. *Puritanism and Liberty.* Chicago: University of Chicago Press, 1951.

QUAKERISM AND CAMBRIDGE PLATONISM

BRAITHWAITE, W. C. *The Beginnings of Quakerism.* Cambridge: Cambridge University Press, 1955.

CASSIRER, E. *The Platonic Renaissance in England.* Edinburgh: Nelson, 1953.

TULLOCH, JOHN. *Rational Theology and Christian Philosophy in England in the Seventeenth Century.* Edinburgh: Blackwood, 1874.

JOHN DONNE

SIMPSON, EVELYN and POTTER, GEORGE, eds. *The Sermons of John Donne.* Berkeley: University of California Press, 1955–62.

SIMPSON, E. M. *Study of the Prose Works of John Donne.* Oxford: Clarendon Press, 1948.

WALTON, ISAAC. *The Life of Dr. John Donne.* London: H. Milford, 1927.

WEBBER, JOAN. *Contrary Music.* Madison: University of Wisconsin Press, 1963.

SIR THOMAS BROWNE

BENNETT, JOAN. *Sir Thomas Browne.* Cambridge: Cambridge University Press, 1962.

DIGBY, SIR KENELM. *Observations Upon Religio Medici.* London: L. Chapman and D. Frere, 1643.

DUNN, W. P. *Sir Thomas Browne.* Minneapolis: University of Minnesota Press, 1950.

HUNTLEY, FRANK L. *Sir Thomas Browne.* Ann Arbor: University of Michigan Press, 1962.

KEYNES, GEOFFREY, ed. *The Works of Sir Thomas Browne.* London: Faber and Faber, 1928–31.

JEREMY TAYLOR

EDEN, C. P., ed. *The Whole Works of the Right Reverend Jeremy Taylor.* London: Longman, Brown, Green, and Longmans, 1847–54.

HUGHES, H. TREVOR. *The Piety of Jeremy Taylor.* London: Macmillan, 1960.

STRANKS, C. J. *The Life and Writings of Jeremy Taylor.* London: Society for Promoting Christian Knowledge, 1952.

WOOD, THOMAS. *English Casuistical Divinity during the Seventeenth Century.* London: Society for Promoting Christian Knowledge, 1952.

JOHN MILTON

BARKER, ARTHUR. *Milton and the Puritan Dilemma.* Toronto: University of Toronto Press, 1942.

DARBISHIRE, HELEN, ed. *The Early Lives of Milton.* London: Constable, 1932.

HANFORD, J. H. *Milton Handbook.* New York: Appleton-Century-Crofts, 1946.

MASSON, DAVID. *The Life of John Milton.* London: Macmillan, 1881–94.

WOLFE, D. M. *Milton in the Puritan Revolution.* New York: Humanities Press, 1963.

JOHN BUNYAN

BROWN, JOHN. *John Bunyan.* London: Hulbert, 1928.

TALON, HENRI. *John Bunyan.* London: Rockcliff, 1951.

TINDALL, W. Y. *John Bunyan, Mechanick Preacher.* New York: Columbia University Press, 1934.

WINSLOW, OLA E. *John Bunyan.* New York: Macmillan, 1961.

THOMAS TRAHERNE

JONES, RUFUS M. *Spiritual Reformers of the 16th and 17th Centuries.* London: Macmillan, 1928.

NICOLSON, MARJORIE. *The Breaking of the Circle*. Evanston, Ill.: Northwestern University Press, 1950.

STRANKS, C. J. *Anglican Devotion*. London: S. C. M. Press, 1961.

WADE, GLADYS. *Thomas Traherne*. Princeton: Princeton University Press, 1944.

ABOUT THE EDITOR

ANNE DAVIDSON FERRY, Lecturer in English at Harvard University, received her B.A. from Vassar College and her M.A. and Ph.D. from Columbia University. Before going to Harvard University in 1958, she taught at Hunter College and Wellesley College. Dr. Ferry is the author of MILTON'S EPIC VOICE, *editor of* SEVENTEENTH-CENTURY MINOR ENGLISH POETS, *and co-editor of* BEGINNING WITH POEMS.

A NOTE ON THE TYPE

The text of this book was set on the Linotype in a new face called Primer, designed by Rudolph Ruzicka, earlier responsible for the design of Fairfield and Fairfield Medium, Linotype faces whose virtues have for some time now been accorded wide recognition.

The complete range of sizes of Primer was first made available in 1954, although the pilot size of 12 point was ready as early as 1951. The design of the face makes general reference to Linotype Century (long a serviceable type, totally lacking in manner or frills of any kind) but brilliantly corrects the characterless quality of that face.

The book was designed by Betty Anderson and was composed, printed, and bound by H. Wolff, New York.